MW00981951

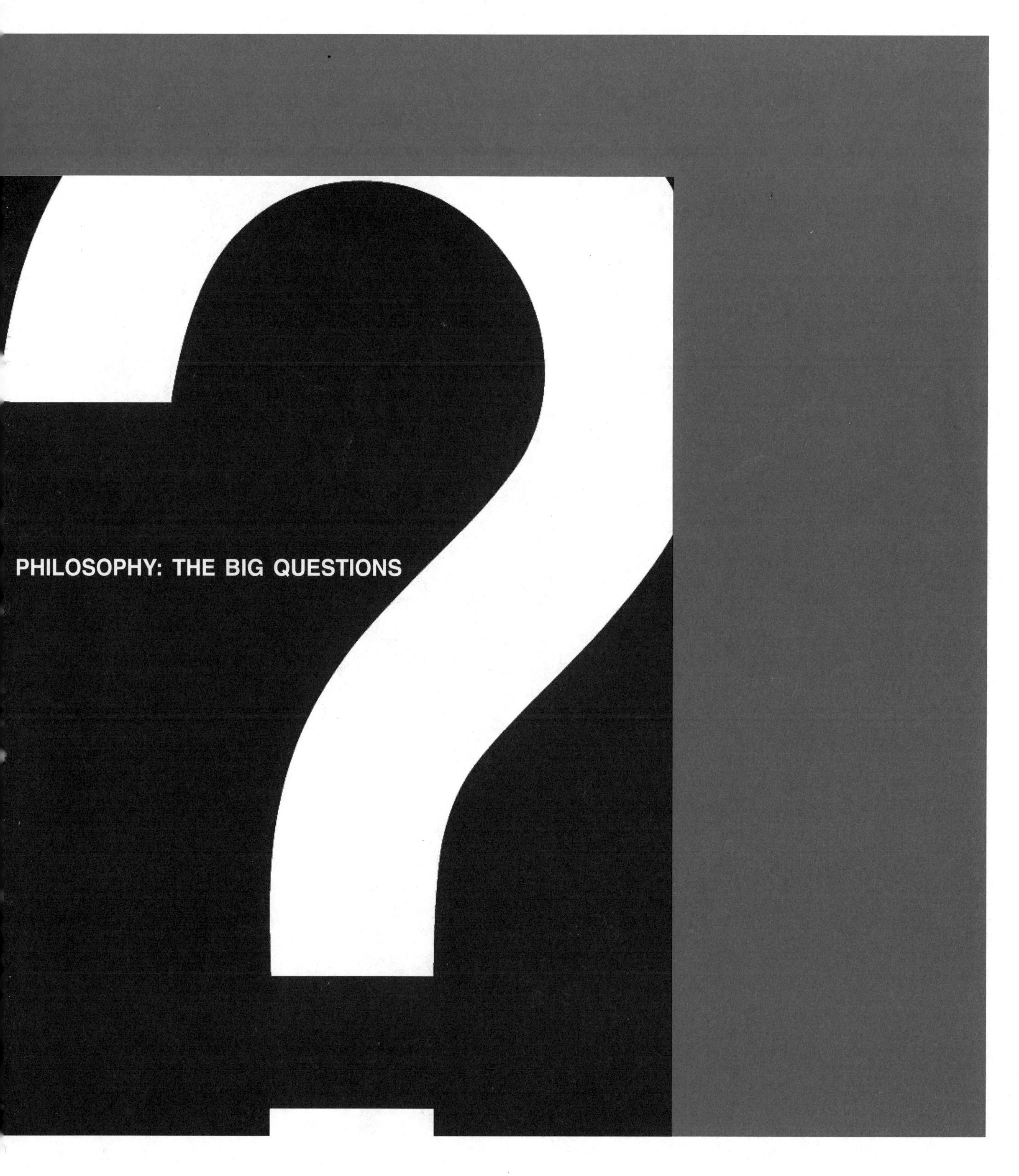
PHILOSOPHY: THE BIG QUESTIONS

PHILOSOPHY: THE BIG QUESTIONS

Frank Cunningham

Daniel Lalonde

David Neelin

Kenneth Peglar

Canadian Scholars' Press Inc. Toronto

Philosophy: The Big Questions
Frank Cunningham, Daniel Lalonde, David Neelin, and Kenneth Peglar

First published in 2003 by
Canadian Scholars' Press Inc.
180 Bloor Street West, Suite 801
Toronto, Ontario
M5S 2V6

www.cspi.org

CSPI gratefully acknowledges financial support for our publishing activities from the Government of Canada through the Book Publishing Industry Development Program (BPIDP) and the Government of Ontario through the Ontario Book Initiative.

National Library of Canada Cataloguing in Publication

Philosophy: the big questions / Daniel Lalonde ... [et al.].

ISBN 978-1-55130-230-0

1. Philosophy—Textbooks I. Lalonde, Daniel

BD21.P46 2003 100 C2003-903230-2

Cover design by George Kirkpatrick
Text design and layout by Brad Horning
Developmental, permissions, and copy editing by James Gladstone

08 09 10 11 12 6 5 4 3 2

Printed and bound in Canada by Marquis Book Printing Inc.

Canada

Table of Contents

The Authors

Daniel Lalonde: Units 1 and 2
Bayridge Secondary School, Kingston, Ontario

Kenneth Peglar: Unit 3
Turner Fenton Secondary School, Brampton, Ontario

David Neelin: Unit 4
East York Collegiate Institute, Toronto, Ontario

Frank Cunningham: Units 5 and 6
Department of Philosophy, University of Toronto

Acknowledgements

The authors would like to thank the editorial staff of Canadian Scholars' Press and the following people for help and advice in the preparation of this book: Andrew Bailey, James Gladstone, David Jopling, Henry Laycock, Alistair Macleod, Amy Mullin, Bob Phillips, Floyd Switzer, Jane Cutler, Kelly Cross, Carolyn La Roche, Kelly Snyder, and Marilyn Wilson.

Prologue

> *"Philosophy begins in wonder."*
>
> Plato

What Is Philosophy?

Philosophy is critical and creative thinking about fundamental questions, such as:

- What is a person?
- What is a meaningful life?
- What is beauty?
- What are good and evil?
- What is a just society?
- What can be known?

These are the six big questions this book will help you think about. If you have ever wondered about them, you are already part philosopher. To become more of a philosopher, skills of critical and creative reasoning are required.

For nearly three thousand years, philosophers in all cultures have applied these skills to the fundamental questions. In this book you will learn how Aristotle, Confucius, Descartes, Sartre, and many others, approached them. You will develop your own reasoning skills as you think about them as well.

> *"Philosophy is the microscope of thought."*
>
> Victor Hugo

Critical Thinking

Critical thinking does not mean just criticizing other peoples' opinions. Philosophers try to give good reasons for their arguments about the fundamental questions and they insist that other people provide sound reasons too. This means:

- carefully defining terms
- expressing yourself in a clear, direct manner
- identifying biases, prejudices, and unsound arguments

- being consistent
- giving reasons that are appropriate to your conclusions

Studying Philosophy

Studying philosophy is more like learning to swim or to ride a bicycle than memorizing periodic tables or studying history. Like swimming or bike riding, philosophy is only learned by *doing* it. Good examples are found in the writings of the ancient Greek philosopher Plato. His ideas were presented as dialogues or conversations among the students of his teacher, Socrates.

These dialogues usually started with Socrates asking a question such as "What do you think makes a society just?" or "What is knowledge?" His companions then suggested various answers and debated each of their merits and weaknesses. They were not professional philosophers but they were learning about important philosophical matters by thinking and talking analytically about them. Socrates' role was to help them by insisting that they define their terms and carefully construct their arguments. To encourage this process, he would sometimes report what previous philosophers had said about these issues. This book will pose many questions and you will be invited to *do* philosophy as you try to answer them.

Theories of the Major Philosophers

Many of the theories of the major philosophers are summarized here. But this is not a history of philosophy. There are many good philosophical histories you can consult, in addition to much useful information that can be found on the Web and in encyclopedias. The theories examined in this text will stimulate your thinking as you build and clarify your own ideas about yourself and your place in the world.

Most of the philosophers referred to are from Europe, starting in ancient Greece about 500 BCE, and include their North American descendents. However, this does not mean that the only major thinkers are from these traditions. In fact, all of the regions of the world have produced important, innovative philosophy, sometimes well in advance of the Europeans. Some of these theorists are described in this book.

Most of the philosophers you will read about in this text are men. As is the case in all too many professions, women have been largely shut out of professional philosophy because of discrimination. That women are the philosophical equals of men is evidenced by that fact that even in ancient times philosophical views of women were recorded. The work of most of the women philosophers discussed in this text dates from the women's liberation movements of the 1970s. Just as these movements paved the way for greater numbers of women to enter law, medicine, politics, and business, so they broke down the barriers in professional philosophy. In philosophy departments in Canadian universities today, it is not unusual to find that over half the majors are women.

Philosophy Expectations

This text addresses the following questions in six units: What is a person? What is a meaningful life? How do you know what is beautiful in visual art, music, and literature? What are good and evil? What is a just society? What is human knowledge?

By the end of each unit, you will meet certain expectations in each of five categories:

- the basics of each philosophical question
- theories advanced by some famous philosophers
- application of philosophy to everyday life
- application of philosophy to other subjects studied in school
- the reasoning, research, and communication skills necessary for philosophical study

Philosophical Questions

Expectations

- compare two or more answers to some of the big questions of philosophy
- give appropriate reasons for your own or others' answers to some of the big questions of philosophy
- summarize some arguments for and against answers to some of the big questions of philosophy
- describe the strengths and weaknesses of the main arguments used to defend answers to some of the big questions of philosophy

- compare philosophical approaches to some of the big questions with non-philosophical approaches

Philosophical Theories

Expectations

- compare answers to some of the big questions by different philosophers
- describe the differences in approach to some of the big questions of philosophy by some major philosophical schools
- describe important similarities and differences among some of the world's philosophical traditions with regard to some of the big questions

Philosophy and Everyday Life

Expectations

- describe what difference the answers people accept to some of the big questions of philosophy should make to your values, behaviour, and life plans
- describe the strengths and weaknesses of alternative responses to questions of applied philosophy
- apply philosophical skills such as precise writing and critical analysis to solve problems that arise in jobs and occupations

Applications of Philosophy to Other Subjects

Expectations

- identify philosophical positions presupposed in some other disciplines
- contrast alternative philosophical viewpoints in controversies discussed in other subjects
- identify examples of fallacies in reasoning in writings from other subjects

Research and Inquiry Skills

Expectations

Using Reasoning Skills

- correctly use the terminology of philosophical argumentation
- define terms central to philosophical discussions of each of the big questions
- identify the main conclusions of some philosophical positions regarding some of the big questions, and the arguments used to support them
- illustrate common fallacies in reasoning

Using Research Skills

- find overviews of a variety of philosophical concepts and theories by accessing such sources as encyclopedias and surveys, and report on their findings
- compile information related to the big questions of philosophy, using the Internet

Using Communication Skills

- discuss your own views in philosophical exchanges in class with others
- clearly explain your views and display use of philosophical reasoning skills in short written papers, using accepted forms of documentation as required

Philosophy's Dangers and How to Avoid Them

Critical thinking about fundamental questions carries dangers with it. Analysis taken to an extreme turns into empty word games and hair-splitting. To avoid this danger remember that critical thinking skills are not ends in themselves, but tools of inquiry. You will use them to build arguments about the questions posed in this text, and to evaluate the positions of others. It is also important that you respect others when they produce good reasons especially when you disagree with their conclusions.

Raising fundamental questions about the meaning of life or good and evil can be a frustrating and disturbing experience. The best way to prevent philosophical anxiety is to keep an open mind.

The authors of this book have been thinking about philosophy and teaching it to high school students like you for many years. Their own views have developed and changed throughout their lives. It is likely that the same will be true for you. By realizing that your philosophical theories are subject to improvement and to change, you will avoid the frustration caused by not being able to find an answer that you need, or the anxious feeling that there is no escape from a conclusion you do not like.

Remember: the point of it all is that you will be *doing* philosophy. We hope that you find it challenging, useful—and fun!

Unit 1

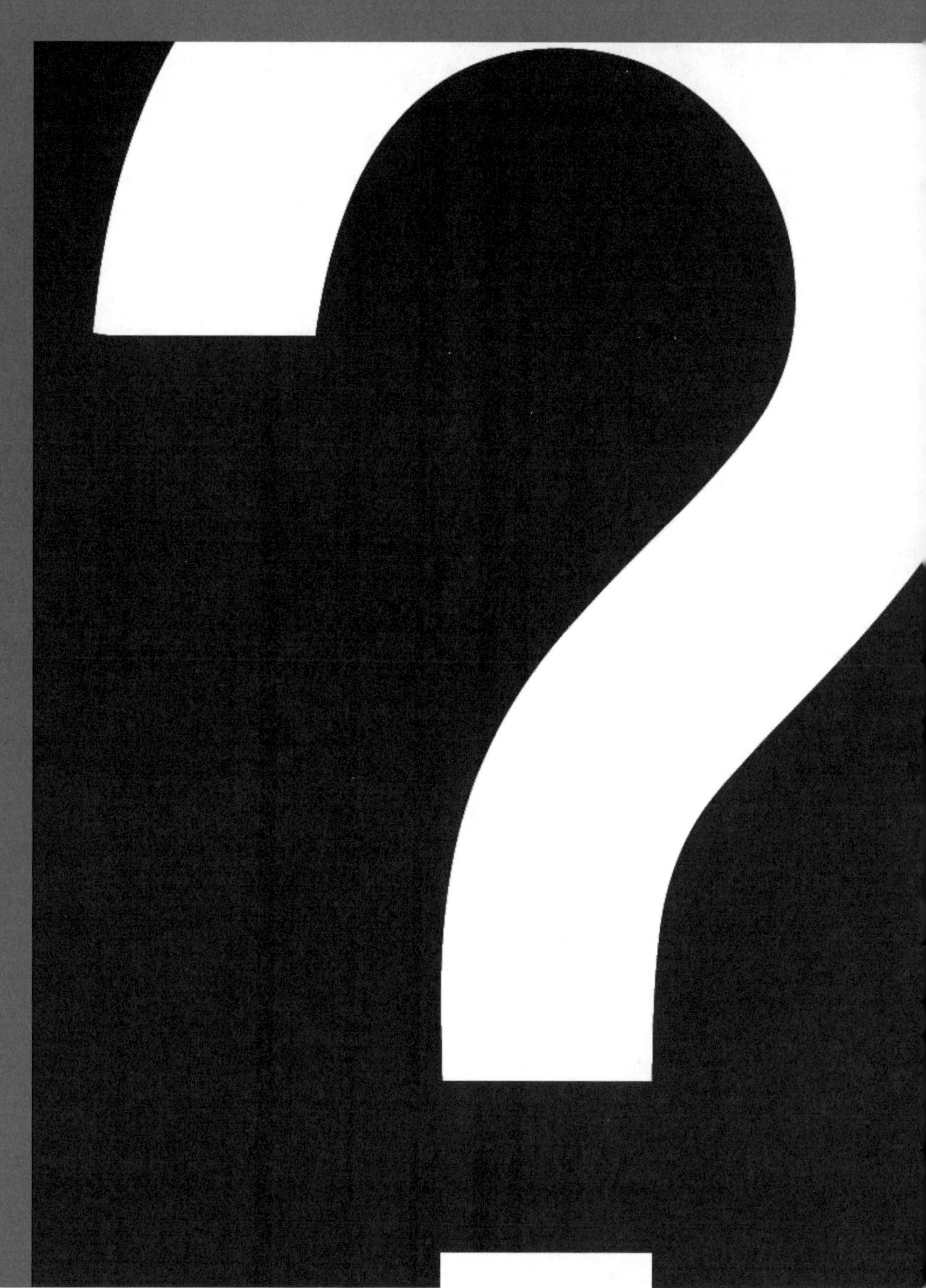

What Is a Person?

The question "What is a person?" does not have as simple an answer as you may think. For centuries, philosophers have grappled with this question only to discover that it raises many more difficult questions. For example, how does your brain, your body, your mind, or your soul play a part in who you are? Are you essentially a physical creature? Are you essentially a thinking thing, a mind? Are you free, or do forces and influences beyond your control determine you? In your life, you have a variety of experiences. If you forget some of these experiences, does that change who you are? What is the most important part of you? Is it the way you feel, the things you do, or the way you look?

Philosophers have also raised questions about whether non-human beings might be considered persons. Think about animals, for example. If animals have feelings and thoughts, and the ability to communicate, does that qualify them as persons? Take computers as another example. If computers play chess, solve complex mathematical problems, and help fly rocket ships, is this a sign that they are thinking? Is thinking sufficient to qualify machines as persons? When (and if) this happens, will it make a difference to what is labelled a person? Will the floodgates then be opened to include all animals and all machines as persons? In Chapters 1–3, you will explore and challenge the answers that some philosophers have given to these questions, while also being encouraged to develop your own answers.

Chapter 1 What Is Human Nature?

Key Words

Nature
Soul
Dualism
Mind
Existentialism

Key People

Plato
Thomas Hobbes
Gilbert Ryle
Albert Camus
Jean-Paul Sartre
Georg W.F. Hegel

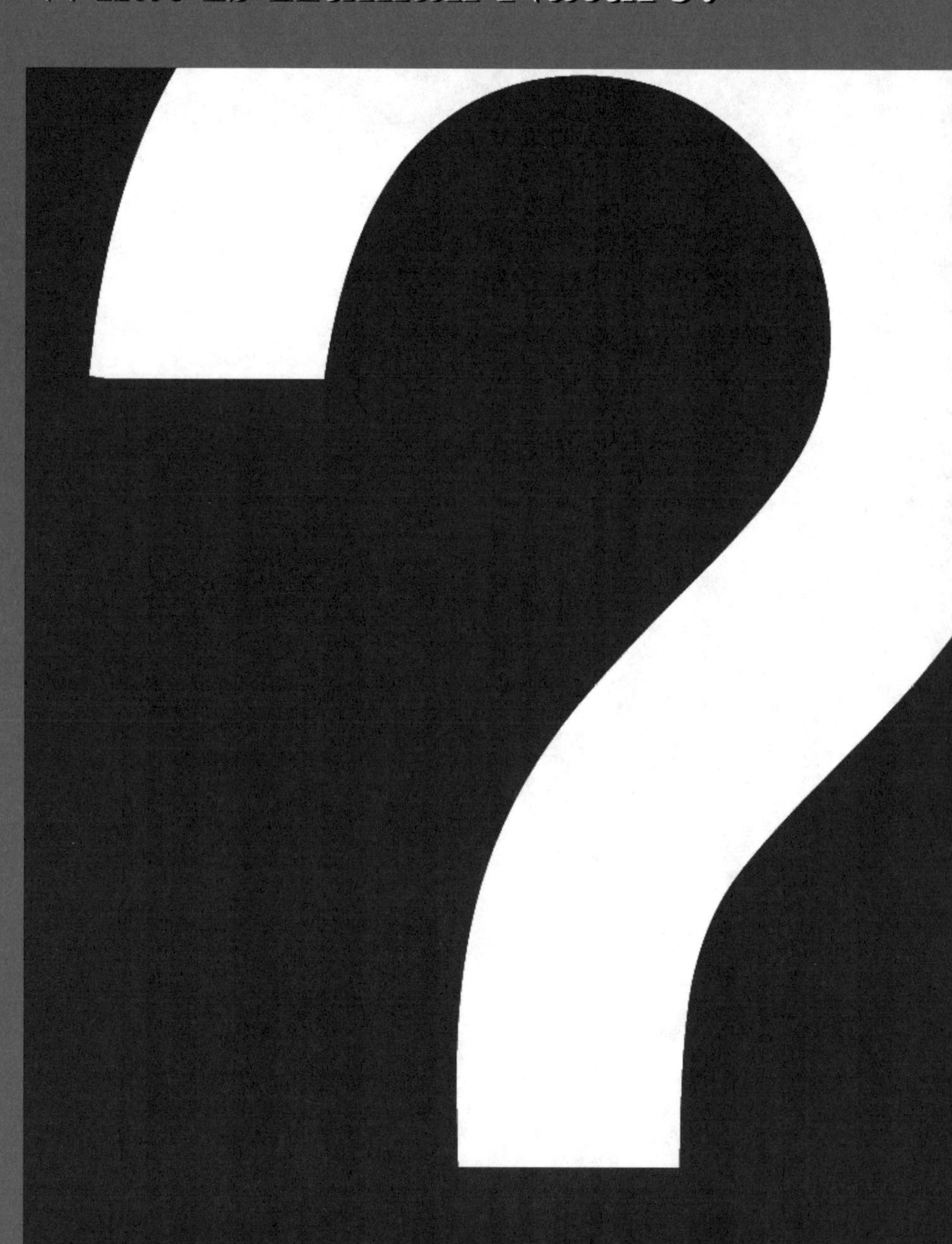

What makes you who you are? What are the features that define your human nature?

What Is Your Nature?

One of the philosophical questions you may ask about life and the universe is "Who am I?" By the time you can articulate this question, you have probably come to understand a few things about yourself. You know, for example, that you are different from rocks, tables, and other people. You probably understand some of the many features that are unique to being human. As a human being, you walk upright, live in family groupings, and probably appreciate laughter and the use of language. But, as you grow in wisdom and knowledge, you may be searching to understand, more precisely, exactly who you are—what is your nature as a human being?

Discussion about human nature can go in several directions. There is, for example, individual nature. This refers to certain exceptional talents that you may have, personality traits, or moral characteristics. Your individual nature usually refers to a collection of strictly human abilities, including such things as the ability to write or play sports. Such a description of your individual nature accounts for the degree or measure to which you possess such skills, talents, or characteristics.

However, there is a distinction between your nature as an individual, and human nature in general. Human nature refers to a general set of distinguishing features that belong to all human beings, regardless of where, when, and how they live. These features—if there are any at all—serve to distinguish human beings from all other beings. You will investigate the character of human nature in this chapter.

What Does the Word *Nature* Mean?

Sometimes the same word means different things depending on how it is used. The word **nature** is found in discussions about things as diverse as blue skies, plants, minerals, and foods. Nature may also refer to genes, and the stuff of which a thing is made. If furniture is made of wood, it may be advertised as all-natural. If someone takes piano lessons, or is learning to play baseball and quickly becomes very good, this person may be described as a natural. So, depending on the context, nature may refer to something external, such as how fruit is grown, or to something internal, such as your genes or soul. Further, nature may refer to the potential you have to become this or that type of person.

You may also say that there are features that are in the nature of a thing. For example, think of a bear that has the potential to hunt and hibernate, or a seed that has the potential to grow into a yellow flower. You may say that these features are typical of the bear and the seed. Likewise, there may be many features typical of humans—that is, things that are in their nature. Walking upright, or the use of tools are two features that may be part of human nature. Many philosophers have also claimed that rationality is a central feature of human nature.

In defining human nature, you may also ask what human nature is *not*. For example, flying is something that does not come naturally to humans. Many humans yearn to fly, but the human body is incapable of flight. Can you think of other features that are not part of human nature? What about killing? Sometimes, people kill other people in war, self-defence, or with criminal intent. Is killing a distinctive feature of human beings' nature, or is it something that is at odds with human nature?

Are There Good and Evil Natures?

Should criminals be punished or reformed? Can a criminal be "cured" of his or her criminal tendencies? Do criminals have a criminal nature that is an unchangeable part of them?

A prominent distinction in philosophy is the contrast between good and evil. You have probably noticed that some people perform good actions, and some people perform evil actions. For example, Paul Bernardo tortured and killed two high school girls in Southern Ontario in the early 1990s. Most people would agree that what Bernardo did was evil. The same could be said about the group of men who destroyed the World Trade Center and part of the Pentagon in Washington, D.C. in September of 2001—acts that took the lives of several thousand people.

There are also people who perform acts that help others. For example, from 1985 to 1987, Canadian Rick Hansen propelled himself around the world in his wheelchair to raise money for spinal cord injury research. Hansen continues to raise money for research, while Bernardo is in prison because of what he did. What motivated these individuals to their actions? Is there

POINT OF VIEW

Thomas Hobbes

Thomas Hobbes (1588–1679) was an English philosopher who believed that humans are born self-interested, only looking out for themselves. In his book *Leviathan*, Hobbes described human life in the state of nature as "solitary, poor, nasty, brutish, and short." By this he meant that, in the absence of a state and a strong political authority capable of maintaining law and order, the members of society, being purely self-interested, would find themselves in a constant state of war with one another. In such circumstances, humans would not be able to lead civilized lives. Moreover, humans would be prevented from protecting even the most basic of their interests. Realizing this, people agree to submit themselves to the authority of a state. Some modern-day followers of Hobbes, such as the Canadian philosopher David Gauthier (born 1932), think that self-preservation also leads naturally self-interested people to support moral education.

something in human nature that makes people do good or evil things? Is human nature inherently good or evil?

What Is Conscience?

You may have seen cartoon versions of the idea of conscience—an angel on one shoulder, a devil on the other. This is a scene common in animation, but also a popular theme in movies. Characters often state that they had to listen to their conscience before making an important decision. The idea of a conscience is prominent in Western culture.

If conscience plays a part in human nature, then what is it, this voice in your head? Conscience may be a function of the mind—a moral barometer. Perhaps a person's mind gauges each action or each possible action the person may commit. The mind then gauges if the action is good or bad, giving the person a good or bad feeling, which may influence whether the person commits the act. In this sense, maybe conscience is just another word for common sense—or reasonable thinking. Alternatively, conscience may be a type of survival instinct, in the same way that an animal could be said to sense danger. Maybe conscience is an automatic way your body looks out for its best interest. But is conscience part of human nature—something with which all people are born?

POINT OF VIEW

Bertrand Russell (1872–1970)

Bertrand Russell points out one problem with conscience: it cannot be trusted. One person will say that his conscience tells him to go to war, while another person's conscience tells her to condemn war. Conscience seems to be responsible for opposite positions. According to Russell, this confusion casts doubt on the reliability of conscience.

For Russell, conscience is related to learned behaviour and is probably not an internal function of human nature. For example, conscience is simply the training in "right" and "wrong" children receive from teachers and parents. You may forget that a teacher told you not to fight, but those feelings may stay with you throughout your life. If you were called to fight in a war, feelings of guilt you may have had while being reprimanded for fighting as a child may cause you to protest that aggression as bad.

If human nature is to help people make decisions about how to live, Russell believed that you can do better than following the unscientific feelings of conscience.

Is Your Nature Defined by Soul?

Perhaps the good and bad feelings that are associated with conscience are really a function of something bigger, like a soul. Some people think that who you are—your nature—is a function of **soul**. The ancient Greek philosopher Plato (427–347 BCE) believed that the soul is what animates the body. He claimed that when a person dies the corpse is not referred to as a person. Rather, the person is spoken of as being "gone." For Plato, soul is a nonmaterial life force, the centre of all that is a person.

The soul is of the nature of the unchangeable,
the body of the changing;
the soul rules,
the body serves;
the soul is in the likeness of the divine,
the body of the mortal.

From Plato's dialogue *Phaedo*

Plato described human nature from a dualistic point of view. **Dualism** is the view that humans are made of two parts: a body and a soul (or mind). Plato believed that the soul is not made of a physical substance, but nonetheless, it is indestructible. The soul exists before birth and continues after the body's death.

Plato further divided the soul into three parts: Appetite, Spirit, and Reason. Appetite is that part of you that desires, lusts, and hungers. At the scene of a car accident, your Appetite may direct you to look at the carnage. According to Plato, your Spirit is that part of your soul that directs you to turn away in disgust or to offer help to the victims. Your Reason is that part of soul that engages in thought, deliberates, and makes judgements and difficult decisions. It is Reason that would organize a rescue operation. Plato thought that the best type of human is guided mostly by Reason.

Plato thought that just as there are three divisions of the soul, so, too, there are three types of people in the world: those whose nature is governed by lusts and desires (Appetite), those who live seeking honour and prestige (Spirit), and those who seek education and wisdom (Reason). Each type of person is guided primarily by one or another division of their soul.

Many people of faith believe that the soul is God-given and immortal, and the single most defining feature of human nature. Like Plato, they believe that the soul is the non-physical centre of a person, linked only for a short time with the physical body.

Why Is Soul Problematic?

As is the case with conscience, any discussion about the soul presents interesting problems. If the soul is not a physical thing, such as the brain, can it be found? If the soul is beyond perception, how can you learn what it does? Such questions are interesting, but if the answers are not obvious, you may wonder whether there is a problem with the questions themselves. It may not be possible to find a plausible and cogent answer to the question of whether or not humans have a soul—an answer, that is, that clarifies how human nature ought to be conceived. If this is the case, you may conclude that the view that humans have souls—an invisible and mysterious entity within each person—is deeply problematic.

PHILOSOPHY IN SCIENCE

Where Is the Soul?

Do humans have souls? If yes, where is the soul located, and how is it found? Dr. Wilder Penfield (1891–1976) wanted to answer this question. Penfield was American born, but lived and worked for most of his life in Montreal, Quebec. Penfield spent his life studying the brain and brain functions. He was fascinated by questions about the soul that were addressed by philosophers such as Plato.

Penfield was interested in proving that the soul is not just reducible to brain activity. He wanted to show that the soul is a special kind of "thing" within people. Penfield discovered that by touching various areas on the surface of the brain with a mild electric stimulant, patients (who were *awake* for the operation!) would respond in remarkable ways. Touching one area could elicit a memory of dancing in the kitchen of a childhood home. Touch another area and the patient might remember the smell of burnt toast. Using an electrode, Penfield found evidence of memories encoded on the surface of the brain. However, he was never satisfied that he had found anything resembling a soul hiding in the brain tissue of his patients. He concluded that the soul must be something nonmaterial.

> *I never witness this heroism [of a patient undergoing brain surgery] without a fresh admiration for the stuff that makes a human being. It is the spirit that ennobles him or her for a lifetime. The combined mechanisms of brain and body, matchless though they be, are nothing without the spirit.*
>
> Wilder Penfield

Care should be taken when you discuss the relationship between the soul and human nature. Humans engage in a variety of activities. These activities could be sorted into a variety of categories of the type described by Plato (Appetite, Spirit, Reason). If soul is thought of in this way, as defined by the variety of activities people pursue, then much of the mystery about the soul is removed. On the other hand, the view that the soul is a mysterious

RESEARCH AND INQUIRY SKILLS

Compiling Information and Using the Internet

When Dr. Wilder Penfield retired from medicine, he began writing books. To write these books, he relied heavily on the information he had gathered over years of researching brain injury and neurobiology. When *you* write, you must begin by doing research and compiling information to make the point you want to make. People compile information on a regular basis and for a variety of reasons. Before going to a movie theatre, you would typically compile information about what movies are playing, which of your friends can come with you, and what time the movie starts.

Though most books, magazines, and Web sites present interesting ideas, not all sources work well for philosophy. Just as there is a difference between a comic book and a novel, sources in philosophy have particular qualities. In your research, you should look for sources that are both reputable and clearly written.

Reputable sources include those that are sponsored or supported by a good publisher, university, or by some other well-established institution. Personal opinion pieces, such as letters to the editor or personal Web pages, sometimes contain factual errors, or express unfair, biased, or prejudiced views.

Practising Your Skills

Using the Internet, write a short biography on the life and work of one of the philosophers mentioned in this chapter.

Be sure to include:

- birth and death dates and places
- the title of a book written by your philosopher
- an interesting event from his or her life
- one way in which he or she has influenced someone else, society, or philosophy in general
- comment on one or more aspects of his or her philosophy

nonmaterial thing that is attached to your body during the time you are alive, and which continues to exist after the death of your body, is much more difficult to defend. Plato's description of the soul as an immortal thing within people is an example of this problematic view.

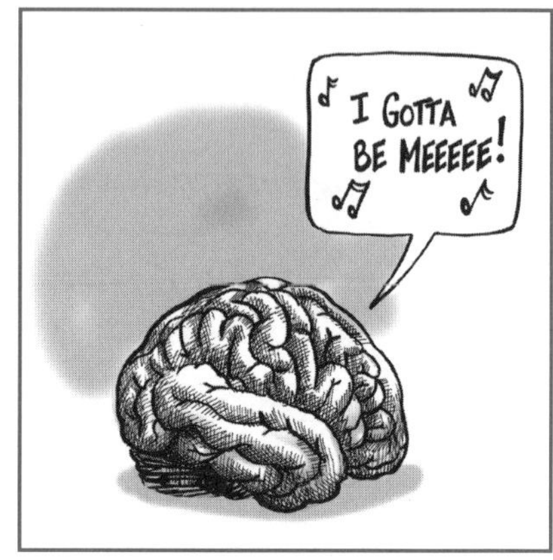

What Is the Mind's Role?

What role does the mind play in defining human nature? When you flex your bicep or bend your leg, something physical happens. Responding to a signal, muscles and tissue change their position. That signal comes from your brain. Think of the last time you changed your mind. Changing your mind is different from flexing a muscle. Like many other things you can do with your body, flexing is an activity of a particular type—namely a physical activity. What type of activity is "changing your mind," thinking, imagining, or even daydreaming?

Many philosophers take the view that the **mind** is the most distinctive feature of human beings, the one thing that sets them apart from other creatures and objects. Wishing, thinking, remembering, reflecting, and reasoning are all functions of the mind: they are sometimes called mental states, or mental events. One way of specifying the relationship between the mind and human nature is to say that it is the non-physical aspects of humans—the mental aspects—that are most crucial to human nature. The problem with this view is that it suggests that human nature can only be expressed by the activities of the mind. Yet, many physical activities also seem to express human nature. If you were to consider only mentality as the key feature of human nature, how would you account for the mainly physical relationship you have with the world outside of your mind?

Mind Is Not a Thing

Remember that dualists think of mind and body as separate things. The British philosopher Gilbert Ryle (1900–1976) claimed that it is a mistake to think of mind as a thing, just as we think of bodies as things. A body has dimensions, such as height and width, so it is safe to assume that the body is

WEB CONNECTION

Mind and Soul

Go to the *Internet Encyclopedia of Philosophy* (www.iep.utm.edu) and look up the words *mind* and *soul*. Create a mind map of each term and discuss your findings with others in the class.

THINKING LOGICALLY

Category Mistakes

Ryle maintained that a mistake is made when the mind is referred to as a thing. He called this a "category mistake." When presenting an argument, it is important to sort the claims that are made into proper logical categories. Consider the following analogy. As a child, you may have played a game that involved putting shaped blocks into shaped holes. A round block has to go into a round hole, a square block has to go into a square hole, and so forth. In a similar way, when you are trying to make a point in an argument that embodies claims that belong to different categories, such as "favourite athletes" or "coolest bands," it is important not to try to put square blocks into triangular holes.

Consider a car that is speeding along a racetrack. You can speak of the type of car it is, or its shape or size, but it would be wrong to ask, "Where is the car's speed?" This feature, speed, is inherent in what the car is doing, and not in the car itself. Speaking of speed as a feature of the car itself is to make a category mistake.

Ryle's point is that sometimes mind is spoken of as if it belongs in the same category as body, overlooking the fact that most mental events (thoughts, feelings, memories) differ in significant ways from bodily events. So important are the differences that Ryle thought that mind and body belong to different logical categories. He thought that while the body can be described as a type of thing, the mind should never seriously be thought of as a thing or substance of a special nonmaterial sort. He recognized that there is a common sense tendency to regard mind and body as different things, assignable to the same general category. However, Ryle thought this common sense notion involves a category mistake.

a physical thing. But what dimensions does a mind have? According to Ryle, it is an error to think of the mind as a thing.

Ryle did not deny the existence of minds. He was, of course, well aware that people have thoughts, beliefs, desires, wishes, and so on. But he noted that these states could not exist without a body. For Ryle, human nature is a complex function of the relationship between mentality and physical activity. The mental and the physical are interconnected aspects of human nature.

Is Human Nature Physical?

If genetic makeup determines human nature, then do you think human nature could be improved by genetic engineering?

Philosophers such as Plato thought that human nature received its fullest expression when it was controlled by Reason. The British writer Thomas H. Huxley (1825–1895) thought that beneath the thin veneer of civilized behaviour, human beings are dominated by animal-like desires that constantly strive for satisfaction and pleasure. A similar view to this is reflected in religious beliefs that take humans to be partly evil. For Huxley, human nature is defined by the struggle to conquer the brute within.

Is human nature a function of purely physical features, such as physical shape or genetic composition? Perhaps the genes you were born with help give you your special talents. You may be a great musician and your friend may be a great athlete. Wherever your talent lies, it may be in your nature to exercise it well. How is this use of "nature" different from Huxley's?

Is There Such a Thing as Human Nature?

Most existentialist philosophers hold that there is no human nature or human essence that pre-exists our appearance in the world, just as the blueprint for a building pre-exists the actual building. Human beings are thrown randomly into an indifferent world, without any higher or God-given plan or purpose. Adrift, rootless, and abandoned, human beings must define and choose themselves from the ground up. They are completely—and terrifyingly—free in this project of self-definition. Each human being is free to make him or herself in any way he or she chooses, free to invent values, and free to confront life and death on any terms he or she chooses. Existentialists hold that most people flee this overwhelming freedom, or deny it, or deceive themselves about it.

Existentialist author Albert Camus (1913–1960) wrote about the Greek hero Sisyphus who was condemned to push a rock up a hill for eternity. Sisyphus would spend all day pushing his rock to the top only to watch it roll to the valley below. For Camus, this myth represented the absurdity of life—unending, frustrated tasks with no final meaning. Still, Sisyphus is admired by Camus as an existential hero for not giving up in the face of his challenges, and for giving a meaning to a condition that is intrinsically meaningless.

Do You Choose to Be Responsible?

Many existentialists, including Camus and Jean-Paul Sartre (1905–1980), were also atheists. Atheists do not believe that there is a God or a supreme being who created the world and gave to humans a purpose and a plan for how to live. Some people of faith may argue that, if there is no God, then there are no grounds for morality: anything goes, anything is permissible. Without God, there cannot be objective moral values, and, therefore, there is no reason to be good.

Existentialists have often argued the opposite to people of faith. Being radically free makes it all the more important to live authentically and responsibly. In some circumstances, this may mean choosing to help others and contribute to society. Cowardice lies in committing suicide and avoiding the challenges of defining yourself and your own values without any objective guidelines or God-given blueprints. Existentialists such as Sartre or Camus believe that each person must take full responsibility for his or her existence.

> *Man is condemned to be free; because once thrown into the world, he is responsible for everything he does.*
>
> Jean-Paul Sartre

What if Your Choice Is Limited?

Existentialists believe that each human being must define and choose her or himself, because there is no God or God-given blueprint that defines each human in advance. However, in a variety of obvious and not so obvious ways, social, historical, and cultural forces seem to influence this project of

POINT OF VIEW

Jean-Paul Sartre

Do you believe you should take responsibility for your own life? This was the view of existentialist philosopher Jean-Paul Sartre. Sartre developed this philosophy of personal responsibility during World War II when, for a time, he was imprisoned by the German forces occupying France. A staunch atheist, Sartre argued that the freedom that is the defining feature of human beings is not a matter of doing anything you want, but of living authentically and accepting responsibility for yourself and the choices you make about how to be.

In 1964, Sartre was awarded the Nobel Prize for literature, but he refused to accept it. He claimed that Alfred Nobel (1833–1896), whose estate funds the annual prize, earned his fortune developing dynamite and a variety of explosives. To be true to his anti-war commitments, Sartre would not associate himself with anything that had to do to with war.

© Hulton-Deutsch Collection/CORBIS/ MAGMA

self-definition. For this reason, some philosophers have argued that human nature is highly dependent upon history and culture, and that an individual's identity is shaped by and imbedded within a larger history and a larger cultural system. The German philosopher Georg W.F. Hegel (1770–1831) for instance, held that human nature could not be understood independently of the relationships among human beings, the various groups to which they belong, and the larger historical and social forces that sweep them along the path of history.

What Do You Think?

What is human nature? Some philosophers define human nature in terms of the soul. Do you think the existence of the soul can be proven? Alternatively, some philosophers hold that human nature is a function of history and culture, including education and moral training. Different still, some philosophers think that there is no such thing as human nature, and that it is the inescapable task of each human being to choose how to be. What do you think?

Chapter 2 What Is Personal Identity?

Key Words
Personal identity
Bundle of perceptions
Continuity
Ad hominem
Mind
Memory

Key People
David Hume
Plato
John Locke
Thomas Reid

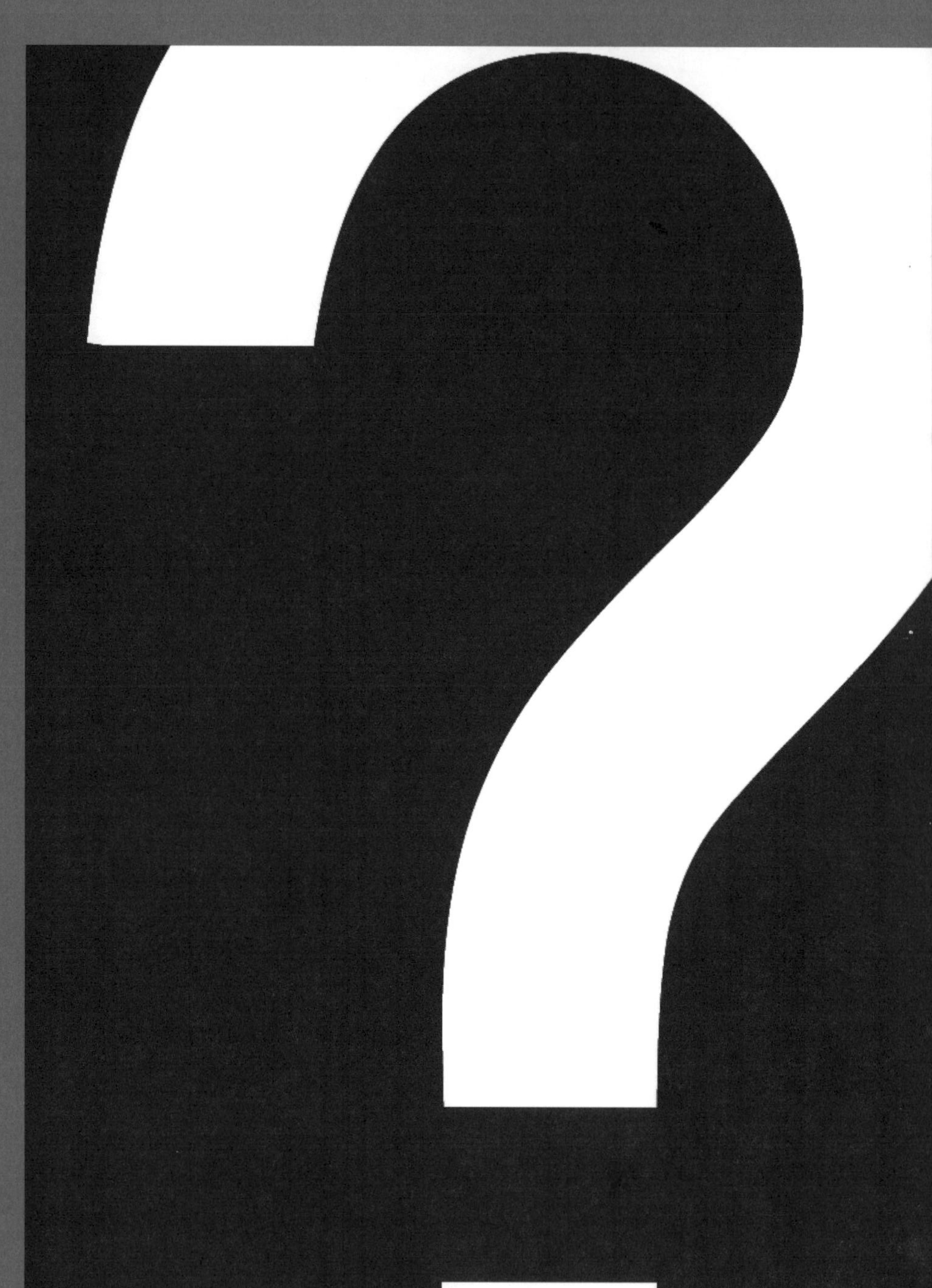

Who Are You?

What makes you distinctly you and not someone else?

Your school has specific features that help you identify the building as your school from one day to the next, and from one year to the next. It is the same with where you live. You have learned the features that identify your school as your school and not an office building. You can also tell the difference between where you live and a grocery store. There are specific identifying features—building blocks—you look for: the colour of the building, the look of the surrounding area, and the name of the road the building is on are all elements you could look for that tell you that you are home.

The philosophical problem of **personal identity** is this: if your physical body, your thoughts, your psychological makeup, and your experiences constantly change over time, then are you one and the same person from one day to the next, one year to the next, and one decade to the next? If so, what is it that makes you the same person over time? If not, then is it better to describe you as a series or number of persons, rather than as one and the same person? Are you today numerically different from yourself of last year in the same way that you are numerically different from your best friend? After all, you and your best friend add up to two distinct people, but do you, too?

Philosophers have had different views on this problem. Some have argued that your identity as a person depends on your physical body and brain remaining the same over time; others believe that it depends on your memories and thoughts; and others think that it depends on your soul. In this chapter, you will explore some of the things philosophers describe as the building blocks that make you the same person over time.

Are You a Bundle of Perceptions?

The Scottish philosopher David Hume (1711–1776) argued that there is no such thing as a unified and substantial self that remains the same over time, and that serves as a kind of anchor for the constantly changing stream of experiences. Hume described the self as a loosely-knit and ever-changing **bundle of perceptions**. There is neither a centre to the bundle, nor a single thread that holds it together and makes it the same from one time to the next. He wrote that the perceptions that make up the self "succeed each other with inconceivable rapidity, and are in a perpetual state of flux and movement."

Is There a Blueprint of You?

Another view is that a person's identity comes from an unchanging blueprint that is independent of changes in your experiences over time. Consider the purpose of a building's blueprint. Before construction workers construct a building, such as a school or a house, they need a blueprint. The blueprint lists what materials to use, the dimensions of the building, where the plumbing and wiring go, and so on. All of the blocks of the building are described in the blueprint. These drawings could be called the *idea* of the building since they exist before the building is built. In fact, long after the building is constructed, the drawings are stored for reference should any repairs to the structure be necessary.

Just as the blueprint is the idea for a building, perhaps there are similar ideas that describe you. Perhaps there is a blueprint (or an idea) that describes you and only you. The blueprint for the CN Tower in Toronto could not be used to build the Peace Tower in Ottawa. Similarly, if there is a blueprint for you, it might only be used to build you and no one else. What do you think your blueprint looks like? What are the ideas that make up your blueprint? And where is the blueprint located?

Do certain things about you stay the same throughout your life? Is it these things that make you the same person from one time to another?

Do You Stay the Same Over Time?

You have considered personal identity in light of Hume's bundle theory, and Plato's theory of Forms. But what if you are constantly changing across your life—changing in physical size and shape, personality, outlooks, beliefs, and opinions? Is there any one thing that stays the same throughout all these

POINT OF VIEW

Plato

© Archivo Iconografico, S.A./CORBIS/ MAGMA

The ancient Greek philosopher Plato (427–347 BCE) believed that every physical object—tables and chairs, for example—has a blueprint or an idea that exists outside of space and time. Plato called these ideas Forms. Although we can think about the Forms, they also exist independently of any mind. Because the Forms are the perfect ideas of every thing that exists in space and time, Plato believed that the Forms are better than the things they describe. For example, a table will eventually fall apart or break. The Form, or perfect idea, of a table will not fall apart. The Form of the table exists in a timeless realm, not subject to change.

Another example of a Form is virtue. While all of us can think about virtue, Plato believed that the Form of virtue exists independently of all minds, and exists whether or not anyone can understand virtue. Plato also believed that there are Forms for concepts such as justice, love, and beauty. As well, Plato thought that there is a Form for a virtuous or perfect person. He did not believe that each person has his or her own blueprint—there is no perfect Form of each individual person. However, like virtue, Plato believed that there must be qualities that apply to what is the Form of a perfect person. What qualities do you think the Form or idea of a perfect person would have?

changes? If so, then what is it? Is there some glue that makes you one and the same person at different times and places? Consider, for example, certain rivers in Africa that are only wet during the rainy season. The rest of the time they are cracked riverbeds. Each year when it rains, a rushing body of water appears. Is it a river when it is dry, or is it just an extension of the land? Must there continue to be water in this place to say that it is the same river? Are there aspects of the river that remain the same in dry and wet seasons?

Take another example. Most baseball fans have a favourite team. Each year, your favourite team trades a number of players. From one year to the next, the only thing that may continue to be the same about the team is a small group of players, the coach, or the owner of the team. So why is it considered to be the same team? Is it the continuity of the team's logo or a particular continuity of certain players? What represents the real identity of the team?

Perhaps the dry African river is still called a river because certain things remain the same—its location, or the fact that year after year, when the water returns, it always flows in the same direction and to the same places. It is similar with your favourite baseball team. Aspects of the team change over time, but other parts remain the same, such as its city of origin, the stadium in which it plays, and the colour of the team's uniforms. **Continuity**, the fact that some things do not change over time, plays a similar role in personal identity. Just as the African river is still a river, whether wet or dry, you continue to live with the same family, have roughly the same colour skin, eyes, and so on. You probably speak at least one language consistently throughout your life. These characteristics, and many others, have continuity. Perhaps it is these that make you one and the same person from one year to the next, and one decade to the next—rather than two or more persons.

> *"You could not step twice into the same river; for other waters are ever flowing on to you."*
>
> Heraclitus

What if There Is No Continuity?

How would your life be different if no aspect of you ever changed?

Some things about you stay the same over time. Other things change. Many physical things about you change, such as how you look and how tall you are. Non-physical things about you also change, such as what you know, how you think, and how you feel. Could enough physical and psychological things change that you have no continuity with your past self at all? The ancient Greek philosopher Heraclitus (c. 500 BCE) described everything as being in a state of flux. But while everything is always changing, the change itself creates harmony. In other words, Heraclitus thought that change was a

PHILOSOPHY IN EVERYDAY LIFE

Is Identity Based on Continuity?

In Central Japan, there is a Shinto temple called the Ise Shrine. Shinto is a Japanese religion, which started as early as 500 BCE. The Ise Shrine was built in about 700 CE. As part of the history and tradition of the Ise Shrine, the building is destroyed every twenty years. In a purification ritual, the shrine is rebuilt with new material. It was last rebuilt in 1993. Through this process the Ise Shrine is perpetually renewed. The Ise Shrine points to many of the issues surrounding personal identity. Is the identity of the Ise Shrine from one incarnation to the next contained within the continuity of the *idea* of the Shrine and what it stands for? Is it one and the same shrine, or is it really a series of different shrines that happen to look like each other and carry the same name?

Is there any building that has great meaning for you? Perhaps you attend a house of worship that holds meaning for you. If the building was torn down and rebuilt, would it still be the same house of worship to you? Would what your house of worship represents remain continuous even though the building had changed?

necessary and useful part of nature. Do you change so often or so fast that you are not the same person from one day to the next? Is there something useful or adaptive about these changes?

Is Identity Based on Your Body?

Probably your first impressions of other people relate to their physical characteristics. Such perceptions may shape your sense of their being the same people over time. To what degree do peoples' physical characteristics make up, or at least contribute to, personal identity?

It has been said that no two people are exactly the same. Even identical twins have some differences. They may have different hairstyles, or a physical feature may be slightly different. One may have a birthmark that the other does not. Think again of the CN Tower and the Peace Tower. There are significant physical differences between these two structures, which is how you can tell them apart. Do your physical features serve to differentiate you

THINKING LOGICALLY

*Personal Attacks (*Ad Hominem*)*

When you are having a heated debate with someone over an issue, it is fairly easy to say something like, "What do you know, you big jerk!" or, "You're just as stupid as you look." Statements about physical appearance, intelligence, or personal attitude have little to do with the issues you are debating. The technical name for such statements is ***ad hominem,*** which is Latin for "to the person." Philosophers agree that such name-calling does not contribute to the argument or serve to clarify the issues.

Name-calling, or making a personal attack, is a fallacy because it leads the conversation away from its central idea. Many focussed conversations are quickly run off course by such personal attacks. An argument about which of your classmates is a better candidate for student council would be quickly confused by a personal attack such as: "Oh yeah? Well, you smell like cheese!" This attack will not help anyone decide who should run for student council. Instead of discussing student council elections, you are provoking someone.

As a philosopher, your responsibility is to identify, illuminate, and eliminate such fallacies wherever you find them. Avoid name-calling and being driven off course by an opponent who resorts to name-calling when they begin losing an argument.

from others? Just as physical characteristics make a building unique, perhaps it is your physical characteristics that make you unique.

Throughout your life, your body is changing. As it changes, do you become a different person? Imagine you awoke tomorrow to find that you had grown 30 centimetres taller, your skin had changed colour, and you now appeared to be 30 years older. What effect would such sudden changes have on you? Are you now numerically one and the same as the person who went to sleep last night, or are you numerically different? Do you and he (or she) add up to two people, or to one?

Is It What's Inside that Counts?

Questions have been raised about how changes to your external appearance may affect your identity over time, but what about changes to the inside of your body? Think about all the changes that surgery can bring about: heart transplants, hip replacements, and artificial limbs. How many parts could be changed inside you before you should be considered a different person?

Consider the following imaginary scenario (what philosophers call a thought experiment, a kind of game with concepts). During a transplant operation, 50 percent of your brain is replaced with 50 percent of the brain of another person. Is the person who wakes up after the operation you, or another person? Suppose it is half a pirate's brain that is transplanted into your body. Is the patient who wakes up after surgery you, or the pirate? What if 100 percent of the pirate's brain were transplanted into your body? Who would wake up then? What if 30 percent were transplanted?

Now consider another thought experiment. Instead of removing your brain, surgeons perform a "mind swipe"—that is, they erase all your memories, thoughts, beliefs, and psychological characteristics. For a brief period you are a complete mental blank, but your body and brain are still intact. The surgeons then install (or download) all the memories, thoughts, beliefs, and attitudes of a pirate from the seventeenth century. Who awakes from this amazing medical procedure? You, or the pirate?

Finally, consider this imaginary scenario. Scientists invent an amazing machine called the Replicator. When you step inside it and push the On button, the machine scans every single molecule in your body and brain, and then stores the information in its memory banks. It has a complete informational blueprint of you. When you push the Go button, the machine draws on this blueprint to manufacture a body (and brain) that is identical to yours: your own personal clone, identical in every way, right down to the smallest freckle. Your clone even has your memories, attitudes, and plans. Now suppose that you learn that you, but not your clone, are about to die in the next week. Should you be worried? Should you fear what is about to happen? After all, your clone will carry on with your plans, will have the same memories that you have, and will have all the same friends. Is what happens next week the end of you, or are you simply continuing in another person who is qualitatively identical to you?

Would You Want to Be Cloned?

If humans could be cloned, would you want to be cloned for more than spare body parts? Would you want your clone to take over all your plans and projects, and keep up with all your friendships, if you were to die?

Would you fear dying any less if you knew your clone would take over when you died?

Many philosophers are concerned with whether or not humans should even consider cloning themselves. Some philosophers wonder if clones would be treated differently from their originals. Would clones enjoy the same rights and privileges of their originals? Some suggest that cloning is like playing God. They say that scientists should let nature run its course rather than engineering clones.

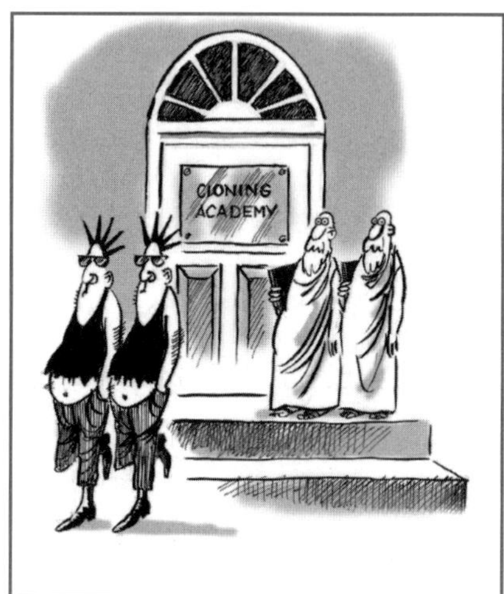

Does Identity Come from Your Mind, Memories, or Experiences?

As you reflect on the problem of personal identity, you may think that you have many more building blocks inside of you than you have on the outside. Consider some things that go on inside of you: thoughts, memories, and experiences. Is personal identity related less to physical properties and more to how your mind or memory works, or to what experiences you have?

Does Identity Reside in Mind or Soul?

Do you think it is possible to have a dream so vivid that you mistake it for something that really happened to you? Is it possible that experiences, such as vivid dreams, change or shape your sense of self? How?

WEB CONNECTION

The Cloning Debate

Should humans be cloned? Use a search engine to find sites related to cloning. Read about and compile different points of view, then decide for yourself.

There are many words used to describe the part of you that animates your body. These include mind, spirit, soul, or life force. These words are also used to describe the place where thoughts, decisions, and feelings occur. Perhaps there is a place inside of you—someplace other than in your brain—where the real you resides. What role does the mind or soul have in explaining personal identity? Some philosophers argue that without that part of you that animates your body, or gives you an ability to perceive the world, you might never be the same person from one minute to the next, and one year to the next.

> *"Give me a dozen, healthy infants, well-formed, and my own specified world to bring them up in, and I'll guarantee to take any one at random and train him to become any type of specialist I might select—doctor, lawyer, artist, merchant-chief and, yes, even beggar-man and thief, regardless of his talents, penchants, tendencies, activities, vocations, and race of his ancestors."*
>
> John B. Watson

PHILOSOPHY IN PSYCHOLOGY

Can You Shape the Self?

John B. Watson (1878–1958), a behaviourist psychologist, claimed that he could shape a person's character, temperament, and sense of self. He claimed that by controlling what types of experiences a child had, he could produce a doctor, lawyer, a beggar, or a thief. He said that the self was not a function of mind or body, but a function of learning and behavioural conditioning. Consider, for example, how different you would be if you were living in Argentina, or raised in Thailand? How different would you be if you were not able to attend school? How do education, environment, and family influence these characteristics? If you have children at some time in your life, do you think the choices you make may influence your children's character and temperament?

How Does Memory Affect Identity?

> *"As far as this consciousness can be extended backwards to any past action or thought, so far reaches the identity of the person."*
>
> John Locke

Most people have fairly clear memories of childhood, of yesterday, or of last week. Your thoughts, feelings, and actions happen in the present and are stored in your memory for later reference. Have you ever wondered what is the purpose of **memory**? Why do you remember the fact that you fell off your bike and cut your knee when you were four, or the fact that you moved to a new house when you were seven? One philosopher, John Locke (1632–1704), was convinced that continuous consciousness was the main building block of personal identity. There are several components to this concept of continuous consciousness: remembering your past is just one. Locke suggested that if you can extend your present consciousness backwards to past events and actions, and in doing so feel concern for those past events and actions, think that they are your own, attribute them to yourself, and take responsibility for them, then you are the same person today that you were yesterday. A continuous consciousness is what keeps you connected to you in the past. So, over time, even though other things about you change, such as your physical body, you are one and the same person.

You probably remember generally what happened yesterday, but you may have trouble remembering all of the details. You may have trouble remembering anything from before you were about four years old. What does it mean when you forget? Imagine that the only knowledge you have of your third birthday party is that, in the family album, there is a picture that looks like you sitting beside a birthday cake. Locke was aware that people forget, misremember, and sometimes suffer from amnesia. According to his theory, if there is a sharp enough break in your consciousness, so that you simply cannot extend your present consciousness backwards to certain past events, and you cannot feel concern for those events, attribute them to yourself, or take responsibility for them, then those events cannot be counted as yours. The youngster in the picture may look like you, but you and he are two distinct persons, if these conditions hold.

POINT OF VIEW

Thomas Reid

Locke's theory of personal identity relies on the concept of continuing consciousness, which is a concept involving many parts. Thomas Reid (1710–1796) interpreted Locke's concept of continuing consciousness somewhat narrowly as being mainly about memory. He criticized Locke's theory and suggested that memory cannot be the main building block of personal identity. Reid proposed the "gallant officer objection" to make his point. Imagine there is a boy, Joseph, who gets into trouble for stealing apples. Some years later, Joseph saves a fellow soldier in a battle. In old age, Joseph becomes a decorated army general. Now imagine that Joseph the soldier can remember Joseph the apple stealer. Reid says that according to Locke, these two Josephs must be the same. The general can remember Joseph the soldier, so the general and the soldier are also the same.

What if Joseph the army general cannot remember Joseph the apple stealer? Reid points out this problem: since there are memories that connect Joseph the soldier to both the apple stealer and the general, all three must be the same Joseph. However, according to Reid's interpretation of Locke's theory, the general and the boy cannot be the same. Reid argues that this is illogical and that it must be something other than comprehensive memory that accounts for personal identity. Reid's objection suggests that, to be the same person at different times, some amount of forgetting may be acceptable. However, in the same way that Joseph the soldier connects to both the apple stealer and the general, you need some thread of memory to be considered the same person from age 8 to age 80. Locke would respond to Reid's objection by pointing out that Reid interpreted the concept of continuous consciousness too narrowly (as involving only memories), but omitted many of its other important features.

What If You Forget Everything?

Reid's objection to Locke's theory was based on the claim (which Locke in fact accepted without reservation) that everyone forgets certain things throughout their lives. But what if you forgot everything, as in cases of profound amnesia? According to Locke, the person who wakes up one morning without *any* memory of his or her past life—and also without any ability to attribute certain past actions and events to him or herself, or any feeling of concern for those past actions, and without any feeling of responsibility for them—is not the same person who went to sleep the night before. There are two distinct persons here, despite the fact that they share the same continuing physical body. There are two distinct and incommunicable consciousnesses: the person whose history leads up to the onset of amnesia, and the person whose history continues from the moment amnesia sets in.

What Do You Think?

Do you think that personal identity depends on just one feature of you, or many features? Perhaps what makes you the same across time is dependent on a set of ideas or a blueprint. Or perhaps personal identity is a function of your environment, life experiences, or memory. Or perhaps you change so much over time that there is no lasting set of features that makes you the same person from one moment to the next, or one year to the next.

Chapter 3 If It Thinks, Is It A Person?

Key Words

Thinking
Self-aware
Person
Particular interest
Dumb brutes
Artificial intelligence

Key People

René Descartes
John Locke
Judith Jarvis Thomson
Michael Tooley
Alan Turing

What Makes A Human Being A Person?

Do you believe that you are a person simply because you think?

A Canadian dollar has many features: it is a metal coin, it is round, and it has words embossed on it. One of the more significant features of a dollar is that it enables you to buy things. A person also has distinguishing features. Some of these features were reviewed when various questions about personal identity and human nature were discussed in Chapters 1 and 2. These features and the questions they raise are probably not the kinds of things you think about every day. One thing, though, is certain—you *do* think every day. Some philosophers believe that thinking is the feature that makes a human being a person.

Keep in mind that, as a human being, you are a biological creature. You have a variety of biological features that relate to being human. Is thinking the feature that, all on its own, makes a human being a person? If this were true, then could other things, such as animals and computers, also qualify as thinking things? Would these other thinking things also qualify as persons? These are questions you will explore in this chapter.

What Is Thinking?

What would you include on a list of things that count as "thinking"? What things would you leave off such a list? Why?

Having clear definitions of the terms you use is one important feature of good philosophy. For example, the word **thinking** can mean many different things. Thinking may relate to remembering facts. You could also say that you are thinking when you are deciding whether a statement is true or false. Like running, or singing, thinking is something you do. It is an activity of a particular type. Running and singing are physical activities. Would you say the same about thinking?

Thinking may also refer to the ability to process complex information, such as adding a series of numbers. Statements about intelligence, wisdom, or being smart may also be included in a definition of thinking. As well as being an activity, thinking could be described as a particular ability—the power of thought. The point is that there is a common way in which the term "thinking" is used that is quite broad and refers to many different types of mental processes.

René Descartes and John Locke

French philosopher René Descartes (1596–1650) and English philosopher John Locke had many views about what thinking is. Descartes wrote, "I think, therefore, I am." Descartes meant that, if nothing else, he knew he existed and that he was a thinking thing—he was **self-aware**. Descartes included several forms of thinking in his definition: doubting, willing, imagining, and feeling.

> *"To be conscious that we are perceiving or thinking is to be conscious of our own existence"*
>
> Aristotle

Locke added different types of thinking activities to his definition, such as reasoning, reflecting, and remembering. Are there other types of thinking that you might add to a definition of thinking?

Beyond definitions of thinking, both Locke and Descartes believed that thinking is what makes human beings unlike other living things. They believed that only humans engage in the types of activities they called thinking. Thinking, for Descartes and Locke, makes a human being a **person**. For them, no other thing—living or non-living—ought to be called a thinking thing or a person.

> *"What am I? A thing which thinks. What is a thing which thinks? It is a thing which doubts, understands, affirms, denies, wills, refuses, which also imagines and feels."*
>
> René Descartes

Defining thinking can take the form of a long list of types of mental activities. How would you relate things such as knowing or intelligence to thinking? How do you use such definitions to help decide who or what does or does not think? Where should the line be drawn between thinking and not thinking? If the power of thought is crucial to being a person, does a definition of thinking help draw the line between persons and non-persons?

Are Some Humans Not Persons?

Do you think a human who is in a coma or unconscious is a person? Why?

If the definition of a thinking thing is limited to beings that are aware of themselves, a problem arises. If a human being in a coma gives every sign of not thinking, should he or she be stripped of the title "person"? According to Descartes' and Locke's definitions of thinking things, it might seem that a human in a coma is not a person. Moreover, all humans spend at least part of the day sleeping. Though dreaming occurs during sleep, dreams are usually disorganized and chaotic, and bear little resemblance to thinking. Some might suggest that sleeping humans are not thinking things. Do human beings lose the right to call themselves persons every night? Do you think it is possible, despite appearances, that people are self-aware, or thinking in some capacity, when they sleep?

Under what conditions could it be said that a sleeping individual is still a person? One consideration may be to emphasize that a person has the *capacity* to think, rather than accepting that a person must always be thinking. A professional ballet dancer is still a dancer when he is eating or sleeping, or engaging in activities other than dancing. If you see the dancer engaged in a non-dancing activity, it would be odd to argue that he is not a dancer just because he is not presently dancing. In a similar way, a sleeper or a coma victim may not be thinking, but perhaps they are still persons because they possess the capacity for thought.

PHILOSOPHY IN EVERYDAY LIFE

Ken Parks: The Sleeping Murderer?

When Ken Parks was six years old he tried to crawl out of his bedroom window. He lived in an apartment six floors from the ground. His mother stopped him just in time by waking him up. As a teenager, Parks would wake up screaming, and often walked around the house in his sleep.

One night, in May of 1987, Ken Parks drove 23 kilometres to the home of his in-laws. There he killed his mother-in-law and seriously injured his father-in-law. He then drove to a police station where he told police that he feared he had just killed someone.

His defence at the 13-day trial was that he was sleepwalking and was not responsible for what he had done. He was acquitted of his crime. He was so convincing at trial that even Parks' wife, the daughter of the victims, believed his story. Parks still does not believe that he killed his mother-in-law, a woman he loved. He is convinced that there was another intruder in the house that night who framed him for the murder and took advantage of the fact that Parks was in the house asleep.

The Supreme Court of Canada acquitted Parks on the basis that he was not fully conscious of what he was doing when the crime was committed. In other words, he killed his mother-in-law when he was not "thinking." Should any "non-thinking" criminal be acquitted?

> *A person is "a thinking intelligent being, that has reason and reflection, and can consider itself as itself, the same thinking thing, in different times and places; which it does only by that consciousness which is inseparable from thinking, and as it seems to me, essential to it."*
>
> John Locke

What Is A Legal Person?

There are other problems with how to view what or who is a person, which have little to do with the issue of thinking. For example, historically, under

POINT OF VIEW

Judith Jarvis Thomson

The American philosopher Judith Jarvis Thomson (born 1929) addresses the contemporary issue of whether an unborn human being—a foetus—is or is not a person. Laws about abortion and the rights of a foetus are contentious issues for debate. Thomson states, "we shall probably have to agree that the foetus has already become a human person well before birth." Thomson suggests that the line between person and non-person should be drawn some time before the birth of a child.

From Thomson's view, you might think that a foetus has "person" rights—specifically, a right to life, as other persons do. However, if a pregnant woman wants to have an abortion, whose right to life is greater, the mother's or the foetus'?

Thomson argues that although a foetus may be considered a person, there are cases when abortion could be permissible. Thomson considers pregnancy due to rape such an instance. On the other hand, she says that "the desire for the child's death is not one which anybody may gratify, should it turn out to be possible to detach the child alive." Her claim is that the right to have an abortion is not a right to kill. If, in some odd circumstance, a foetus survives abortion, no one has the right to kill it. In this sense, the idea of a person's rights seems to rely upon biological aspects of the foetus—its ability or inability to survive on its own, outside of the mother, and not on thinking or consciousness. Thomson's argument is not whether or not a foetus is a person, but rather, a consideration of whose rights should be prioritized in the specific cases of rape or incest.

Where do you draw the line when it comes to deciding when a foetus is a person? Would your decision be based strictly on biology, or would you take into consideration the possibility that the foetus thinks, or its potential to be self-aware after it is born?

the law, the definition of a person sometimes did not depend on thinking at all, but on gender or race. At one time, Canadian women were not allowed to own property. Inherent in such rules was the fact that women were not considered (by men) as rational or as capable as men. Canadian law stipulated that only landowners could vote. For this reason, women were not able to vote until 1918.

POINT OF VIEW

Michael Tooley

The Australian philosopher Michael Tooley (born 1941) goes beyond discussions of whether a foetus is or is not a person—although he claims they are not. He also claims that small children are not persons. For Tooley, a person must have a concept of self that continues over time, as well as a **particular interest** in his or her own continued existence. He claims that children, when they are very young, may have an interest in avoiding pain, but they do not yet understand themselves as existing in the future.

Children (and foetuses) may still have rights, though not as persons, but under some other definition. Young children and foetuses simply do not meet any of the complex capacities that go with being a person. It is simply a mistake to consider humans as persons from the moment of birth, or earlier.

Do Animals Think?

Can you think of a time when you saw an animal, a pet, for example, that appeared to be thinking? Have you ever seen an animal do something that was almost "human"?

Where should the line be drawn between persons and non-persons and between thinking and non-thinking? How many elements of "thinking" must a non-human exhibit to be considered a person? This is a difficult question to answer. However, some arguments for or against the existence of non-human thinkers (and the questions of whether or not they deserve status as "persons") merit some consideration.

Imagine that one morning you hear the newspaper delivery girl ring the bell on her bike as she throws the morning paper onto your lawn. By your side, your trustworthy dog Jake lifts an ear and bolts out the front door. He retrieves the paper and drops it at your feet, like always. When Jake responds to the sound of the delivery girl and retrieves your newspaper, or when he responds in a friendly way to you and viciously to a stranger, is this an indication of thinking?

Some philosophers, including Descartes, have thought of animals as **dumb brutes**: "dumb" because of their inability to express themselves in the linguistically complex ways that humans do; "brutes" because animals are typically used for heavy labour, beyond the capacity of human beings. Descartes also described animals as unconscious machines. He argued that because animals are not capable of language or complex problem solving in a variety of situations, they can neither be called thinking things nor persons.

Think of creatures such as snails or sea cucumbers. They may be considered "non-thinkers." However, there are some animals, such as police dogs, who seem to think at least as well as human children. Some of these animals, when trained in an appropriate way, are able to discover concealed drugs, or follow instructions to apprehend a criminal, rescue someone, or even alert a fellow officer to danger. Owls are often described as "wise," foxes as "clever," and snakes as "sly." Are these just empty expressions or have humans observed behaviour in some animals that warrant these labels? Could it be that some animals, such as police dogs, are thinking things?

Michael Tooley argues that there are some adult animals that deserve rights persons because their thinking is at least as complex as—and maybe in some cases more complex than—the thinking of human infants. He points out that some animals seem to have an interest not only in avoiding pain, but in their own future. A bird building a nest, for example, might be seen as planning for the future, thinking ahead. On the other hand, could this type of behaviour be only instinct and not thinking?

Do animals think at all? Certainly, some animals seem to feel and respond to commands. What differences are there between how human beings think and how animals think? For Descartes and Locke, whether or not a human being is a person depends in part on whether or not he or she is considered a thinking thing. Descartes believed that a human being is a person if he or she is always thinking. Locke held thinking in the same esteem, but focused on the capacity for thought rather than whether or not a person is always thinking.

If you apply the narrow definitions of person penned by Descartes or Locke, you could conclude that animals do not meet all of their criteria, and that neither chimpanzees, police dogs, nor sea cucumbers qualify as "thinking things." On the other hand, you could reject what Descartes and Locke imply, and, instead, argue that some animals, such as police dogs, or hunting animals, such as wolves or hawks, are indeed thinking things. Where do you draw the line between animals that are thinking things and those that may be more properly labeled "dumb brutes"? How many elements of your definition of thinking match the behaviour you observe in animals?

There are two questions at hand:

1. Are animals thinking things?
2. Should animals be considered persons?

Though an animal may be called a "thinking thing," there may still be reasons for offering or rejecting some rights or entitlements as a person. If you conclude that the difference between animal and human thinking is minor, should animals be treated as persons? Can you think of some conditions under which animals should be given consideration as persons?

Do Computers Think?

Locke and Descartes were not alive to witness the invention of computers. But do you think that they would believe computers are thinking things?

Computers are a relatively new invention in human history. Their invention has raised some interesting philosophical questions: Are computers thinking things? Do they have the potential to be thinking things? Should they be considered persons? The world's first supercomputer, ENIAC (Electronic Numerical Integrator and Calculator), was built during World War II. It was designed to predict the accuracy of military weapons. When testing missiles, designers had to figure out how far a missile could travel, taking into account wind speed, air pressure, terrain, and other factors. These complex calculations involve so many variables that it took humans days of calculations

PHILOSOPHY IN SCIENCE

Please Buy Me a Hamburger!

Descartes believed that the only things that should be called thinking things are human beings. Scientists conducting research with bonobo chimps (a type of primate) may have reason to disagree with him. "Buy me a hamburger" is a request that was made by a 14-year-old bonobo chimp using a speech synthesizer linked to a special keyboard designed for chimps. The bonobo, named Panibasha, has a vocabulary of about 3,000 words and has taught many of the words to her one year-old son.

For centuries, primates such as bonobos were thought to be savage and wholly animal, lacking in any human traits as thinkers. Scientists felt comfortable drawing a distinct line between primates and human beings. According to recent genetic research, bonobos share at least 99 percent DNA with humans and have very similar blood chemistry.

In the wild, bonobos are known to make and use tools, solve problems, and use medicinal plants to treat illness. They have also been observed vocalizing distinctive sounds to each other—signs of a robust communication system, if not a language *per se*. Moreover, bonobos raised and trained in research labs have been taught to use signs for words, such as hug, shoe, person, good, and smell. They are known to understand complex concepts, such as "more" and "less." And some have been trained in American Sign Language, and can create complex phrases that resemble human language. This research, going back three decades and continuing to this day, seems to show that bonobos are capable of more complex thought than humans have given them credit for. This may suggest that bonobos deserve being considered as persons.

for each missile fired. However, ENIAC could complete this type of task in less than thirty seconds.

ENIAC was a gigantic monster when compared to the size of today's notebook computers. Weighing 30 tons and filling an entire room, it contained hundreds of vacuum tubes and looked more like piles of cash registers than today's sleek electronic models. Today, all of ENIAC's functions could fit on to one microchip. ENIAC was retired in 1955, but while it operated, it replaced many human thinkers by doing the same work faster and more efficiently. Should ENIAC's abilities qualify it as a thing that thinks?

POINT OF VIEW

Alan Turing

In your lifetime, do you think computers will exist that can out-think a human being or be called a thinking thing? Around the same time that ENIAC was built, the British mathematician Alan Turing (1912–1954) predicted that by the year 2000 computers would be spoken of as thinking things. Turing's work with the British military intelligence service was aimed at stopping German U-Boats from sinking the British fleet during World War II. The German military used a machine called Enigma to communicate in codes that the British could not understand. Turing was instrumental in cracking the complex code of the Enigma machine. He believed that someday a machine might be created that a human could not out-think.

> *"I believe that at the end of the century the use of words and general educated opinion will have altered so much that one will be able to speak of machines thinking without expecting to be contradicted."*
>
> Alan Turing

> *"If Deep Blue can't find a way to win material, attack the king or fulfill one of its other programmed priorities, the computer drifts planlessly and gets into trouble. In the end, that may have been my biggest advantage."*
>
> Garry Kasparov
> (speaking after the 1996 Chess tournament)

Are Computers "Dumb Brutes?"

Machines, such as ENIAC and Deep Blue, are programmed to perform tremendous feats of information processing. However, some people claim

PHILOSOPHY IN EVERYDAY LIFE

Deep Blue

In 1996, and again in 1997, chess grandmaster Garry Kasparov played in a tournament against a supercomputer named Deep Blue. Deep Blue was built and programmed to play chess. Although smaller than ENIAC, Deep Blue was big enough to fill a small moving van. Its 20 processors could contemplate two hundred million chess moves per second and anticipate a win faster than a human mind. Kasparov commented that he was playing the match against Deep Blue to preserve human dignity. He was concerned that if Deep Blue were to win, it might mean that human beings would no longer be alone at the top of the thinking food chain.

Kasparov won the tournament in 1996. However, he lost to Deep Blue during a 1997 rematch. Kasparov and his supporters were devastated. After losing in game two of the 1997 match, Kasparov, convinced that it was impossible for a machine to beat him, complained that he thought a human was helping Deep Blue.

that what computers do is not thinking. Like animals, computers are described as "dumb brutes." Are they thinking or just working a different kind of muscle? Descartes' definition of animals (as non-conscious biological machinery) could be applied to computers. However, computers have other features that draw attention to their similarity to human thinkers. Like human minds, computers have a storage area, a processor that handles information, and a retrieval system for representing or communicating the things they know. The popular term for the capacity computers have that resembles human thought is **artificial intelligence**.

You have probably read stories or seen movies in which robots are depicted as having a sense of humour, or being cruel, or performing acts of kindness, or exhibiting artificial intelligence in some other way. Certainly, humans have not yet created a robot or computer that is self-aware. Do you think that humans will create machines that exhibit self-awareness, or that exhibit real (as opposed to merely "artificial") intelligence? Inventors have fabricated machines with memory, processing abilities, and other fantastic human-like features. Is self-awareness the type of feature that could be fabricated? Do you think that self-awareness will remain a distinctive feature of human beings, and ultimately the key ingredient associated with being a person?

Are Animals and Computers Mindless Workers?

Computers and animals have a number of limitations—things they cannot do—that make them different from humans. Animals do not build skyscrapers or use money. Computers lack the ability to enjoy a milkshake or a movie. Computers do not fall in love, and animals do not study philosophy.

Animals are able to perform some complex tasks and obey certain commands. Computers are also credited with solving difficult mathematical problems with incredible speed. However, some people argue that performing such tasks does not involve any activity that deserves to be called thinking. Such tasks may be simply mindless mechanical actions. Complex though this behaviour may be, it should not be confused with thinking—the sort of thinking that might be related to self-awareness, the sort that might be regarded as crucial to being a person. Perhaps Deep Blue does not really understand the game it plays. Perhaps moving a chess piece from one spot to another on the chessboard has no meaning for it. Similarly, a parrot repeating clever comments has no grasp of what the words mean.

> *"Here the question is not whether we will ever build machines that will think like people but whether people have always thought like machines."*
>
> Sherry Turkle

Our interest in the status of animals and machines may have something to do with the way in which we value them. Perhaps you consider animals to be friendly or loving. And perhaps, though this is less likely, you think of computers as more than just good at math, or useful tools in business. These human attitudes make it tempting to think of animals and computers as persons. Or to hold that animals and computers ought to be invested by the state with certain rights.

What Do You Think?

It is difficult to devise a complete definition that describes thinking. Yet, thinking is one of the features that has been identified by philosophers as important to personhood. Descartes and Locke believed that human beings are the only true thinkers. However, some people would argue that human beings are not the only thinkers. Computers and animals seem to be capable of complex mental processes. Is this all that is needed to say that they have the capacity to think? There is a further question. Even if humans concluded that animals (and perhaps computers too) have the capacity to think, would this mean they should be regarded as persons? If yes, how would you define what a person is? And what are the crucial things you would want to include in a definition of thinking? Where do you think the line should be drawn between person and non-person, or between thinker and non-thinker?

Unit 2

Chapter 4
Does God Exist?

Chapter 5
What Is a Good Life?

Chapter 6
What Is a Purposeful Life?

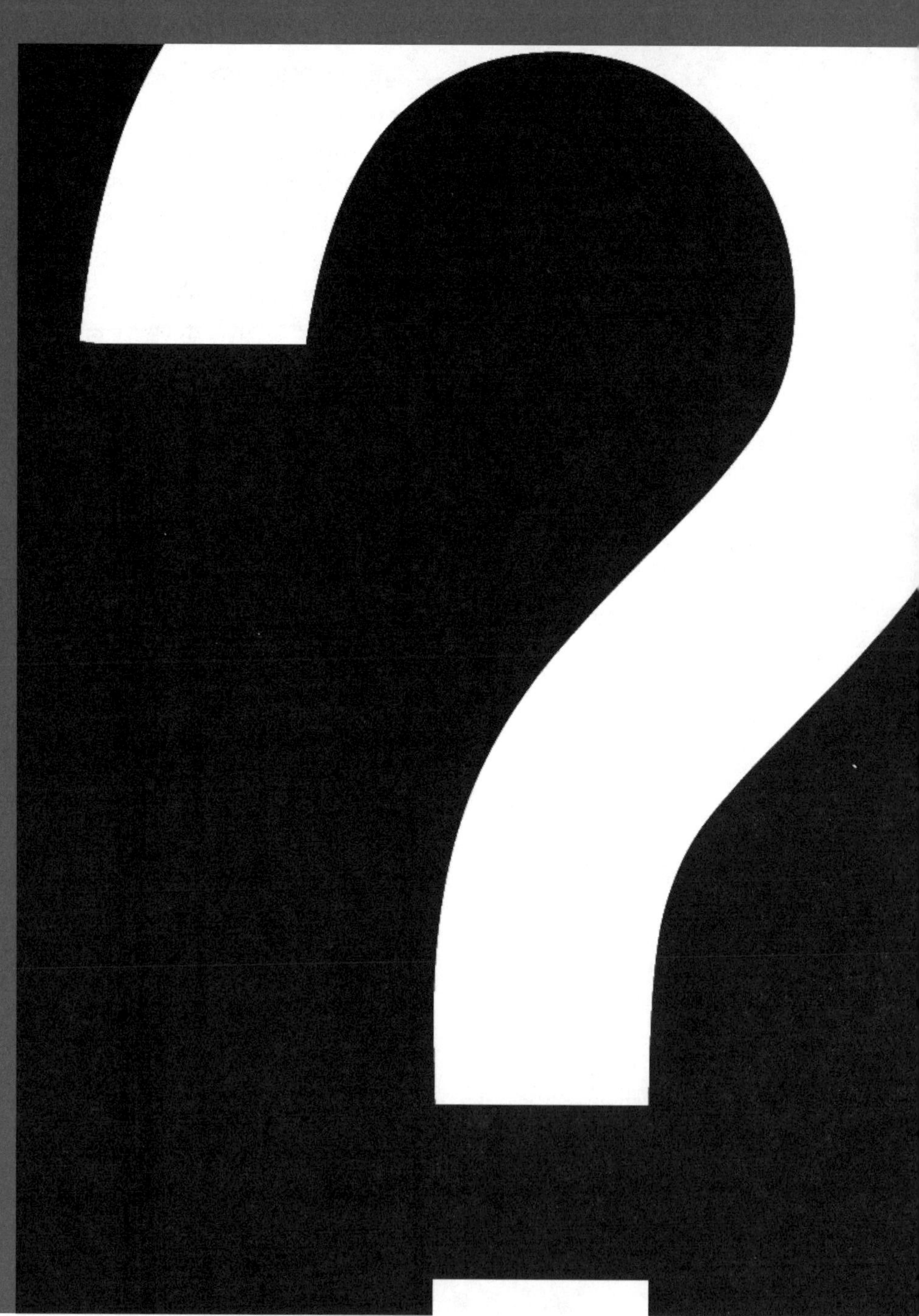

What Is a Meaningful Life?

What is the meaning of life? Why are you here on Earth, now? These questions are among the most important you will ask in life whether you continue to study philosophy or not. The ancient Greek philosopher Socrates (470–399 BCE) stated, "The unexamined life is not worth living." The American civil rights activist Martin Luther King, Jr. (1929–1968) said, "If a man hasn't got something in life worth dying for, he isn't fit to live." These strong statements underline the importance of addressing questions of this type in your life.

What role, if any, does God play in your life? For many Canadians, of many backgrounds, belief in God is central to what makes life worth living. What role does God play in making life meaningful? Philosophers ask questions about what people mean when they talk about God.

If you examine your life, what do you think are the good things about it? Perhaps you think you are happy or healthy. Does happiness come from pursuing pleasurable activities, or something more meaningful? Do you have a duty to others in your community, or are you looking out for yourself? In Unit Two, you will investigate the nature of God, what makes a good life, and the nature of the purposeful life.

Chapter 4 Does God Exist?

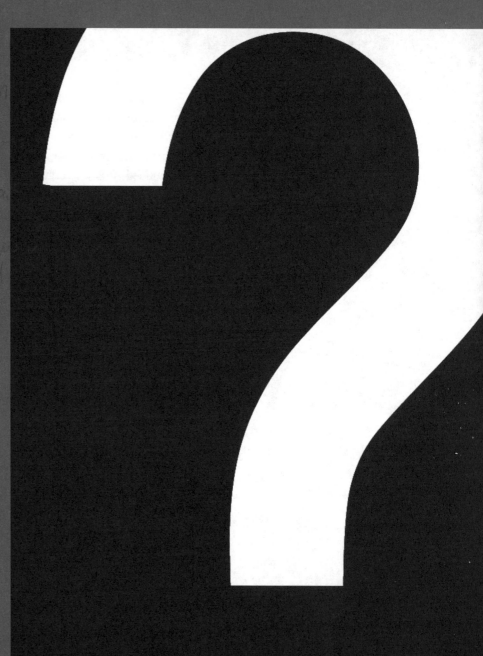

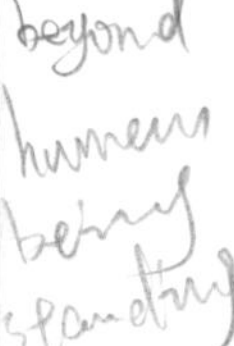

Key Words

God
Faith
Theist
Deism
Agnostic
Atheist
First cause
Design
Experience
Fideism

Key People

Blaise Pascal
Francois-Marie Arouet de Voltaire
Karl Marx
Mary Daly
Friedrich Nietzsche
David Hume
Aristotle
St. Thomas Aquinas
William Paley
St. Augustine
Mohammed
Søren Kierkegaard

Did God Create Everything?

It is the night of the new moon, which means the sky is dark except for the stars. You look up to see as far as you can. It is natural to feel small compared to the vastness of the big night sky. The night sky can fill you with awe and wonder about where nature originated. One of the first philosophical questions people often ask is, "Where did I come from?" A common answer is that God created everything. However, philosophers are interested in whether or not there is evidence in support of the existence of God. Is there truth in any of the different ideas about God that exist in the world?

In this chapter, you will explore some arguments that attempt to prove God's existence. You will also consider whether God, or the idea of God, brings meaning to life.

How Do Philosophers Think About God?

Over the last thousand years, much of Europe and (and later) North America has been dominated by Judeo-Christian ideas of God. This is because people who followed Christian or Jewish beliefs settled much of Europe. Prominent Western philosophers (Judaic, Christian, and Islamic) discuss God from a monotheistic perspective. Monotheists claim that there is one God who is creator of the world and a guide to living a meaningful life.

Polytheism is common in many non-Western religions. Polytheistic religions believe that there are many gods. These gods are said to contribute to different aspects of the lives of those who believe in them. (For example, there may be a weather god, a harvest god, or a god of war.)

Still other religions, such as Buddhism, believe in a spiritual dimension to the universe without positing the existence either of a single God or of several gods. In this chapter, **God** is referred to in the singular, not with the intention of supporting or rejecting one or another approach to religion, but to avoid complexities that are not easily dealt with in such a brief discussion.

Are Logic and Faith Separate?

Are faith in God and philosophy incompatible? Explain your view.

Philosophers use reason and logic as they ponder serious questions. As in math, logical arguments have to add up. The formulae you learn in math are carefully designed to offer accurate results. **Faith**, on the other hand, does not depend on argumentation of the sort math requires. Many people who have faith in God may believe that there is evidence that adds up that supports their beliefs. Their "evidence" may involve certain feelings rather than equations or proofs. The Christian philosopher Blaise Pascal (1623–1662) distinguished between the God of philosophy and the God of faith in his claim, "It is the heart which experiences God, and not the reason." Pascal argued that, while it may be reasonable for philosophers to undertake rational investigations into the existence of God, reason has no role to play in matters of faith.

> *"Faith is the substance of things hoped for, the evidence of things not seen."*
>
> Hebrews 11:1, *The Bible*

What Is Faith?

Theists are people who believe in God. The religious beliefs of theists around the world vary greatly, as do treatments of faith, and descriptions and depictions of God. For theists, faith is a particular way of knowing. Faith is about hope and feeling, rather than logic, reason, or evidence. However, philosophers argue that even people of faith look for evidence to sustain their faith, whether in the form of warm feelings, dreams, or visions. Despite the apparent conflict between faith and logic, many people of faith look for reasons for their beliefs—ways of defending their beliefs. In fact, many forms of religious belief claim that there is some sort of evidence of divine activity in the world.

Whether there is or is not a God, do you think that believing in God gives meaning to life? Why?

POINT OF VIEW

François-Marie Arouet de Voltaire

Do you believe that you can prove the existence of God? French philosopher François-Marie Arouet de Voltaire (1694–1778) thought that God's existence could be proven using reason and logic. However, Voltaire held a position known as **Deism**, which involves belief in a God that is unlike the God of religion or faith. Voltaire thought that God is a disinterested figure who set the universe in motion in the first place, but, afterwards, saw no reason to interfere in its operation. According to Deism, God does not answer prayers and plays no role in the religious activities of humans.

Does Theism Make Life Meaningful?

Traditionally, humans have seen themselves as God's creation. Consequently, the meaningfulness of people's lives has been closely tied to what it was thought God expects of, and desires for, his creatures. Many religions also teach that there is an afterlife. This belief, too, is relevant to questions about the meaning of life, in that a person's actions in this life have a bearing on what rewards he or she can expect in the next life.

Are there Alternatives to Theism?

There are people, called **agnostics**, who neither accept nor deny God's existence. They believe that it is not possible either to prove or to disprove the existence of God. On this view, judgement ought to be suspended on such matters.

There are people who do believe that God does not exist. They are called **atheists**. In philosophical history, atheism usually involved rejection of the God of Christianity, though there are atheists within other religious traditions. Most atheists think that their atheism is compatible with the possibility of a meaningful life.

PHILOSOPHY AND WORLD RELIGION

The Upanishads

Most of the world's religions have a book of scripture that is used by believers as a guide to how life should be lived. These books, such as the *Qur'an* and the *Torah*, embody the doctrines and philosophies of a particular religion. For members of religious groups, life is more structured and focussed if they follow the directions given in such texts. It may or may not be as simple as it sounds, but to some degree, people of faith claim to find the meaning of life in the rules and instructions presented in scripture. By relying on the answers to questions about God provided in such texts, they claim to discover the meaning of life.

The Upanishads are an example of a collection of religious scriptures. The literal translation of the word Upanishads is "sit down close," because students who learned them sat close to their teacher. The Upanishads form part of the holy Hindu scriptures. They were considered required reading for early philosophers studying sacred Sanskrit literature. Like much of Indian philosophy, the Upanishads were transmitted by oral tradition for hundreds of years. A teacher recited the Upanishads to students, who were required to memorize each word and sentence perfectly. By about 800–900 BCE, the Upanishads were compiled in written form.

The Upanishads' central theme is the relationship between the self (Atman) and God (Brahman). The authors of the Upanishads explore other concepts, such as the nature of sleep and dreams, human rights, and the afterlife. In one parable about the self (Atman), a group of ten people are unable to find the tenth person, because each person in the group fails to count him or herself. This parable teaches that self-knowledge is the ultimate good. According to the Upanishads, self-knowledge is only attained by philosophical thinking and selfless service of others.

Most religious groups claim that God inspired the writing of sacred texts and that, consequently, they are a guide to living a meaningful life. Philosophers point out that religious texts vary a great deal in their content. For this reason, philosophers are sceptical of the view that appeals to scripture as proof that God exists.

> *"Religion is the sigh of the oppressed creature, the heart of a heartless world, and the soul of soulless conditions. It is the opium of the people."*
>
> Karl Marx

Marx's Appeal to the Working Class

The German philosopher Karl Marx (1818–1883) did not think that religious belief originated in the rational recognition of the existence of God. Rather, he thought that religion's origins were rooted in the miserable conditions that most people endure in oppressive societies. In such societies, small minorities of powerful people control the economy, while others are forced to work for low wages in poor conditions. He thought that, under such conditions, many turn to religion for comfort in the same way that others turn to opium, alcohol, or other drugs. Religion gives meaning and purpose to life for the poor and oppressed by providing people with what little morality and humanity they may find in the world.

Marx's main objection to religion was that it fosters the idea that hard lives are inevitable, and that God allows social inequalities. Working people are consequently kept from engaging in the revolutionary activity required to eliminate domination of societies by oppressive, minority classes.

POINT OF VIEW

Mary Daly

Do you think that it is fair or just for God's name to be used to rule over people? Philosopher Mary Daly (born 1928) would say no. Daly advanced a feminist argument about God. She believes that women are undermined and deceived in many cultures that conceive of God as male. A male God creates and maintains stereotypes of male power and domination in society. If God is male, she says, men easily find value, or define themselves as valuable and powerful—like God. Women, on the other hand, are automatically placed below God, because they lack "maleness." She believes that women can regain the authority they ought to have by harnessing their creative spirit. She notes that the Biblical creation story describes both men and women as created in God's image. Too many cultures, she believes, ignore the role of women in creation.

Nietzsche's Criticism of Religion

German philosopher Friedrich Nietzsche (1844–1900) had a less flattering opinion of people than Karl Marx. He believed that most humans are no better than cattle and need a god-like figure to look up to. He described the average person as having a herd mentality. He believed that, whether or not God exists, people need to create one to give them someone or something around which to focus their lives. Like cattle that follow the farmer to the barn for food, people need a shepherd to follow.

A popular argument for the existence of God holds that humans have the potential to be good. If goodness of this sort cannot be traced to genetic, it must have a divine source: there must be a God. Indeed, if there were no God, there would be no reason to be good.

This is quite unlike Nietzsche's view. He believed that, whatever the motivation for people being good, it should be rooted in human reasons rather than being based on the authority of religious leaders, whom he saw as cynically manipulating the foolish masses of people. To offend the religious philosophers, to shock people into questioning their religious beliefs, and to underline the fact that by his times religion was in fact ceasing to give people a sense of meaning, Nietzsche declared that "God is dead."

Hume's Criticism of Miracles

The philosopher David Hume (1711–1776) was critical of the types of evidence or proof presented by world religions in support of their creeds. In particular, Hume made several claims about the nature and treatment of miracles. He pointed out that all religions use miraculous events to establish credibility of their religious doctrines. Miraculous events in the New Testament are thought to point to the truth of Christianity. Such events in the *Torah* are taken as evidence of the truth of Judaism. The *Qur'an* recounts miracles to establish the credibility of Islam.

Hume's difficulty is this: the argument from miracles is supposed to establish the exclusive truth of a particular religion. If it were conceded, for example, that the miracles proclaimed by Christianity really did occur, and if these miracles were viewed as evidence of the truth of Christianity, then the truthfulness of the claims about the occurrence of miracles presented in all other religions would have to be denied. There seems to be some similarity in the claims about the occurrence of miracles presented by all religions. On what basis, then, should such claims be accepted as true when they are made by one religious group, while rejecting such claims by other groups? Hume also noted that such miracles do not happen "in our days." Since this points to the possibility that claims of miracles recorded in the past may have been fabricated, Hume remarked, "it is nothing strange, I hope, that men should lie in all ages." The hypothesis that the reports were simply concocted is therefore plausible. Hume argued that human senses are more reliable than the testimony of people from the distant past, and that it is best to be sceptical of such accounts. He pointed out that the truth of claims of miraculous events may be verifiable only if they could be confirmed "by the immediate operation [upon the heart] of the Holy Spirit."

Hume also claimed that "no testimony is sufficient to establish a miracle, unless the testimony be of such a kind, that its falsehood would be more miraculous, than the fact, which it endeavours to establish." For example, he said that claims of people being raised from the dead probably involve deceit on the part of the witness, or deception of the "witness" (perhaps because the person was not really dead to begin with). On this basis, Hume claimed that most accounts of miracles recorded in scripture can perhaps be dismissed either as fabrications or as erroneous reports.

Though Hume was sceptical of miracles, and how they are used as proof by religions, he indicated that "reason is insufficient" to convince us of the truthfulness of any religion. Consequently, faith, in its strange operations, may lead people to believe things that are contrary to reason and experience. Hume, for one, was not likely to fall for what he called such "superstitious delusion."

> *"I flatter myself, that I have discovered an argument of like nature, which, if just, will, with the wise and learned, be an everlasting check to all kinds of superstitious delusion, and consequently, will be useful as long as the world endures. For so long, I presume, will the account of miracles and prodigies be found in all history, sacred and profane."*
>
> David Hume

Can Philosophy Prove that God Exists?

> *"If God set before me the Eternal, unchangeable Truth in his right hand and the eternal quest for Truth in his left hand and said, 'Choose,' I would point to the left hand and say, 'Father, give me this, for the eternal, unchangeable Truth is for thee alone.'"*
>
> Gotthold E. Lessing

Can you prove the existence of God? Do you think proof is even necessary?

The idea of God has played a central role in philosophical discussions about the nature of humans, the universe, and, really, everything, since philosophy began. For example, Aristotle (384–322 BCE) observed that things in the universe, such as the Moon and planets, are moving. He argued that, because there was motion of objects in the universe, there must be a Prime Mover—something that started everything moving. He believed this Prime Mover must be divine, since the movement in the universe appears so complex. Do you think that Aristotle's argument is a good one?

Other philosophers have devised a variety of arguments in attempts to prove God's existence. If such arguments are to be compelling, they will not rely on statements heavily influenced by emotional responses, or those based on perceptual illusions. For example, having warm feelings or seeing a light in a dream cannot be taken seriously as proof that God exists and is interacting with the person having these experiences. Such experiences may just as readily be caused by indigestion or restless sleeping patterns. On the basis of the "feel" of human experiences, how can people distinguish between experiences having ordinary explanations and those said to involve an encounter with the divine?

While some philosophers present arguments to prove God's existence, other philosophers come up with objections to these proofs. What follows are some common arguments philosophers have presented for and against God's existence.

PHILOSOPHY IN PHYSICS

What Started Everything?

Physics has its own explanation for the beginning of everything. The popular scientific theory, called the big bang, is presented by some as an account of the origin of the universe. According to the big bang theory, all matter in the universe was once compressed into a small mass called a singularity. The singularity is theorized to have been 10^{-35} metres across—a very small dot of compressed matter. The theory suggests that, before the big bang, there was no time and no space; therefore, the Big Bang was the universe's first event.

In a car race, when a referee waves a flag to start a race, she is telling the drivers to "start now." If there was no time or space before the big bang, you cannot speak of a "now" in which the universe began. For this reason, some physicists suggest that the question of what happened before the big bang is irrelevant since there was no "before."

Some physicists are not satisfied with this explanation and suggest that singularities are caused by black holes in other universes. These scientists suggest that the process of creating universes is infinite and has no knowable beginning. Like giant chickens, universes give birth to other singularity eggs, which themselves grow into giant universe-sized chickens.

Can God Be Proven by First Cause?

Which came first, the chicken or the egg? A chicken's egg needs a chicken to lay it. But then, a chicken has to grow from a chick. And, of course, a chick comes from a chicken's egg. This is an old problem, which can also be applied to humans, planets, galaxies, and so on. Is such a problem worth solving? When people ask questions about the origin of the universe, what do they really want to know? Life may be thought to be more meaningful if its origin is discovered. Some have argued, for example, that the big bang theory explains the origin of the universe. This theory suffers similar problems as the chicken/egg approach. If you accept the big bang theory, then the next question is, What preceded the big bang? Questions like these do not have easy answers, but it may still be worth searching for a **first cause** of everything—eggs and big bangs.

Is God the First Cause?

Christian philosopher St. Thomas Aquinas (1225–1274) called God the uncaused first cause. He said that the chicken/egg cycle could not have an infinite history. In his argument, there has to have been a first egg, or a first chicken. More generally, Aquinas argued that there has to be someone or something powerful enough to begin everything. He called this first cause God.

Is there a First Cause?

Some critics of Aquinas's first cause theory argue that it assumes there can only be one cause of the universe—God. Think if you were to find a bag of money under your pillow. You would be justified in asking a questions such as like, "Where did this come from?" or, "What caused this money to be here?" You know from experience that things (especially bags of money) do not just appear. You may never know what caused the bag of money to be under your pillow, but you can speculate that there are any number of causes. You can also speculate that any of these causes may be the true cause. Just as the money might have appeared from any number of causes, or in any number of ways, the origin of everything in the universe may also have other causes. Aquinas makes the assumption that this first cause was God without considering other possibilities, for example, the Big Bang hypothesis.

Another problem seen in Aquinas's approach is that it assumes the universe can be traced back to its origins in some one "thing"—the first cause (singular). But what if there were many things that caused the universe all at once? And there is also the possibility that there was no first cause at all, and that the universe is actually infinite or has no beginning. In defence of Aquinas's view, it is argued that he was not invoking the existence of God just to explain how the universe got started, but to explain why there is anything at all. That is, he was arguing that we must appeal to God to answer the question, "Why is there something rather than nothing?"

Viewed this way, the defenders of St. Thomas point out, the arguments about many different things causing the universe or its having always existed misses the point, which is to ask why anything exist in the first place. Similarly, the defenders maintain that it is much more plausible to conclude that an eternal Being, that is, God, is the cause of the existence of finite things, than to conclude that these finite things somehow came out of nothingness. Philosophers of religion continue to debate this question.

Do you believe that the complex design of the universe proves God's existence? Why?

Can God Be Proven by Design?

The British mathematician Sir Isaac Newton (1642–1727), like Aristotle before him, sought to explain the motion of the objects in the universe. Newton adopted a mechanical model and determined that the parts of the solar system (the Sun, the planets, their moons, and so on) worked like the parts of a clock. Like a clock's parts, Newton believed that parts of the universe moved in a mathematically precise and predictable way. The hands on a clock predictably move from one minute and hour to the next. Similarly, the Moon moves around Earth in roughly a twenty-eight-day cycle.

Very accurate analogue watches depend on a human designer who carefully assembles each delicate part. Hundreds of parts must work carefully and precisely together so that time is kept accurately. Each little wheel has a purpose in the overall function of the watch.

One peculiar characteristic of structures in the universe, is how well designed they seem. Like clock parts, each planet's proper orbit in the solar system is affected by the weight and gravitation of other planets. Many parts of the universe, such as stars and planets, seem to move in a precisely predictable way and direction. That is, the stars and planets do not suddenly stop, reverse their direction, or move erratically through space. Instead, their movements follow a regular path. This suggests that, as in the case of a watch, someone or something has designed their movements.

Is God the Designer?

What accounts for such curious design in the universe? William Paley (1743–1805) suggested that, just as watches are complex structures, so, too, are body parts such as the human eye. Just as structures like watches have designers, so, too, must body parts like eyes. A being who could design something as complex as the human eye must be much more powerful than a human designer. In fact, the complexities of the universe continue to baffle and amaze scientists. Paley concluded that this designer must be God. This argument for the existence of God is called the **Design** argument.

Is the Design Flawed?

However, sometimes a watch breaks. This may be because of an imperfection in the workmanship. A little wheel is not installed correctly, or another human

PHILOSOPHY IN NATIVE STUDIES

Are Creation Stories Proof of God?

The Haida Nation of the Queen Charlotte Islands (Haida Gwaii), in British Columbia, believed that humans emerged from a giant clamshell with the help of Raven, a significant character in the Haida culture. Raven heard voices and helped the humans escape from the shell and encouraged them to come into this world. Like the Haida, cultures around the world have creation stories to explain the existence of humans.

Accounts of a miraculous or supernatural creation that exist in various cultural and religious traditions usually suggest that humans did not come into being through evolution, or spontaneously out of the air. Creation stories, such as the Haida Raven story, suggest that humans came about in a purposeful way, under the direction or by the power of a designer. What should be thought of such stories? Do different cultures invent creation stories to satisfy a deep-seated need, or do these stories provide trustworthy pointers to divine creative activity? Certainly, the stories lack the elements necessary for real history.

There is reliable anthropological evidence that creation stories—fantastic and unbelievable if treated as history—are to be found in many cultures. You may agree that these stories do not prove the existence of God. But that leaves many interesting questions. What is the difference between a myth and real history? How do you account for the existence of human creation stories that defy common sense? What purpose do such stories serve?

error is made. How can flaws in the human body be accounted for? Since they are part of God's creation, should we assume that humans will run as perfectly as the parts of the universe? However, birth defects, psychological problems, criminal tendencies, and so on, are all examples of apparent flaws in the design of human beings. Weather disasters are usually called "acts of God," because they are beyond human control. Should human flaws—those that are not subject to human control—also be regarded as features of God's design for the world?

Is there No Design?

A criticism of the design argument is implicit in Charles Darwin's (1809–1882) theory of evolution. Darwin accepted the possibility of God's existence, but he thought the Christian belief in a perfect creation and design is contrary to the ordinary observation that living things are constantly evolving. Instead of supposing that a divine creator designed nature's structures and life forms, Darwin suggested that they evolved over millions of years into what is seen on Earth today.

Do you believe that human visions of God prove God's existence? Explain your view.

Can Experience Prove the Existence of God?

In religious records, there are many stories of people interacting with angels, spirits, or even God(s). For many people of faith, these reported **experiences** are evidence of God's existence. For people of faith, participation in the religious life through faith and spiritual exploration is the key to understanding how God makes life meaningful.

St. Augustine's Experience with the Divine

For example, the Christian philosopher St. Augustine (354–430) wrote of weeping in his garden in need of personal guidance. He recounts that he heard a voice that instructed him to "Take up and read, take up and read." Augustine tells of going to his books and reading the first thing that his eyes fell upon, which happened to be a verse from the New Testament: "But put ye on the Lord Jesus Christ, and make not provision for the flesh. . . ." He had a similar life-altering experience while reading the work of Cicero, an early Roman philosopher. Until that time, Augustine had been a half-hearted Christian and philosopher. These experiences gave him the courage to put all his energy into both disciplines. As a Christian philosopher, Augustine dealt with theological questions about existence, the nature of God, the universe, and the problem of evil. As a philosopher of the first millennium of the Common Era, he is called the greatest and last of the Christian Fathers, having spent his life defending and promoting Christianity and establishing it as the most prominent religion in Europe.

Mohammed's Experience with the Divine

The Muslim prophet Mohammed (c. 570–632) also described an encounter with the divine. Until he was in his forties, Mohammed was considered nothing more than a successful businessman. During his lifetime, people in his community worshipped God (Allah) indirectly through three goddesses. Various spirits, which dwelt in trees, rocks, and mountains, were also the objects of some worship. Mohammed was concerned by the lack of unity in Arab religion. He was also concerned by the prevalence of such "sinful" things as violence and adultery. He began spending time secluded in a cave near the city of Mecca. It was there that his meditations were rewarded by revelations from Allah. The Muslim holy book, the *Qur'an*, is the collection of Mohammed's revelations.

Mohammed was persecuted and ridiculed. His claim that there was only one God was a criticism of local religious leaders who encouraged worship of many different gods and goddesses. After three years of preaching his ideas, he had only a few dozen followers who believed in his visions. Today, there are more than one billion Muslims and more than 40 countries whose primary religion is Islam. Because of his visions, many people see Mohammed as the great prophet of Islam and Allah as the one true God.

Is It a Trick of the Mind?

Aside from Mohammed and St. Augustine, many people describe encounters with God, spirits, angels, or other supernatural phenomena. Some people treat these experiences as proof that God, or a spiritual dimension, exists beyond human reality. However, there is no consensus among those who claim to have these experiences about either their content or their supernatural significance.

Some philosophers dismiss these experiences altogether as tricks of the mind. Sometimes such experiences are ordinary or familiar, despite the fact that those who have them attach supernatural significance to them. For example, you may dream that you have a disturbing conversation with a friend. If, the next day, you really do have such a conversation, you may mistakenly conclude that your dream was an omen of some sort. In truth, the chances are high that, on any given day, you may have disturbing conversations with any number of people. Even when the experiences are in some way out-of-the-ordinary, this may be more coincidence than providence.

Another reason to be sceptical of claims about supernatural encounters is that the testimony of those who have such experiences cannot be corroborated. For example, if a suspect is to be successfully prosecuted in a court of law, judges and juries expect the witnesses to offer the same

WEB CONNECTION

Gods and Religions

Use a search engine to find sites about different faiths and different views of God. Gather information about how some religious organizations defend their ideas about God. Are their beliefs based on faith or logic? Present this information to your class.

account of the crime. Rarely will the testimony of one person against another hold up in court without corroborating testimony or evidence. As another example, lab scientists cannot publish findings of a great cure or discovery without first replicating their findings several times under controlled conditions. Spiritual reports usually refer to experiences that defy this type of scrutiny—they cannot be measured or repeated at will to give such reports general credibility.

Is It Common Sense?

Some philosophers may dismiss claims that supernatural encounters prove God's existence. Such claims are questioned by philosophers because they defy common experience and common sense. Some critics may argue that at least as many reports of UFO and Elvis Presley sightings exist as supernatural encounters! If you believe in people's claims that God exists on the basis of their out-of-the-ordinary experiences, to be consistent should you also believe in UFO and Elvis sightings? Under what conditions would you believe such claims? How would you react today if a stories such as St. Augustine's or Mohammed's were presented on the nightly news?

If human reason is flawed, can humans understand a perfect God? Why?

Can Reliable Belief in God be Based on Faith Alone?

People of faith hold that a faith approach to the question of whether or not God exists provides a legitimate basis for belief. This, despite the sharp difference that is conceded to be between faith and logic. Their view is known as **fideism**. Danish philosopher Søren Kierkegaard (1813–1855) believed that faith is not only superior to logic, but that it is essential to knowledge of God. Reason or logic relies on human understanding and the powers of the human mind. Since humans are imperfect, Kierkegaard thought people are mentally unable to reason about a being as perfect as God. Also, since God is by definition beyond human understanding, logical argument is a foolish way to try to apprehend God. Kierkegaard described faith as transrational. This means that faith is above logic and reason. Faith may not prove God's existence in a philosophical way, but, for some philosophers, this is unnecessary.

> *"To believe in God is to yearn for His existence and, furthermore, it is to act as if He did exist."*
>
> Miguel de Unamuno

Kierkegaard thought that people must take a leap of faith if they are to know God at all. Faith, he says, leads to a perpetual striving of each person for a truer understanding of him or herself through God. Reason, on the other hand, makes people trust in human mental abilities, which are flawed. If, with a view to proving God's existence, you depend on reason or, the experiences of others, or on what religious leaders teach, you deny your self. Kierkegaard meant that you would be attaching your belief to something outside of yourself rather than relating yourself directly to God. Faith comes with an uncertainty that must be accepted with courage and conviction. Kierkegaard believed that faith involves choice for freedom and makes people wholly responsible for their lives.

What Do You Think?

Ideas about God have had the attention of philosophers for a very long time: Does God bring meaning to life or can you live a meaningful life without God? Many philosophers have tried to provide proofs of God's existence. The first cause, design, and other arguments were reviewed in this chapter. For yet another attempt see the ontological argument in Chapter 18. Other people argue that what is available as proof of God's existence can only be secured through participation in the religious life, or through direct experience of God in such things as visions. Do you think that any of the ideas in this chapter have proved or disproved God's existence? Do you think that philosophical inquiry, with its emphasis on the need for evidence and rational argument, can contribute to answering definitively the question, Does God exist? Alternatively, does God's existence come down to a matter of faith at the expense of more logical approaches?

Chapter 5 What Is a Good Life?

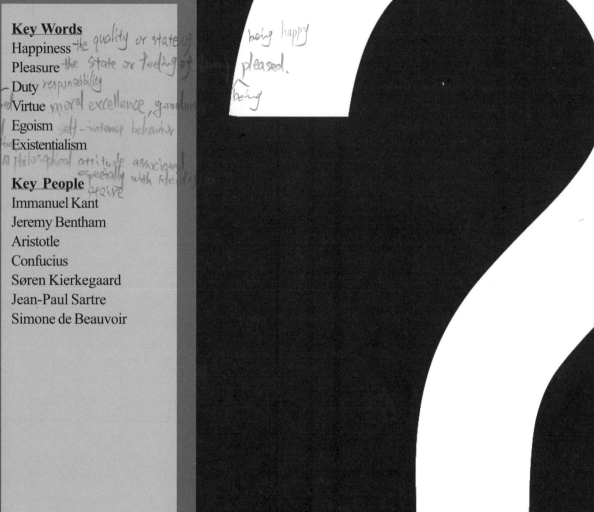

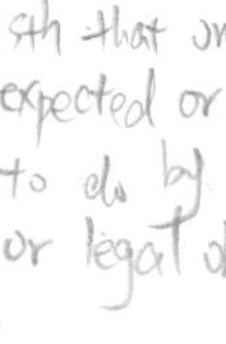

Key Words

Happiness
Pleasure
Duty
Virtue
Egoism
Existentialism

Key People

Immanuel Kant
Jeremy Bentham
Aristotle
Confucius
Søren Kierkegaard
Jean-Paul Sartre
Simone de Beauvoir

How Do Philosophers Discuss the Good Life?

> *"He who has a why to live for can bear with almost any how."*
>
> Friedrich Nietzsche

If you had to rate your life right now, would you say it is satisfying and meaningful? What would improve your life?

Imagine that a friend passing by greets you with, "How's life?" You remark, "I'm fine, thanks," but your friend rushes away without awaiting a response.

When you say, "I'm fine," what do you mean to communicate to your friend? Perhaps you mean, "Things are going well, and though there are some things I might complain about, all things considered, life is good." Philosophical discussions about a good life are about the quality of your life and not whether you have been good or bad. A good life could be defined by how much happiness you have, or how much pleasure you derive from life. A good life may refer to the fact that you are living up to your duties or responsibilities, or even that all of your wants and desires are satisfied.

In this chapter, you will explore many features that different philosophers believe are part of a good life. You may find that some of these features of a good life seem to go together. You may notice that happiness goes hand-in-hand with pleasurable experiences, or that getting what you want, and looking out for yourself, both can be pleasurable and cause you to feel happy. However, to simplify a philosophical discussion of the good life, each feature of a good life should be considered for its own sake, independently of the other features. Consider whether a good life is simply a matter of carrying out one's duties, or of the pursuit of pleasure alone, and so forth. For example, if you think the good life is one that is happy, then it may make sense for you to pursue happiness and nothing else—to live life as if the only reason for doing anything is to secure long-term happiness.

Should a Good Life Be Happy?

What makes you happy? Some of your friends may think that making a lot of money would make them happy. Others may find happiness in doing well

POINT OF VIEW

Immanuel Kant

What is the purpose of everything you do? For the German philosopher Immanuel Kant (1724–1804) it was a combination of both virtue and happiness. Kant thought that it was both natural and necessary that humans should be happy. Kant wrote that humans have an "inclination" to happiness, and are naturally drawn to happiness. However, as happiness comes from the things that people do, Kant believed that people have a duty to do things that will guarantee lasting happiness. He described this duty as an imperative that people become aware of when they consider rationally the choices they have to make. "Imperative" specifies the important things that a person should do to ensure happiness. Kant thought it was important for people to do virtuous things. Such things should not be done out of inclination (or in order to experience the good feeling which often accompanies doing the right thing), but because they are things that ought to be done (in response to an imperative). Kant believed that actions from duty rather than from inclination were more likely to contribute to lasting happiness.

Do you do things only because you expect or hope that they will make you happy or because they are the right things to do? What you think will make you happy may not in fact make you happy. Happiness often results from doing the right thing. Kant believed that people should do their duty because that was the right thing to do, not in order to achieve happiness. Kant contrasts those things that are done to secure happiness, and those things (like doing your duty) that may, in the event, result in happiness.

What relationship do you think there is between doing your duty and feelings of lasting happiness in your life?

at school and work. Still others may find happiness in religion and moral living. The happiness that philosophers often associate with living a good life is not simply about having a collection of enjoyable feelings throughout your life. For example, you may have been to a movie recently and really enjoyed it. The feeling of enjoyment you experienced may have lasted as you shared the funny or interesting parts of the film with friends. After some time though, the feeling of enjoyment associated with seeing the movie probably passed.

Some philosophers refer to a pursuit of **happiness** in life that is long lasting and more satisfying than the happy feeling that passes when the weekend is over. A doctor will likely feel a deeper happiness from the life-saving work she or he does every day than in getting a birthday card once a year. People who really enjoy their work may find happiness in the success they have in what they do for a living.

Is Pleasure a Necessary Feature of a Good Life?

Does the pursuit of pleasure give you a good life? If yes, what kind of pleasure? If no, why not?

You may think that pursuing lasting happiness is impossible, or not worth the effort. You may spend a long time unhappy trying to achieve a number of goals that could lead to lasting happiness. Some people would rather pursue something more immediate, and perhaps less difficult to achieve. Filling up the moments in your day-to-day life with immediate pleasures may seem like a more fulfilling endeavour, for the time being, at least. This approach, on the whole, sacrifices choices or actions you could take to secure the lasting happiness discussed earlier.

Jeremy Bentham on Pleasure

British philosopher Jeremy Bentham (1748–1832) associated the good life with **pleasure**. Bentham used the word *happiness* in a different way than many other philosophers use it. For him, the word *happiness* was interchangeable with the word *pleasure*. He thought of happiness as a passing feeling of a certain sort rather than as something deeper or more lasting. For Bentham, the good life is one in which pleasurable feelings are experienced in regular or predictable ways throughout people's lives.

LADIES AND GENTLEMEN.... MY NAME IS JEREMY BENTHAM AND I AM MOMENTARILY HAPPY TO BE HERE!

More specifically, Bentham felt that whether a life was a good one or not could be determined mathematically. If you calculate the amount of pleasure you feel and subtract any pain you are feeling, the sum indicates how well your life is going. If you experience more pleasure than pain in life, your life is a good one. But, if you have more pain than pleasure in your life, it is not a good life, so far as Bentham is concerned. For example, perhaps you would like to find a great job for the summer. You might go from place to place delivering resumés and finding an occasional employer to interview you. There is likely nothing incredibly pleasurable in doing all of this job-search work. The benefit comes later when you get the job, and likely not until you have worked for a time and receive a pay cheque. If the pay cheque makes you happy enough to more than make up for all of the pain of working and job searching, a Benthamite might conclude that you are having a good life.

Different Types of Pleasure

According to Bentham, not all pleasures are the same. Does playing in the snow have the same value as eating your favourite ice cream? For Bentham, not all pleasures are equal. When Bentham spoke of calculating the good life mathematically, he recognized that, while pleasures do differ in value, people may sometimes get the math wrong. Which types of pleasure would you pursue to achieve the good life?

> (The following verse was written to help people remember the value of pleasure.)
>
> *"Intense, long, certain, speedy, fruitful, pure—*
> *Such marks in pleasures and in pains endure.*
> *Such pleasures seek, if private be thy end:*
> *If it be public, wide let them extend.*
> *Such pains avoid, whichever be thy view:*
> *If pains must come, let them extend to few."*
>
> Jeremy Bentham

Some things may produce pleasure for one person and not another. In grading or valuing pleasure, Bentham suggested that you consider several features of the pleasures you pursue: their intensity, duration, and certainty.

POINT OF VIEW

The Cyrenaics

The philosopher Aristippus (c. 5th century BCE) lived in Cyrene (now North Africa) and believed that the only worthwhile pleasure was immediate pleasure. His followers started a school in his hometown, and the group became known as the Cyrenaics. The Cyrenaics held that since thinking about the future or contemplating the past usually causes stress, people should pursue simple and immediate sensual pleasures. Cyrenaics thought that you could only be sure of what is happening now in your life, and that you should therefore live for the moment. Can you think of problems that may arise from thinking this way?

That is, how intense will the possible pleasure be, how long will it last, and how certain can you be that it will occur? You may also consider the availability of the pleasure.

For example, consider a shopping trip. Could you rate the intensity of the pleasure of shopping on a scale from 1 to 10? Likely, any feeling you derive from such an event may only last a short while. Whether or not you experience any pleasure may depend on such things as who goes with you and how much money you have to spend. Bentham also believed that you should consider some of the consequences of the pleasure. Will there be pain after the pleasure? Will it produce further pleasure? Will the pleasure you have extend to others? In the case of shopping, the anticipation of the pain of running out of money, or being unable to pay the credit card bill may diminish the intensity of the pleasure. The likelihood of further pleasure may be limited by how much money you have left. However, the pleasure may be extended if, perhaps, you are buying a present for a friend.

Does the Good Life Involve Doing Your Duty?

Many people borrow money, for lunch, perhaps, or for some other reason. If you borrow without a promise to pay back the money, do you have a duty to do so?

Firefighters and police officers are trained to run toward danger while most other people flee. They have done a good job if they have done all they can to save a life or quell a dangerous situation. Police officers and firefighters have a duty to serve and protect the public. Often their jobs seem neither pleasurable nor happy. Nevertheless, it could be thought that they live a good life. Does doing your duty have a role to play in the living of a good life?

Living a life of duty can mean a number of different things. Sometimes duty relates to things people should do because of the roles they play. For example, a father has a duty to care for his children and a teacher has a duty to teach well. Doing your duty might also have to do, more narrowly, with standing by the promises you make. And in philosophy, **duty**, in a common moral use of the term, is a matter of doing the right things at the right time. This means that, in given circumstances, your sense of "duty" would enable you to identify the thing that ought to be done in just that situation. Anyone might be expected to do the same thing in precisely the same situation. For example, the duty of any bystander who can swim would be to dive in the water and save a drowning child. The act of diving in to help, in this situation, is the right thing to do.

> *"For example, it is always a matter of duty that a dealer should not overcharge an inexperienced purchaser, and wherever there is much commerce the prudent tradesman does not overcharge, but keeps a fixed price for everyone, so that a child buys of him as well as any other."*
>
> Immanuel Kant

What Are the Duties in Your Life?

Are there times when fulfilling your moral duty is more important than fulfilling another duty, say, to your teacher or employer? Why?

It may seem that doing your duty involves discharging heavy responsibilities and making personal sacrifices. Duty is also a possible ingredient in a good (or satisfying) life. In seeking out the good life, should you stand ready to do your duty for duty's sake?

Bear in mind that sometimes duty refers to a role you play (hall monitor, tax collector, etc.) while another definition of "duty" refers to the types of moral behaviour you ought to be engaged in (helping others, saving lives, etc.). In some cases, your duty may overlap with the roles you are playing. A doctor, for example, plays a particular role in the healthcare system, while a doctor also has a duty to ameliorate suffering. Again, your various moral duties may conflict with the roles you play. Your duty or role as a loyal employee may conflict with your moral duty to be honest should it turn out that your employer is cheating customers. Usually, when there is a conflict between role-related duty and moral duty, it is your moral duty that overrides any other role-duty you may have.

PHILOSOPHY IN EVERYDAY LIFE

Is Duty Important?

How important is duty in the daily life of a community? In May of 2000, more than 2000 people became ill and seven people died in the small town of Walkerton, Ontario when they contracted the deadly virus E. coli. This disease can destroy kidneys and cause diarrhea and death. The virus, which is usually contracted from uncooked meat, was found in the town's drinking water. Lawsuits and investigations pointed fingers in several directions. Politicians, the provincial health officer, and local water officials were all called to testify at a provincial inquiry into the Walkerton tragedy.

How were opportunities for the living of a good life diminished by the failure of various officials in Walkerton (or elsewhere in Ontario) to carry out their duties? How important is doing your duty at your place of work, in your community, or in your family?

POINT OF VIEW

Aristotle

© Bettman/CORBIS/MAGMA

For Aristotle (384–322 BCE), the good life is one of happiness, or what he called "living well," to distinguish it from a life of mere pleasure. The good life for him is the ultimate end of life and one worth leading for its own sake. This rules out pleasure, he thought, since while some people may be satisfied leading the life of brutes, most look for something else in life than accumulating pleasures. Evidence for this is that people will often sacrifice pleasures to acquire knowledge or to act in a just or courageous way. Knowledge, courage, and justice are among virtues. So, like philosophers in some other traditions, Aristotle thought that a good life must be a virtuous one.

To live well or be happy, Aristotle argued, people must also develop their special talents (for instance, to be a good craftsman, or political leader, or scientist, and so on), and they must exercise their talents in a virtuous way. Because one of the virtues is temperance, this requires avoiding excesses. For instance, courage is a mean between recklessness and cowardice. This is sometimes called "the golden mean."

> *"Thus, the virtues are implanted in us neither by nature nor contrary to nature: we are by nature equipped with the ability to receive them, and habit brings this ability to completion and fulfillment."*
>
> Aristotle

> *"Virtue is more to man than either water or fire. I have seen men die from treading on water and fire, but I have never seen a man die from treading the course of virtue."*
>
> Confucius

What relationship is there between someone's duty and the "virtues" he or she may acquire? Some philosophers, such as Kant, warned that as virtues develop in a person (such as courage or perseverance) they may "become extremely bad and mischievous." For example, speaking of one particular virtue ("coolness," which for Kant could mean "calmness" or "presence of mind"), Kant wrote, "the coolness of a villain makes him not only much more dangerous but also immediately more abominable in our eyes than he would have been … without [that coolness]." We would congratulate a friend for developing "coolness," "presence of mind," or "calmness" in a crisis. These same features would make a villain all the more frightening and dangerous. Kant's statement suggests that people have a responsibility not just to acquire virtues but also to exercise those virtues in ways that are consistent with carrying out moral duties.

On the viewpoint of the Chinese philosopher Confucius, virtues properly understood cannot be dangerous in the way Kant feared. His theory of the good life, called in Confucian philosophy *Dao,* is that it must be a life of virtue, or *De*. Chief among the virtues are:

- **Humanness** (*Ren*), including such virtues as benevolence, charity and kindness
- **Righteousness** (*Yi*), which includes loyalty and conscientiousness. It also includes a version of the golden rule—as Confucius put it: "What you don't want, don't do to others."
- **Propriety** (*Li*), which means acting in accord with the rules of moral action as they have been learned and handed down through the generations in things such as rites (of mourning, sacrifice, marriage, festivals, and so on), and norms of respectful behaviour, as toward someone's parents.

According to Confucius, then, a good life must be a virtuous life and a virtuous life will make for a good life. Such a life will not be one of self-sacrifice, according to him, because a virtuous life actually helps people to

POINT OF VIEW

Confucius

© Bettman/CORBIS/MAGMA

Confucius (551–479 BCE) was born of an educated, but not rich family, in a small village in the state of Lu (in today's Shantung Province). From an early age, his thoughts turned to questions of what makes a good and virtuous life and how education can help to form moral character. He was especially interested in the qualities of a good ruler or public administrator. To the displeasure of some rulers of his time, Confucius advocated benevolent rule and moral leadership over force. As he once put it in advice to leaders, "Your job is to govern, not to kill."

For a time, Confucius held public office as the Minister of Justice for the state of Lu and was promoted to the rank of Grand Officer. He left this post to travel, learn about other places, and to try to win people over to his opinions. In the course of these travels he attracted many followers. Confucius' students put together his main philosophical writings in the "Discourses" or *Analects*. Confucius's influence extended far beyond his lifetime. By the Han Dynasty (in the first century CE), Confucian works were made the basis for the civil service examinations for magistrates and bureaucrats of the Chinese government. In 1684, the Emperor Kangxi of the Qing Dynasty declared him the "Grand Master of all Ages."

lead a personally rewarding life. Indeed, one of the virtues is doing one's best, or *Zhong*. But this must always be with consideration of others, or *Shu*.

Can a Good Life Fulfill Your Wants and Desires?

What are some of the things (talents, possessions, conditions of life) that you desire? How should they be gained? Does it matter whether you cheat or steal?

When viewed cynically, a life of virtue and duty may be represented as self-serving, in the sense that you develop greater virtue and strength of character for yourself. Even so, it is difficult to get away from the fact that, in pursuing virtue or duty, both your conduct and your motivation involve acting in the service of others. A more direct approach to self-satisfaction may require more selfishness on your part. You may wonder why you should help others at all. Perhaps the good life should be motivated by a desire to cater to your own wants and needs without any concern for the good of others.

Should People Live Selfishly?

One proposal for the good life is called **egoism**, which claims that the good life is one in which self-interest is the only fundamental object of pursuit in life. On this view, your only duty in life is to look out for yourself. Living this way means that everything you do is motivated first by your own wants and needs. You should show no consideration for the needs of others, unless doing so provides some benefit for you. For example, you may give to a particular charity, not because the charity will benefit from the gift, but simply because you expect to be perceived as a better person for your generosity.

In the course of being a good egoist, you may find that your interests coincide with the interests of others. For example, you may not litter because you like living in a clean community. If (as seems very likely) this desire is one that most people share, depositing your garbage in a trash can will make a contribution to helping others. But, if you are a single-minded egoist, you will do so not for their sake, but from self-interest.

Egoism can be credited with helping to resolve one problem: it helps people take responsibility for their own well-being, and prevents their dependence on others for the means to living a good or meaningful life. However, you do not need to be an egoist to deal effectively with this problem. People can be encouraged to take responsibility for their lives even when it is clear that there is much more to the good life than pursuing one's own interest in the narrow and single-minded way egoism requires.

A group of egoists rushing madly for the last seat on the bus will find that only one of them can get a seat. In such circumstances, each of them may be committed to doing everything he or she can to secure his or her own interest at the expense of the others. If egoism is to be held as a valuable approach to the living of a good life, should egoists represent it as the approach everyone

PHILOSOPHY IN SOCIAL PSYCHOLOGY

Would You Help?

Have you ever witnessed someone being bullied and stood by doing nothing? If so, it may be plausible to suppose that you were motivated in this situation by a selfish desire of some sort—the desire to avoid personal injury, perhaps, or the desire not to expose yourself to other risk. Social psychologists speak in situations of this type of the "bystander effect." There are some cases where hundreds of people witness a crime that might have been prevented if only one or two people had intervened.

Social psychologists suggest that, when people are in a crowd, and no one else is helping, they have a tendency either to evaluate the situation as beyond their ability to help, or to convince themselves that the situation is not as serious as it looks. On the other hand, when one person is the only witness to a similar event (a crime, or someone falling down), he or she is more apt to stop and help. This points to the conclusion that the motivation underlying what people do (or fail to do) is not simply a matter of how selfish or how altruistic they are. It is also significantly affected by the presence or absence of other people.

should adopt? Yet, paradoxically, the egoist may be more disposed to preventing others from doing what is in their interest.

What would happen if everyone adopted egoism as the preferred way of living their lives? Would this give you more freedom to pursue your own interest—that is, more freedom to live the life of the successful egoist? Probably not. You would probably find that the people around you now had, as egoists, a firmer commitment to getting what they want at your expense. The greater the success they have living their lives as egoists, the greater the likelihood that they will constantly be getting in the way of you living a good or meaningful life.

The narrow pursuit of self-interest—which is what a consistent egoism calls for—is also at odds with the recognition of very basic moral duties. Suppose you discover a seriously injured person by the roadside. Suppose also that you are on your way to an important job interview for which you have been instructed not to be late. It is clearly in your self-interest to make it to the interview in good time. Should you not, therefore, as a good egoist,

POINT OF VIEW

Søren Kierkegaard

The Danish existentialist philosopher Søren Kierkegaard (1813–1855) believed that existence should not be taken for granted. People should honour their existence by taking full responsibility for their lives. He made the bold claim that, "it is impossible to exist without passion." Kierkegaard was suggesting that you can only really know yourself and have a good life if you commit fully to life and the things that you do. The term **existentialism** reflects the idea that for people truly to "exist," they must strive to give their lives meaning no matter how hard this is to do on one's own. Existentialists hold that people are completely free since they are capable of taking personal responsibility for all of their actions and that they should do so. Many people, however, do not recognize their freedom, and some are afraid of it. For example, some people would rather make the claim that their happiness is dependent on the actions and decisions of God, their political leaders, their employer, and so forth. Existentialists insist that a meaningful life requires people to overcome this fear and exercise their freedom to take responsibility for their own happiness.

simply continue on your way, passing up the opportunity to offer help to the injured pedestrian? Cases of this kind pose very awkward questions for the egoist. Most people would agree that there are times when your own interests should be put aside for the sake of others. Do you have a duty, at times, to serve the interests of others at the expense of your own interests?

Are You Responsible?

Does fate or bad luck play a role in whether you have a good life?

Some philosophers believe that, to have a good life, people have to assume responsibility for their choices. Whether they find success or failure in their personal endeavours, they must take responsibility for their actions. People who do not take control of their lives and who are not willing to assume responsibility for the way their lives go cannot achieve true happiness. Of course, the context of your life may also be worth some consideration. Some

PHILOSOPHY IN SOCIOLOGY

Do You Learn from Your Environment?

In contrast to existentialism, some psychologists believe that the good life is not the result of a person's effort, but, rather, how people were trained as children. Psychologist John B. Watson is famed for his theory on how people learn. He once stated provocatively, "Give me a dozen healthy infants, well-formed, and my own specified world to bring them up in and I'll guarantee to take any one at random and train him to become any type of specialist I might select—doctor, lawyer, artist, merchant, chief, and yes, even beggar man and thief, regardless of his talents, penchants, tendencies, abilities, vocations and race of his ancestors." Watson believes that people are not genetically bound to intelligence, or goodness, but that such features are acquired by learning them.

Social learning theory, developed by Albert Bandura, suggests that people learn how to behave by watching the behaviour of others. People dress like their favourite celebrity, not because they possess the same talent, but because they desire the rewards given to a celebrity. According to Bandura, people observe the consequences others receive for their behaviour. He says that people are likely to repeat those behaviours that have favourable consequences. Like Watson, Bandura thought that people's actions occur as a natural outcome of their environment, not from choosing to pursue one thing or another.

At the heart of social learning theory is the idea that people behave the way they do, not out of an intrinsic desire or passion, but because they see others rewarded for the same behaviours. The good life, according to social learning theory, is one in which you behave in such a way to earn rewards. Accordingly, you are who you are, not because of choices you make about who you are, but because of the influence your environment has on you.

people may find the means to happiness through luck or by accident. No matter how much responsibility you accept for your actions, you cannot help where you are born, for example, or whether or not a rich aunt dies and leaves her fortune to you.

What Controls Your Good Life?

Existentialism was developed against people who claim that the basis for a meaningful life lies outside the person whose life it is. For example, existentialists do not believe that the goodness of a good life is traceable either to God or to the process of evolution. If your life is thought to be good because God created you, then the meaning of your life is the meaning God intended it to have, and not the meaning you bring to your own life. It may make sense, in this context, to blame everything wrong with your life on God instead of taking responsibility for your own life. Similarly, if (according to the theory of evolution) humans are evolving creatures motivated by the "survival of the fittest," could blame the way his or her life turns out on genetic or environmental factors. In both cases, a person is tempted to relinquish responsibility for the way his or her life goes by blaming it all on "outside" factors over which he or she has no control. Control belongs to God in the one case, and processes of nature in the other.

> *"Judging whether life is or is not worth living amounts to answering the fundamental question of philosophy."*
>
> Albert Camus

Is Freedom a Burden?

Jean-Paul Sartre (1905–1980) was both an atheist and an existentialist. He thought that, without God, or another external reason to live, humans were left with a great and terrible responsibility. Sartre believed that people are free to do what they choose and that there is no good external reason not to lie, cheat, or steal. He believed that the freedom humans can be a burden to them. He described humans as, "condemned to be free." The good life emerges, not from an external source, such as from God or nature, but from the commitments and choices that you make.

POINT OF VIEW

Simone de Beauvoir

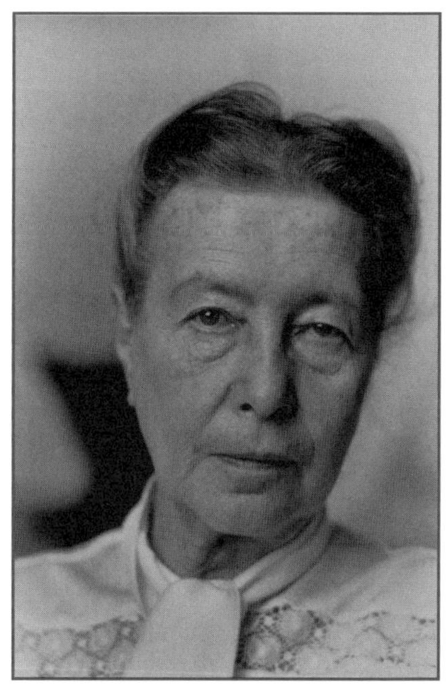
© CORBIS SYGMA/MAGMA

French philosopher Simone de Beauvoir (1908–1986) was a long time companion to Jean-Paul Sartre and supported much of what he wrote. In many important ways, de Beauvoir's philosophy is considered separate from Sartre's. She agreed with the concepts of responsibility and freedom as Sartre described them. She added that a person must also be aware of context. In some cases, circumstances may impede or prevent a person from expressing the kind of freedom important to the good life. Specifically, de Beauvoir refers to how women are treated in the world. She says that women are often objectified, treated as objects that belong to men, and therefore cannot easily be said to be free. That is, there are conditions created by men that get in the way of a woman's ability or opportunity to express her freedom to choose her path in life.

In her book *The Second Sex*, de Beauvoir encourages women to realize and transcend (rise above) their circumstances—move beyond being objects in relationships. She says that true personal freedom depends on a relationship in which the freedom of others is considered important. Only under these conditions will women be free to live the good life.

What Do You Think?

Life is filled with choices and opportunities. You may choose to work hard and earn a good wage, or gamble and hope for riches. You may seek to help others throughout your life, or look out only for yourself. You may find a good life in any number of pursuits. You will probably think that certain choices would make you happier than others. What do you think is the key feature of a good life? Do you think a good life should be measured on a daily basis, or at the end of your life? What difference would this make? How will what you have read in this chapter change your behaviour and approach to the good life?

Chapter 6 What Is a Purposeful Life?

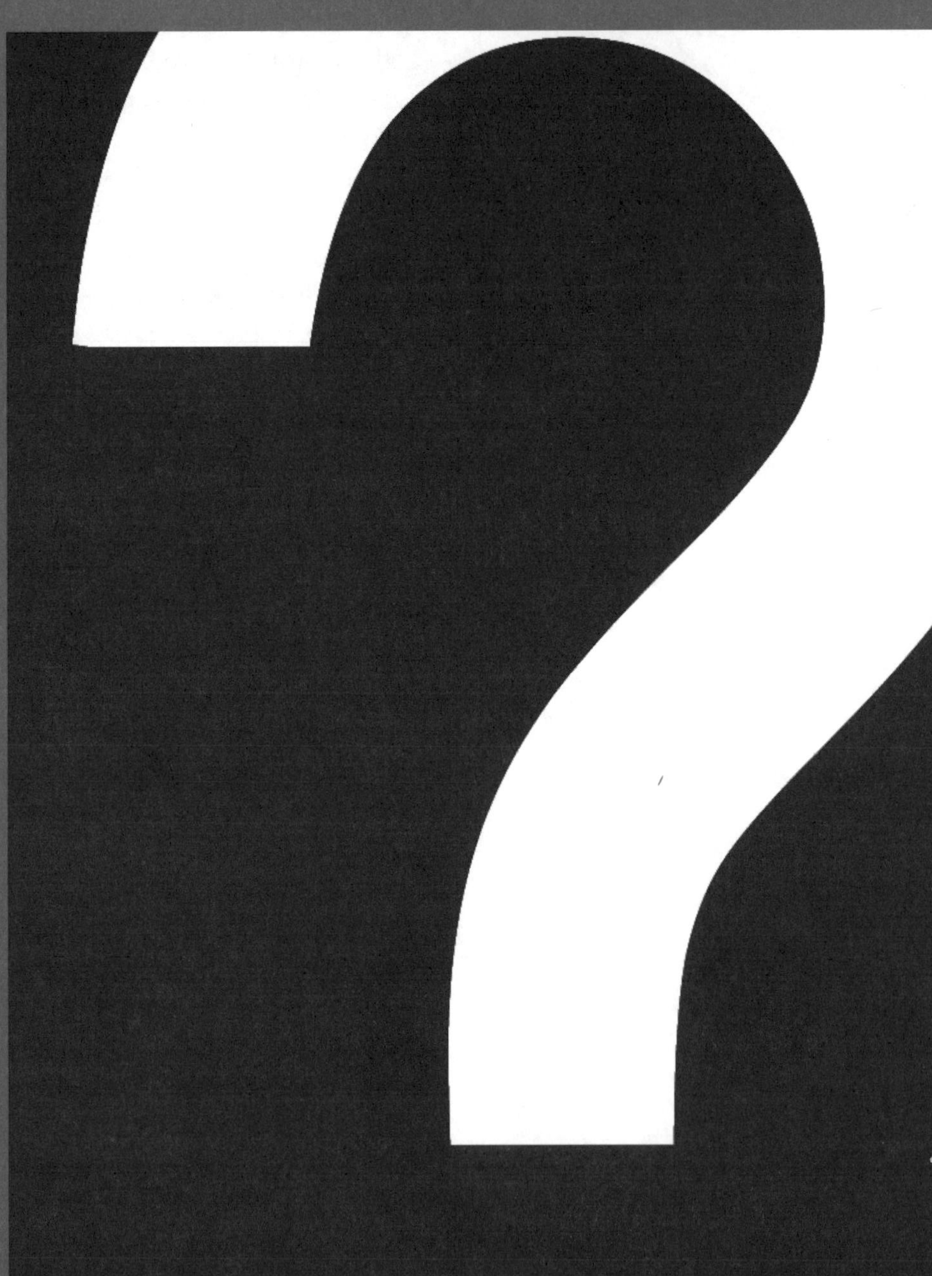

Key Words

Purpose
Function
Artifact
Cosmic purpose
Biological purpose
Sociological and historical function
Communitarianism
Fatalism
Intrinsic value
Hedonism
Egoism
Virtue
Duty
Existentialism
Virtuous happiness
Nihilism

Key People

Karl Marx
Søren Kierkegaard
Henri Bergson
George Santayana
Michael Sandel
St. Augustine
Jeremy Bentham
John Stuart Mill
Jean-Paul Sartre
Aristotle

What Is the Purpose of Life?

The journey of life is a struggle to do meaningful things. Are there specific things you ought to pursue to guarantee yourself a purposeful life? Is there an overarching end all humans should pursue? Or is living a meaningful life a matter of pursuing an assortment of unrelated ends—ends that reflect the distinctive interests or tastes of individuals? Perhaps people live meaningful lives when they are useful to the community. Or is it best to work out the purposes of God in human lives? Do you think that human lives are best spent developing intellectual powers? Have you ever wondered whether a fated future lay in store for you? What if you find that many of the ends you pursue are determined by events in your environment? Or are you, in the end, like a pirate on a wide-open ocean—free to roam, scavenging from island to island for treasures that will eventually make your life fully meaningful?

> *"Our minds are finite, and yet even in these circumstances of finitude we are surrounded by possibilities that are infinite, and the purpose of human life is to grasp as much as we can out of that infinitude."*
>
> Alfred North Whitehead

This chapter does not try to answer these major questions of the meaning of life. It is left for you to try solving these questions and to discuss them with your classmates, friends, and teachers. The chapter will help you consider these questions by distinguishing the different ways that people may have purposes.

What Does Purpose Mean?

The word ***purpose*** has different meanings. Each relates to the question of the meaning of life differently. The meanings are: as a tool or artifact, as a function, and as an intentional plan of life.

Purpose as Artifact

When you talk about the purpose of something, how do you usually use the word? Consider a hammer and one of its main purposes: pounding nails into wood or other hard materials. A hammer can be used, of course, for other purposes—as a paperweight, for example. A hammer, though, does not have purposes of its own. Whether as a paperweight or "pounder," the hammer is considered an **artifact**—a thing that is used for a particular purpose or in a particular way by someone.

Slavery

Sometimes people are used as if they are artifacts. The most terrible example is slavery. In many periods of history, prisoners of war were condemned as slaves. Slaves, or prisoners of war, were often used as labourers to cater to the needs of certain groups within the slave owning—or the victorious—society.

In 15th century Europe, Portuguese slave traders imported hundreds of African men and women to Europe to be used as servants and slaves. African men and women were hunted like animals and forced onto ships where they were destined for the slave trade in Europe. Slavery spread to North America as the colonies grew and the need for labourers grew. By 1860, there were nearly four million slaves in the United States. Slavery was a business during this time, and slave traders would hold auctions where humans were sold in the same way that you might sell goods, or livestock.

Wage Slavery

Another example of people being used as artifacts is as forced labourers. Canada is not innocent of using its citizens as forced labourers. From 1914 to 1920, more than 8,000 Canadians, many of Ukrainian descent, were used as forced labourers on the development of lands now known as Banff National Park (in Alberta), and for mining coal in Nova Scotia. These workers were not exactly slaves, but some of them were considered enemy aliens during World War I when Canada was fighting the Austrian army. Before the war, many people of Ukrainian descent had emigrated from Austria to Canada and (some historians say) were perceived by the Canadian government of the time as a threat to national security. Similarly, at the end of the 19th century and the beginning of the 20th, Chinese men were employed to build the Canadian railroads in near slave-like conditions.

The German philosopher and socialist revolutionary Karl Marx (1818–1883) believed that in a capitalist society all workers are used as artifacts. He lived during the Industrial Revolution. People were moving in large numbers to big cities from rural areas either for the promise of paid work or in pursuit of wealth and prestige. Marx observed the establishment of an elite class of rich business owners. Their wealthy lifestyle was made possible by the hard work of members of a poverty-stricken working class. Marx believed that these workers were unable, under the harsh working conditions that prevailed, to pursue purposes of their own. In such circumstances, humans are treated as "mere instruments," used in the service of other people's ends, rather than as individuals with purposes of their own.

Many people would say that a person who is used as an artifact by someone else is not leading a meaningful life. What about when such people* like *their controlled lives? Imagine a slave who does not complain about being a slave or even thinks it proper to be one? Or what about a working person who is happy not to be his or her own boss and believes the employer must know what is right? Are these people leading meaningful lives?

Purpose as Function

When we say that the purpose of the heart is to pump blood, we do not mean that the heart is an artifact of the body. Rather, the body is a complex organism, each part of which—heart, kidney, eyes, hands, and so on—performs a crucial function in sustaining the organism as a whole. Performing its function is each body part's purpose. This sense of purpose is often what people have in mind when thinking about the purpose of an individual's life. Here are three examples.

Cosmic Purpose

The idea that the entire universe or cosmos is like a single organism is most often tied to religious views. For example, in mainstream Christian thinking, God created the world and organized its parts for human survival and so people could come to know, love, and unite with Him. Exactly how all the parts of the universe serve this end, and, indeed, the full nature of the end itself, may be mysterious to people. But through sacred writings, rules for how to live and what to believe to serve God's **cosmic purpose** are known.

Depending on what parts of the scripture one attends to, or how they are interpreted, there may be different rules for different people: for men and women, children and adults, members of religious orders and lay believers, and so on. Following these rules and embracing the right beliefs makes for a purposeful life in the sense that people are performing functions God intended.

Debates over the meaning of life in this sense, or in similar senses for other religions, take place both among philosophers who are religious and those who are not. The atheist Jean-Paul Sartre (see Chapter 5) denied that there is any God, and the agnostic Hume (Chapter 4) did not think we can know if there is one. So, for them, appeal to a religiously ordained cosmic function is impossible. Kirkegaard (Chapter 5) was religious, but he did not think that we can have any knowledge of divine plans; so we must still find a way to make meaning for ourselves.

If there is no cosmic purpose, is human life meaningless?

Biological Purpose

The idea of a function most clearly applies when thinking about biological organisms, as in the heart example described earlier. The meaning of a human life from this perspective of **biological purpose** is its function or role in perpetuating the human species. This means producing and caring for offspring.

Sometimes this idea is combined with one of the other views about the function of a human life. For example, many religions place a strong emphasis on the importance of producing and caring for children. But the purpose that is supposed to provide meaning is different in the religious and the purely biological cases. On religious views, producing children is part of a larger, God-given plan. From a biological perspective, the goal of producing children is simply to reproduce the species. The urges that lead people to want to reproduce are "programmed" into them in by evolution as instincts, just as in other animals.

There are philosophers who take theories of evolutionary biology very seriously. They try to make their views about things, such as knowledge and ethics, compatible with these theories. However, very few of these philosophers think that the meaning of life is simply to fulfill the biological urge to procreate and to protect and nurture one's children. Instead, they try to find ways to recognize the importance of biological instincts while seeking other sources of human meaning. Some theorists claim to follow the evolutionary ideas of Charles Darwin (1809–1882). They do not apply Darwin's ideas to the evolutionary transformation of one species to another

POINT OF VIEW

Henri Bergson and George Santayana

Henri Bergson (1859–1941) and George Santayana (1963–1952) were philosophers who tried to relate their philosophical theories to evolution and the biological nature of humans. Neither argued that the meaning of life should simply be identified with performing biological functions.

Bergson saw evolution exhibiting the workings of a "vital force," which he thought was God acting through nature. Through time, this vital force reached its most complex form in the freedom of human individuals.

Santayana held that people are essentially biological entities, driven by such things as the need for food and avoiding physical dangers. However, humans physically possess powers of intuition, or "animal faith." These powers enable us to perceive the essences of things, appreciate beauty, and adopt attitudes of kindness toward each other.

(Darwin's main focus) but to social relations within the human species. Herbert Spencer (1820–1903) advanced a theory sometimes called "Social Darwinism." His aim was to justify competition in economic affairs and utilitarianism (see Chapter 12) in ethics on the grounds that their evolution was as important for the survival of humanity.

Traditional Roles

A third candidate for a basic function in life is a combination of sociological and historical rather than biological or religious factors, though they may all interact. The most important human function from this perspective is to act in accord with the roles inherited from the traditions into which someone is born. If, in the tradition of your family and society, it is generally expected that young men follow in the profession of their fathers and girls of their mothers, then a meaningful life for you is to do so. If your father is a construction worker or a doctor, this is what you should aspire to be. If your mother is a nurse or a full-time housewife, then you are acting in accord with your proper function if you follow her example. If the main traditions of your community are religious, say Orthodox Jewish, Shiite Islamic, or Protestant

Christian, a purposeful life for you requires performing the rituals of your inherited religion, attending a certain denomination of temple or church, and raising your children to do likewise.

The traditional approach to the function of life is often associated with conservative thinkers. Examples are the political conservative Edmund Burke (1729–1797), who condemned the French Revolution for trying to destroy all the traditions of the old regime in France and the poet T.S. Eliot (1888–1965), who was critical of the demise of religious and traditional values that he saw resulting from secular and Enlightenment values.

Communitarianism

However, not everyone who looks to tradition for meaning is a political conservative. Those in the "communitarian" school of social and political philosophy—**communitarians**—do not usually locate themselves on the political right wing. One example is the American philosopher Michael Sandel. He believes that a loss of commitment to community service and civic engagement central to the founding traditions of his country has opened the door to economic selfishness and social isolation of individuals. (His communitarian and civic republican theories are described in Chapter 15.) Like other communitarians, Sandel criticizes a view of a meaningful life where people see themselves as pure individuals, unrelated to the traditions of their families, communities, or nations. According to communitarians, only identification with these social things gives meaning to people's lives.

Describe what a meaningful life, for you, would be: (a) in accord with religious function; (b) in accord with biological function; (c) in accord with your traditions. Do you think that any of these lives would really be meaningful?

Purpose as a Life Plan

So far we have regarded purposes as artifacts and as three kinds of functions. These share the feature that the meaning they are supposed to give to human lives exists outside the wills of individuals. On another sense of purpose, a meaningful life is one that people create for themselves. This sense is the one intended in phrases like "doing something on purpose."

FATALISM

The idea of acting on purpose carries with it the idea of acting freely. When people decide to conduct their lives in a certain way, this is something that they choose to do, rather than something that they are forced to do. But on the doctrine of **fatalism,** all human actions are predetermined—whether by God or by laws of nature. People are deluded if they think they act freely. An example of a fatalist on religious grounds was the Christian theologian Jonathan Edwards (1703–1758). From the Eastern philosophical tradition, a fatalist religion was Ajivikas, which existed in India from the 6th century BCE to the 16th century AD. Baron Paul Henri D'Holbach (1723–1789) argued for fatalism on scientific grounds.

> *"In short, the actions of a man are never free; they are always the necessary consequence of his temperament, of the received ideas, and of the notions, either true or false, which he has formed to himself of happiness ..."*
>
> Baron D'Holbach

Some critics of fatalism agree that if God or natural forces cause everything, then there could be no human freedom, but they deny that everything is caused. For example, St. Thomas Aquinas (1225–1274) argued that among the powers God gave to humans is the power of freedom of choice. The Ancient Roman philosopher Lucretius (99–55 BCE) concurred with earlier Greek philosophers who thought that everything that exists is composed of physical atoms (these were the Epicureans). Though Lucretius thought that free will was possible because sometimes atoms spontaneously violated natural laws.

Other philosophers claim that human freedom is compatible with thorough-going determinism. This was the view of St. Augustine (354–430). He maintained that God's all-knowing, all-powerful nature exists in an eternal realm, while human actions are in the realm of time—finite in nature. For this reason, human actions may be freely undertaken within the finite world, even though in the ultimate reality of eternity, they are predetermined.

Most of the pro-scientific, empiricist philosophers (see Chapter 18) agree with John Stuart Mill (1806–1873), who saw no contradiction between believing that everything that happens has a cause and believing in human freedom. On this view, people are free when what they do is caused by what they themselves decide to try to do. How their decisions are themselves caused is irrelevant to the question of whether at the time of acting their actions are a result of their decisions (however they came to make them) or are forced on them by external circumstances.

RESEARCH AND INQUIRY SKILLS

Look up "determinism" in a dictionary or encyclopedia of philosophy to study the positions reviewed above.

In addition to doing things to stay alive or to fill time, people engage in an enormous number of activities aimed at some particular purpose: to be good at a sport; to enjoy or create music; to gain knowledge about a subject; to engage in school, city, or national politics; to teach others; to invent something; to advance a cause, such as environmentalism or neighbourhood improvement; to perfect a hobby, and so on. Philosophers do not deny that any of these specific activities or the many others like them may contribute to a meaningful life. However, they have different ideas about why and how people may engage in these activities to make them meaningful.

Intrinsic Value

Before calling attention to these different ideas, an important feature of a meaningful life must be emphasized, about which most philosophers agree: to be part of a meaningful life, activities must be engaged in *for their own sakes*. The activities must have what many call ***intrinsic value***. Someone could set out to be a good athlete to get an athletic scholarship, or to make money as a professional athlete. For philosophers, there is nothing wrong with engaging in sports for these purposes. However, this does not make for a meaningful life when the sports are only a means to other purposes.

In turn, getting a scholarship or making money are usually not thought of as things done for their own sakes, but for other ends: to acquire an education; to lead a comfortable and secure life; to acquire skills that are useful within society; and so on. It is these ends that qualify for a meaningful life, rather than the means taken to get them. Of course, being a good athlete could be thought of by someone as a goal in itself in addition to whatever other goals it serves, or even if it serves no other goal at all. In this case, being a good athlete would contribute to a meaningful life.

Meaningful Lives as Good Lives

Philosophers differ on just what makes activities undertaken for their own sake parts of a meaningful life. Some of the differing views about what constitutes a good life that were summarized in Chapter 5.

- For hedonists, a life of pleasure is meaningful. In its purest form, **hedonism** counts any activity as meaningful, provided people derive pleasure from it. But most hedonists rule out activities that harm others (for instance, dare-devil driving, or bullying) or that harm oneself (smoking, pigging out on junk food, and so on). Thus, the utilitarian Jeremy Bentham (see Chapter 5) distinguished between higher and lower pleasures. Bentham's follower John Stuart Mill went further to say that it is "better to be Socrates dissatisfied than a fool satisfied."
- Egoists—those who follow **egoism**—think that a selfish life can be meaningful. Many philosophers disagree with egoism, arguing that selfishness backfires. Egoism causes people to lose friends and, in losing the respect of others, also losing respect for themselves. So if a meaningful life should be a satisfying one, the selfish person will usually not succeed in leading one just because he or she acts in a selfish way. Philosophers, such as Aristotle, Confucius, or Kant, who see a good life as one of **virtue** or **duty** may concede that some selfish people can be satisfied, but they do not think that satisfaction is an essential part of a meaningful life. Rather, acting virtuously and doing one's duty to others is necessary for this.
- For **existentialists**, like Jean-Paul Sartre, what is most important are the *ways* that life activities are entered into. For a meaningful life, according to existentialists, people must take full responsibility for the lives they choose for themselves. People should not follow tradition or let others decide for them. Sartre tells a story drawn from his experience as a leader of the underground Resistance to German military occupation of France during World War II. A young man who was torn between joining the Resistance or remaining in his home to care for his aging mother asked Sartre for advice. Sartre thought the young man wanted advice in order not to struggle with this difficult

and important matter himself. Sartre refused to advise him, saying the young man would have to take responsibility for his own decision.

Do you think that Sartre was right or wrong not to advise the young man?

- According to the theory of **virtuous happiness,** advanced by Aristotle, people lead meaningful lives when they fully develop and exercise their special talents—as a carpenter, a teacher, a political leader, a parent, or to whatever they are especially suited—in association with others and in a virtuous way. St. Thomas Aquinas agreed with Aristotle, but added to Aristotle's "worldly" virtues (wisdom, courage, temperance, friendship, and justice) the "religious" virtues of faith, hope, and charity. Aristotle contrasts his view of a life of happiness with pursuing fame, fortune, or political power, which, though many seek them, do not make for a genuinely happy or meaningful life.

Imagine that you and some friends are very talented inventors who form an engineering company and are deciding what to invent. Recognizing that your skills are mainly in the area of electricity, you consider two options: (1) to create a grid for a fully heated and lit 18-hole golf course, that could be used by rich golfers to play their sport 12 months a year and in any weather, or (2) to figure out a way to affordably store the Sun's energy in massive quantity.

With option (1), you would make enormous amounts of money, be famous (at least in the world of golfers), and you could use your fame and money to gain political power if you wanted it. With option (2), you would make enough money to be comfortable, but you would not become famous (since, let us suppose, you would only be a member of a large team working over many decades). Nor would you gain any political power. However, your contribution on option (2) would be much more challenging than the golf course project, and it would solve the entire world's energy problem forever.

Which choice would you make?

Life's Purpose and Philosophy

So far we have not addressed two possibilities:

- that there are many purposes to life
- that life has no meaning at all

When thinking about all the different purposes that people have in life, or the different things that they think makes life meaningful, it is tempting to conclude that there are many different ways that life can be meaningful. Taken one way, the philosophers whose views were summarized in this chapter can agree with this. For example, consider religious theories that hold that a meaningful life is one that serves God's purposes. These theories recognize that different people can serve the same divine purposes in different ways. Or, from Aristotle's view, since happiness requires developing someone's special talents, and since different people have different talents, happiness will be found in a variety of ways.

But taken another way, this conclusion challenges the possibility of knowing what a meaningful life is at all. If the meaning of life is associated with a good life, and if there is no way to decide among the different theories of the good life—hedonism, egoism, existentialism, virtuous happiness—then what is a meaningful life cannot be known. However, do not jump to this conclusion too quickly. It is exactly the task of philosophy not to give up on the power of human thought to solve basic problems, even those that pit some philosophical positions against others.

When people say that life has no meaning or purpose at all, it is important first to figure out what sense of purpose they have in mind. If they think of purpose in the sense of an artifact, and believe that most people are forced to serve other people's ends, this does not mean that life is necessarily meaningless, but that social domination makes a meaningful life hard to achieve. If they think of purposes as functions, and believe that neither cosmic, biological, nor traditional functions confer true meaning, they forget that meaning in the sense of deliberate life plans may still be possible.

If, however, it is thought that people are forever doomed only to be artifacts and that nothing else—neither functions nor plans—gives life meaning, then they are committed to a view in philosophy called **nihilism** (literally, "nothingness"). But even in this case, it is not certain that someone must be driven to complete despair. Some philosophers try to derive a sense of the meaning of life from nihilism itself. One example is existentialism. For existentialists, confronting the absurdity of life can lead someone to realize the important of affirming their own freedom, thus, making life not so absurd after all.

What Do You Think?

This chapter reviewed the different things that "having a purpose" might mean:

- being a tool for someone else's use;
- performing some function, such as serving God's plan for the cosmos, the biological function of perpetuating the human species, or performing traditional social roles;
- acting in accord with a life plan of one's own. In this case philosophers agree that a life plan must be intrinsically valuable, but disagree over what its goal should be: pleasure, serving self interest, freedom, leading a virtuous life.

Which of these purposes do you think is most desirable for people to have? Which purposes are realistic? Give examples from history or from fiction of people whose lives can be said to have purposes in each of these ways.

Unit 3

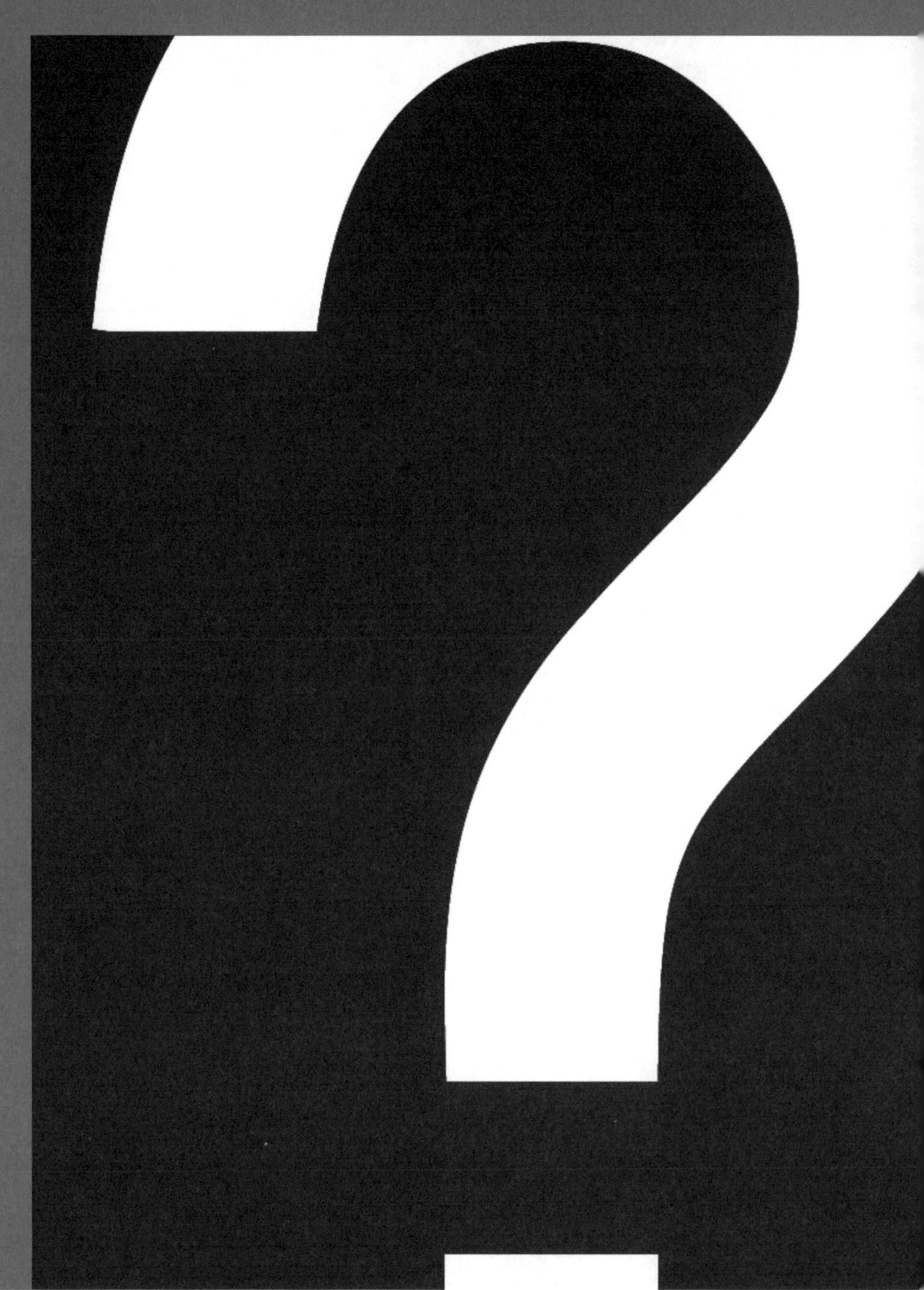

How Do You Know What Is Beautiful in Visual Art, Music, and Literature?

You are surrounded by things that you are told are beautiful. Many of these are called works of art. However, just about anything can be called an artwork. But what makes them beautiful or works of art, and who decides? Is beauty only in the eye of the beholder, or is there such a thing as objective beauty?

We often question other people's taste in the arts. Just as often, people defend their personal taste of what is good by saying, "I know what I like!" What is taste and how do you know if yours is good? Beauty and the arts, their nature and purpose, have intrigued philosophers since ancient times and perhaps as far back as prehistory. Why are beauty and the arts so special and problematic? This unit suggests methods to answer these questions and helps you build your own meaningful theories of beauty and the arts.

Chapter 7 What Are Beauty and the Arts?

Key Words
Aesthetic
Beauty
Aesthetic judgement
Disinterest
Aesthetic experience
Imitationalism
Emotionalism
Formalism
Instrumentalism
Institutionalism
Content
Context
Style

Key People
Clive Bell
Plato

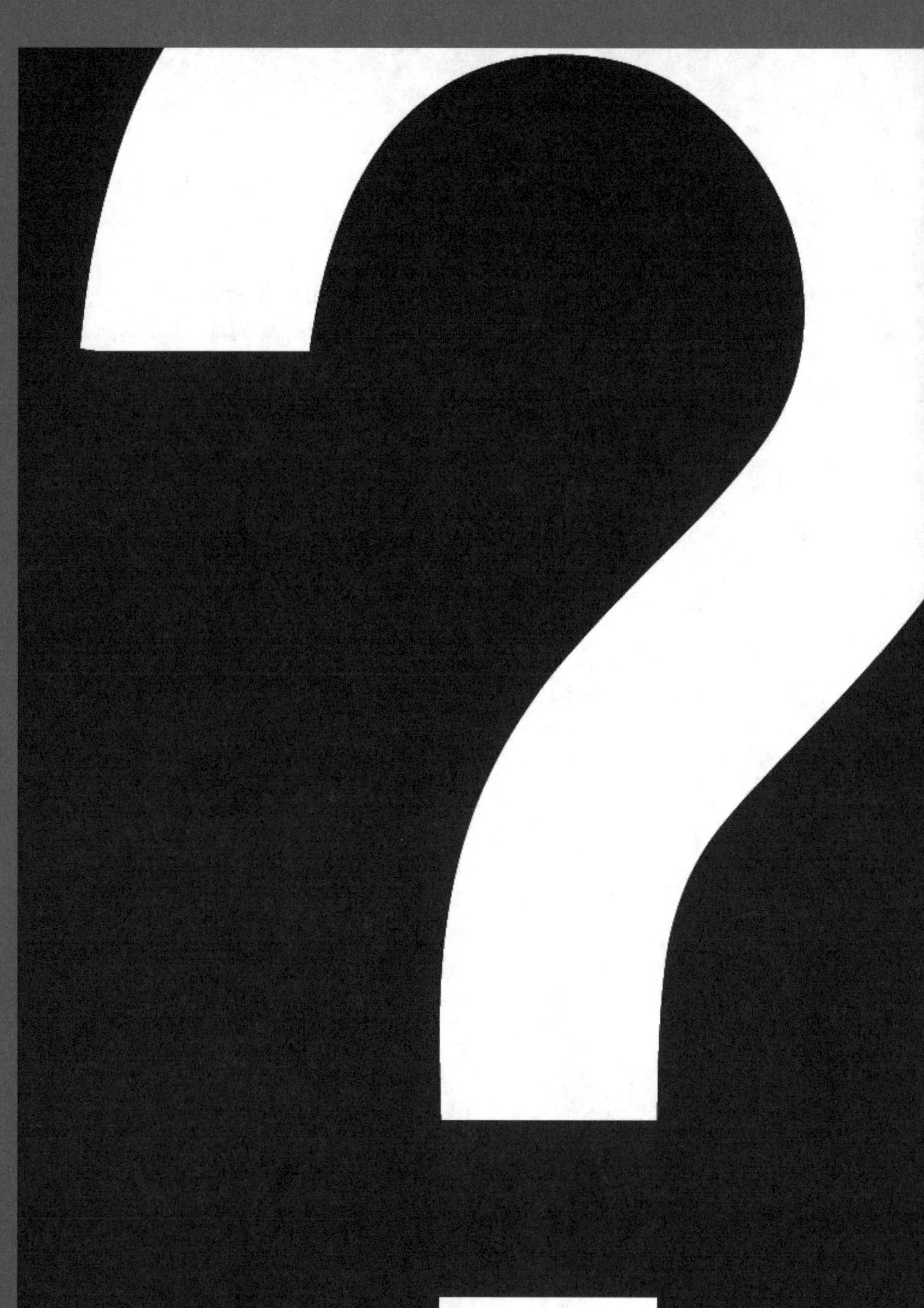

What Is Beauty? What Is Art?

A central task for philosophy is to clarify the meanings of words and how they are used. This chapter will help you sort out the meanings and uses of some terms related to beauty and the arts. For example, the words *pleasure*, *quality*, and *content*, among others, have special uses within beauty and the arts. What is beauty, how do you experience it, and what is a work of art? These are questions this chapter will address as it guides you in laying the groundwork for a personal theory of beauty and philosophy of the arts.

Are Beauty and the Arts the Same Thing?

If something is called a work of art, is it necessarily beautiful?

To understand the similarities and differences between beauty and the arts, it is useful to define the meaning of aesthetics and philosophy of the arts. Aesthetics is the branch of philosophy that deals with the nature and appreciation of beauty. **Aesthetic**, from the Greek word for perceive, means something is perceived and appreciated at a higher, more intense level of awareness than ordinary experiences. An aesthetic experience is one that is caused by something that is beautiful, such as a painting, a dance movement, a piece of music, or a natural event, like a sunset. Philosophy of the arts investigates the problems that arise when you try to define what an artwork is. Thus, the separation between aesthetics and philosophy of the arts is this: when you consider what beauty is, the subject is aesthetics; when you consider what objects are beautiful, and why, you are in the realm of philosophy of the arts.

Aesthetics and philosophy of the arts overlap in several ways because much of what is called art is considered beautiful and vice versa. Objects of nature, such as flowers and sunsets, and human-made objects, like ceramic teapots and sports cars are examples of this overlap.

In Western culture, until the end of the 19th century, the art-viewing public generally expected that all artworks would be beautiful. Ideas of art and beauty were closely related. However, that is no longer the case. Today, definitions and descriptions of art and beauty are matters of considerable debate.

What Is Beautiful?

Everything from parties to pop songs, paintings to haircuts, cheeseburgers to Ferraris, is called "beautiful." What qualities make each of these items beautiful? Are any of the qualities you have identified common to all the items?

Most people agree that the idea of beauty exists, but people do not always see eye-to-eye on what object or quality deserves the label "beautiful." It does not seem to make sense to say that a song, a loved one, or a sunset are all beautiful. These are such different types of things and yet they are often called beautiful. In the first case, a song is an art object that someone creates, while a loved one is a person whose character or appearance is being judged. A sunset is a natural event that has nothing in common with the first two.

Most philosophers agree that people respond to beauty with both their intellect and emotions. It is the nature of these responses that is examined here.

How Is Beauty Defined?

You have read that the notion of beauty is applied to many different things, such as songs or sunsets. In aesthetics, the first task is to determine what beauty is. Here are two different but related dictionary definitions of beauty to consider:

1. **Beauty** is that quality or combination of qualities that causes a person to experience great pleasure through the senses, intellect, or notion of morality.
2. **Beauty** is found in objects that cause aesthetic pleasure.

What Is Quality?

What qualities do you think are necessary for an object to be called a work of art? For example, what are the qualities of a song, a film, or a poem that you look for when you try to decide if it is really a work of art?

Look at the keywords in the first definition of beauty. Quality is the standard you set about something when you compare it to other things like it. Because you make judgements and comparisons every day, quality can include everything that you experience. Colour, shape, smell, surface texture, and sound are some common qualities about objects that you experience. Other qualities you experience are thoughts and ideas. Likewise, you get a sense of the quality of thoughts and ideas when you measure them against the ideas of others. People tend to rate the beauty of these qualities by the measure of their agreement with them or preference for them. In other words, your likes and dislikes of the qualities of a particular object or idea may help you decide if you think something is beautiful. You are unlikely to declare something beautiful if you do not like it. While it is your emotions that initially tell you what you like and do not like, your intellect, your reasoning ability, and your experience also influence your preferences. Your opinions are called value judgements. When you form an opinion about the beauty of something, you make an **aesthetic judgement**.

> *"Ars longa, vita brevis. (Art is long, life is short.)"*
>
> Anonymous

What Is Pleasure?

The next keyword in the first definition of beauty is *pleasure*. Within the subject of aesthetics, pleasure requires explanation. In everyday use, pleasure means enjoyment, satisfaction, and gratification. You can take pleasure from eating an ice-cream cone on a hot day or by watching a movie, but in either case, are you experiencing beauty? What follows is one way that will help you measure if you are experiencing beauty when something gives you pleasure.

People generally agree that the special pleasure derived from beauty is different from everyday pleasures, for instance, how you feel when school is over for the day. The pleasure derived from beauty is caused by a heightened awareness of what you are experiencing. Buddhists say that while you are in this state of heightened awareness, you become one with the object that you contemplate. This does not mean that you are lost in a foggy daydream. Rather, your full attention is concentrated on the object you are experiencing. This kind of emotional response or special pleasure is rare and highly prized. The next time you have an ice cream cone or watch a movie, ask yourself if the experience of this pleasure reaches this level of heightened awareness. Then compare these everyday experiences with the response you have to something more commonly called beautiful, like a scenic panorama or a piece of instrumental music.

What Is Aesthetic Pleasure?

This is where the second definition of beauty becomes useful: beauty is found in those objects that cause aesthetic pleasure. The word *aesthetic* describes the experience of heightened awareness or pleasure. Some writers have used words such as *sublime* and *transcendent* to describe this kind of intense and heightened pleasure. Look them up in a dictionary and see if they adequately describe how you feel about the sensations that beauty causes in you.

> *"Art transforms us from the world of [everyday] activities to a world of aesthetic exaltation. For a moment we are shut off from human interests ... We are lifted above the stream of life ... [into] a world with intense and peculiar significance of its own ... In this world the emotions of life find no place. It is a world with emotions of its own."*
>
> Clive Bell

The English art critic Clive Bell (1881–1964) said that people respond to beauty in art with "aesthetic emotion." Read the quote to learn how he described it. When Bell uses the word *peculiar*, he means special, not strange. It is a rare, remarkable, and extraordinary emotional response.

How Do You Experience Beauty?

> *"But those who are capable of reaching the independent contemplation of abstract beauty will be rare exceptions, will they not?*
>
> *They will, indeed."*
>
> Plato

Recall how the first definition of beauty suggests that you experience beauty through your senses, your intellect, or your sense of morality. It is important to bear in mind that just because there are three different ways in which people experience beauty, it does not necessarily follow that there are three different kinds of beauty. Beauty is a singular concept. While your notion of beauty may apply to many different things, you are referring to the same quality in all those things. In this sense, beauty has only one meaning.

The first way in which people experience beauty is through the five senses: sight, smell, sound, taste, and touch. You make aesthetic judgements about sensual, or sense beauty every day. Less frequent are statements about intellectual beauty, which is the second way people experience beauty. People are often less aware of the beauty of logical and insightful thinking. An example of this kind of beauty is a mathematical proof. It is not so much getting a correct answer, but the ordered thinking process itself that is beautiful. Another kind of intellectual beauty is the beauty of an idea. Everyone has experienced the heightened pleasure of thinking a really good idea. This is sometimes called the "Eureka! experience," after the ancient Greek engineer and mathematician Archimedes (c. 287–212 BCE).

> *"I affirm that the beautiful is the good."*
>
> Plato

The third way in which you experience beauty takes place when something appeals to your notion of morality—the beauty of a good person, for example. There are plenty of models of good people, including Mother Teresa, Mohandas Gandhi, and Dr. Martin Luther King, Jr. The special quality of their lives, their unselfish good works, their strength of character, causes admiration and awe in people. Many philosophers, including the ancient Greek philosopher Plato (427–347 BCE), have connected, even equated, beauty and goodness. Zeno (333–263 BCE), another ancient Greek philosopher, said: "Only the morally beautiful is good." Plato did, as well. Think of a member of your family or community who is beautiful in the moral sense.

What is the connection between the arts and feelings? Begin by using your personal experiences, then generalize your answers to include all of the arts and all feelings. For example, think about the connection between a song that you listen to and the feelings that it evokes in you. How does what you feel about the song affect what you think of the song?

How Do You Know You Are Experiencing Beauty?

One of the problems with the concepts of beauty and aesthetic pleasure is this: How do you measure the intensity of the pleasure you are experiencing? Only you will know if your pleasure is heightened enough or distinct enough from other types of pleasure to be aesthetic. In other words, how do you know when you are experiencing beauty? Perhaps, like Buddhists suggest, you need to feel at one with the art object to experience beauty. Maybe it is difficult to know if you are experiencing beauty. However, some philosophers have suggested ways that may help you to experience beauty. Two of these ways are education and disinterest.

Some philosophers argue that you have to educate yourself in what is beautiful. They suggest that you examine what others have called beautiful and match their judgements with your own. In this way, you constantly add to your store of experience and heighten your appreciation of beautiful things.

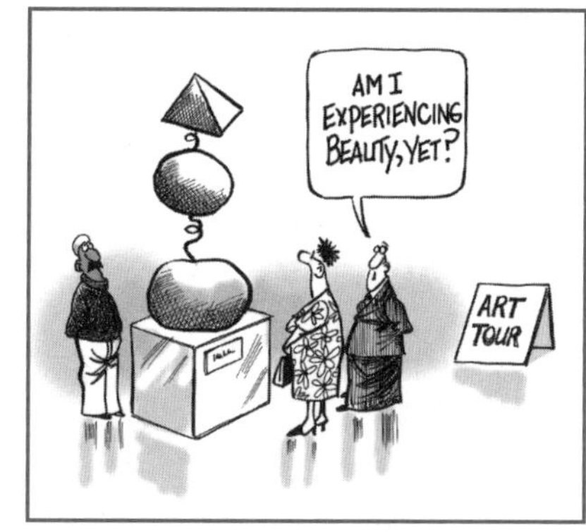

What Is Disinterest?

Disinterest is another way that some philosophers suggest you can have an authentic aesthetic emotional response, to experience beauty. **Disinterest** means that you voluntarily detach yourself from your everyday desires, opinions, and thoughts that might interfere with your aesthetic enjoyment of the artwork or natural object. The point of disinterest is to allow yourself to experience an object or event without bias or prejudice of any kind. Only in this neutral, detached state can you freely respond to your perceptions.

The viewer deliberately begins this process of disinterest. For example, you go to an art gallery with the intention of experiencing one or more of the

Colour Plates

Artworks by Mary Pratt (born 1935), Ken Danby (born 1940), and Jeff Wall (born 1946) are representational or realistic. Search the Web for examples of their work. Keep their style in mind as you view the colour plates.

Search the Web for examples of the work of Betty Goodwin (born 1923), Liz Magor (born 1948), and Greg Curnoe (1936–1992). Using the terminology you have learned in Unit 3, describe the style of their work.

Plate 1

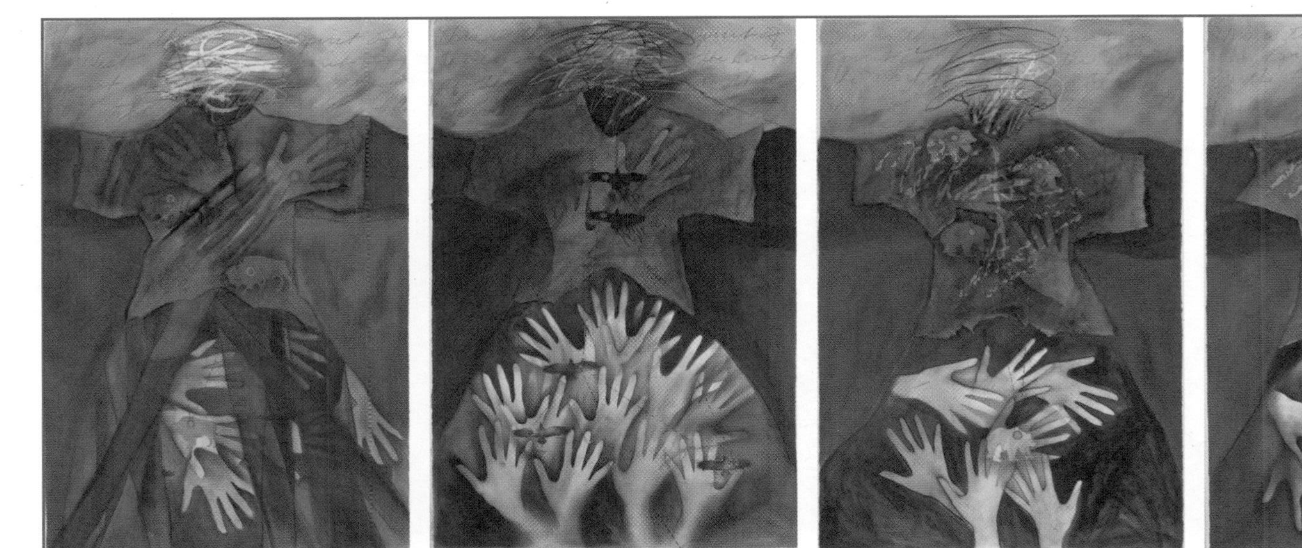

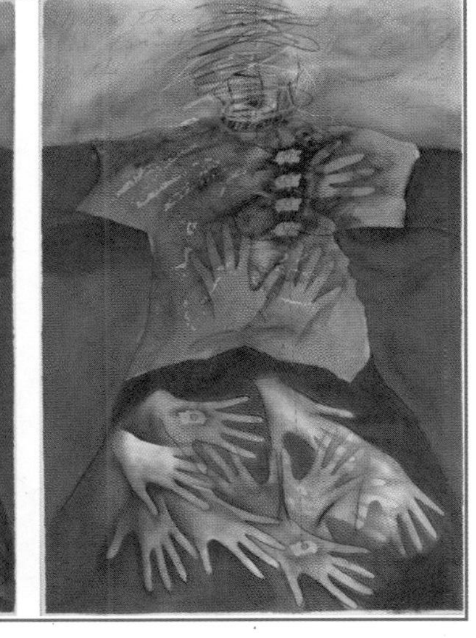

Joane Cardinal-Schubert is a member of the First Nations of Alberta, Canada. One of her goals is that viewers of her work will understand Native issues in terms of their own culture. "I try and create things that are going to be a mirror for people ... where their own knowledge and memory can take off, so everyone can relate to it on some level." The four directions in the title are the points of the compass. War shirts were thought to protect their wearer in battle. The outlines of animals and hands are symbolic as well.

In a group with your classmates, brainstorm several possible meanings of these images. Write a short metaphorical narrative or poem that explains the content.

CARDINAL-SCHUBERT, Joane (born 1942), ***Four Directions—The Warshirt Series—My Mother's Vision: This is the Spirit of the West, This is the Spirit of the East, This is the Spirit of the North, This is the Spirit of the South****, 1986, oil (mixed-media) on rag paper, 4' x 12', © Canadian Museum of Civilization, artist Joane Schubert-Cardinal, catalogue no. V-B-545 a-d, images no. K95-43, S94-13659, S94-13660, S94-13661. Reproduced with permission.*

Plate 2

Compared to the representational paintings you searched, there is more latitude here for possible meanings. Note that this is an abstract piece because the formal properties depict a recognizable shape, the profile of a walking woman, although there is little other realistic detail. Describe it. How many women are there? What are the dominant colours used? One of the women is in outline. Why? What, if anything, does the horizontal yellow line signify?

The pictorial detail and the titles of Mary Pratt's and Ken Danby's paintings make it easier to understand their meaning than Michael Snow's work.

SNOW, Michael (born 1929), ***Venus Simultaneous****, 1962, Oil on Canvas and Wood, 200.7 x 299.7 x 15.2 cm, Art Gallery of Ontario, Toronto. Reproduced with permission.*

Plate 3

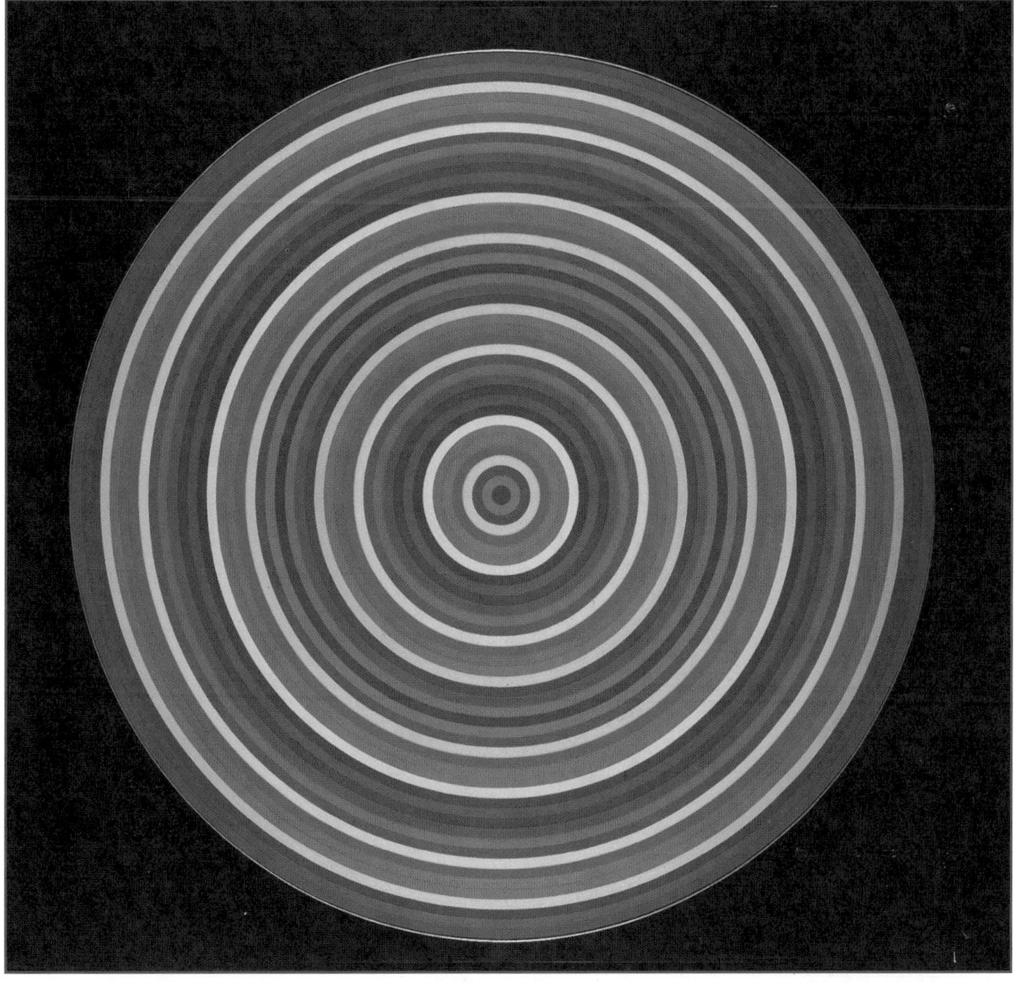

This is a nonobjective or nonrepresentational work. There are no references to anything you might experience in everyday life. Not even targets look like this painting. What do you think it means? The formal properties of Jeff Wall's images provide a clear and realistic frame of reference from which to derive meaning. With Michael Snow's painting, the formal properties remain the same, but there are fewer realistic references from which to grasp a meaning. With Claude Tousignant's painting, the same formal properties of the visual arts are present, but there are no visual references to any real-life experiences. This painting represents only thin concentric circles of alternating hot and cold colours. The title suggests a reference but it may not be relevant to your experience. With no connection to anything real, the viewer is invited to experience the essence of the artwork's formal properties—the line, shape, and colour—alone. In other words, form in the non-representational arts is not used as a means of depicting any thing. The art object is stripped of any instrumental value. It becomes an end-in-itself. Perhaps that is what the picture means. It just is. Perhaps this is what intrinsic value is.

*TOUSIGNANT, Claude (born 1932), **Gong-88**, 1967, Liquidex on canvas, Outside diameter: 233.5 cm, Art Gallery of Ontario, Toronto. Gift from the MacLean Foundation, 1968. Reproduced with permission.*

Plate 4

This is a photograph of graffiti. Describe the style and content using specific terms you have learned in this unit. This image is spray-painted on a building that the painter does not own. Does this make him or her an artist or a vandal?

PEGLAR, Kenneth, ***Graffiti 1****, colour photograph. Reproduced with permission.*

PHILOSOPHY IN EVERYDAY LIFE

Is It Art if It Is Morally Objectionable?

Have you had this experience? You hear a new music recording that grabs your attention. As you listen, you realize that the lyrics promote violence against women. You believe the content is morally objectionable. Should you continue to listen with disinterest? Can you continue to listen with disinterest? There are other elements to the song, like the vocal performance and the music. Maybe you can put the lyrics aside and decide if the other aspects of the song are art. Alternatively, perhaps you cannot separate the lyrics from the music. Which instance applies to you?

Can you think of similar instances in film, literature, or visual art that cause you to question whether you should approach the work with disinterest?

artworks aesthetically. You purposefully prepare yourself for the experience by actively concentrating on the work of art. You deliberately shut out your everyday cares and concerns. It takes practice to do this. Your state of disinterest may last only a few seconds or minutes at a time, before something—a thought or concern about the world—intrudes.

Do you think that disinterest is necessary to have an aesthetic emotional response? Compare how you respond to a novel you are reading solely for pleasure, with your response to one you have to read for school. Even if you are enjoying the book, do your responsibilities as a student affect your disinterested pleasure?

Some critics and philosophers maintain that you should be selective about what you choose to experience with disinterest. This is especially true of material whose content is morally objectionable, such as depictions or descriptions that are obscene or pornographic. Other examples are culturally and racially difficult images including scenes of Nazi or other atrocities, war, and suffering.

What Are Theories of Art?

You have explored ideas related to defining beauty and how to experience beauty. Now focus your attention on the philosophy of the arts. Art objects are so varied that no single description or theory can account for their importance. Philosophers and critics have offered several different views by which you can judge the merits of an artwork based on its aesthetic qualities. An aesthetic quality is any aspect or component of a work of art that causes you to respond to it in a particular way. This response is called an **aesthetic experience**, which is a heightened, intense feeling.

Three aesthetic qualities are considered here: literal, design, and expressive.

Any artwork that is a realistic depiction of life, that is true-to-life, shows literal qualities. Artworks with strong design qualities are considered models of composition. Composition refers to the way the elements and principles of design are organized to produce the artwork. Expressive qualities are the emotion, mood, meaning, or ideas communicated to the viewer.

It is likely that artworks will possess all three aesthetic qualities in some combination or other. Philosophers and critics have argued for centuries about which of these qualities is the most important for understanding and judging the merits of artworks. Here are five widely held theories of art: imitationalism, emotionalism, formalism, instrumentalism, and institutionalism.

What Is Imitationalism?

Imitationalism, also called mimesis theory, states that a successful artwork imitates or looks like something in the real world. *Mimesis* is the Greek word for imitate. Artworks of this type exhibit true-to-life qualities, such as a painting of a lake that looks similar to a real lake.

One problem with imitationalism: it suggests that works of art not depicting life-like objects, people, or scenes are not worthy of your attention or admiration. Imitationalism also excludes instrumental music. Instrumental music, which is organized sound in time, is non-visual and non-verbal. It does not represent or imitate anything.

What Is Emotionalism?

Emotionalism states that the most important aspect of an artwork is its expressive qualities—the feelings, mood, ideas, and meaning it communicates

POINT OF VIEW

Clive Bell

Clive Bell was a formalist. He believed that the form or structure of the object, the way the elements and principles of its design are arranged, is what makes it an aesthetic object. In his 1914 book, *Art*, he wrote: "What quality is shared by all objects that provoke our aesthetic emotions? … Only one answer seems possible—significant form. In each, lines and colours combined in a particular way, certain forms and relations of forms, stir our aesthetic emotions. These relations and combinations of lines and colours, these aesthetically moving forms, I call 'Significant Form'; and 'Significant Form' is the one quality common to all works of visual art."

While Bell specifically identifies visual art, his theory applies to the other arts. For Bell, when the form of an object is significant, that object is beautiful. It is also likely to be an artwork.

to the viewer. This view is most favourable to music and nonrepresentational visual art—art that does not depict anything in the real world.

What Is Formalism?

Some philosophers, such as Plato, insist that the beauty of an object and its value as an artwork is found in its form, or formal properties. This view is called **formalism**. In philosophy, form is more than the shape of an object or the arrangement of its parts. Form also embodies function or purpose, the essence of an object. The form of a table, for instance, is the sum of all the components and conditions necessary for an object to be a table. Buddhists call this essential nature of an object its *suchness*. In the case of a table, it means sturdy legs, a flat horizontal surface, and so on. If all of these conditions are present in the same object, then that object is a table.

In the arts, form is the particular arrangement of the elements and principles of design of that art form. The formal properties of painting, for instance, are shape, colour, and balance, to name three. Four properties of music are pitch, sound quality, rhythm, and duration. Poetry, sculpture, dance, architecture, this textbook, all possess form as a necessary condition of their existence.

What Is Instrumentalism?

The fourth theory of art to consider is **instrumentalism**. This theory states that the most important feature of an artwork is its usefulness. If it serves a practical function, like teaching or furthering an ethical, religious, or political viewpoint, it is worthwhile. Artworks, including novels, films, paintings, and opera that depict scenes or events in the lives of religious and political leaders are examples.

What Is Institutionalism?

Institutionalism refers to the community of philosophers, critics, and gallery owners who determine which objects should be called artworks. An object that these experts consider worthy of being exhibited is an artwork.

What Is a Work of Art?

> *"Music is the art ... which most completely realizes the artistic idea, and is the condition to which all the other arts are constantly aspiring."*
>
> Oscar Wilde

You have considered beauty and theories of art. But what about artworks—what makes something a work of art? The phrase, "work of art," is used to label a wide variety of objects and events with many different characteristics. However, it is worth repeating that something that is beautiful is not necessarily a work of art, and likewise, whatever is not beautiful can still be a work of art.

Because there are so many art forms, many philosophers think it is impossible to define the word *artwork*. They say the best that can be attempted is a description or a method of identifying what an artwork is. However, first it is useful to distinguish between the content, context, and style of works of art.

What Is Content?

Content is what the work of art is about—its subject matter: the story, person, event, or object that is depicted. However, does a poem, dance,

WEB CONNECTION

Nonrepresentational Art

Search the Web for artworks whose content is nonrepresentational. For example, view the artworks in the style of *Pavane* (1954) by Canadian Jean-Paul Riopelle (1923–2002). Also, find examples of American Richard Diebenkorn's (1922–1993) *Ocean Park* series.

movie, picture, or sculpture have to have recognizable content to be an artwork? Until the beginning of the 20th century, generally, the answer was yes. In Western culture, as recently as one hundred years ago, the content of the visual arts usually was clear. By today's standards, even daring visual artists of their day, such as Claude Monet (1840–1926) or Vincent Van Gogh (1853–1890), depicted recognizable scenes. Artworks were always about something: people, events, places, or nature. The 20th century brought many innovations in the visual arts, such as abstraction and non-representation. Composers write instrumental music that has no apparent melody or recognizable harmonies, yet it has a powerful effect on our emotions. Choreographers create abstract dance works whose impact on the audience relies on body motion alone. Because of this, using content to define art, in any of its forms, is one of the major problems in the philosophy of the arts.

What Is Context?

Like everyone, artists live and work in particular circumstances. **Context** refers to all of the circumstances surrounding the making of a work of art. Context includes the ordinary, day-to-day events in the artist's life. However, context also includes much broader considerations: the artist's culture and nationality and the major historical events that took place during his or her lifetime. For example, World War II had a profound and lasting effect on 20th century art. Just as important may be an unhappy childhood, a supportive friend, or a chance meeting with someone in an art studio in your school.

PHILOSOPHY IN EVERYDAY LIFE

What Is Your Context?

Take a moment to reflect on your current context. Where are you reading this: on a bus, at home, in a noisy cafeteria at school? Is your location or the fact that this is homework affecting your concentration or understanding? Consider your context the next time you make or enjoy an artwork. What effects do your current circumstances have on your work? Does context also affect disinterest?

What Is Style?

The third aspect of the arts, **style**, is how the artist uses the elements and principles of design: shape, sound, word order, movement, perspective, rhythm, and balance, among others. Style is affected by context. For example, an artist's formal art education, or the lack of it, affects the style of the artwork. The influence of other artists is another context that affects style.

What Are the Criteria of an Artwork?

You have a sense of how content, context, and style affect works of art. Now try this exercise to understand what criteria you believe are necessary to make an object a work of art. Brainstorm a list of qualities or properties that are common to all works of art. From this list, determine those criteria you believe are the necessary conditions or components of a work of art. Also look for connections with content, context, and style. Begin with this statement: X is an artwork, if and only if, X …

After creating your list, read the following sample list, compiled from several brainstorming sessions. X is an artwork, if and only if, X:

1. is an artifact, an object made by a human being
2. is original, one-of-a-kind, not a copy
3. has no practical value
4. evokes an aesthetic, emotional response
5. is physical and can be experienced by the senses
6. is called an artwork by an art expert

7. has an audience
8. has significant form
9. is intended by its maker to be an artwork
10. has been considered an artwork for a period of time
11. is made by someone who calls her or himself an artist
12. is located in an art gallery
13. shows evidence of skill or technique
14. is rare

What Belongs on Your List?

Now identify which items on your list best fit X, your hypothetical work of art. Examine each criterion for its strengths and weaknesses. Prioritize the items on the list to determine which are the strongest commonalities for all artworks.

In the sample list above, each item has merit and raises intriguing issues.

For example, at first glance, number 1 seems reasonable. However, number 1 excludes the possibility that as-yet-undiscovered extraterrestrial beings may make art. It also excludes animals. Should it? Ninety-eight percent of a chimpanzee's genetic code is the same as a humans'. What level of experience and education is required to be the expert in number 6? Consider number 9 and look at the image of Marcel Duchamp's sculpture *Fountain*, on page 141. Should this piece be called art because the artist Marcel Duchamp says it is?

Listing criteria points to two things: the problem of deciding what an artwork is, and the need for a thorough analysis of all the possibilities to form a meaningful, personal theory of the arts. You need to ask yourself which items belong on your personal list of essential criteria.

> *"What I am arguing ... is that the very expansive, adventurous character of art, its ever-present changes and novel creations, makes it logically impossible to ensure any set of defining properties."*
>
> Morris Weitz

What Do You Think?

There are no easy answers to the issues raised in this chapter. You have explored aesthetics—meanings of beauty, and how it is experienced through your senses, morality, and intellect. You have considered if education and disinterest help increase your experience of beauty. The philosophy of the arts introduced you to five theories of art: imitationalism, emotionalism, formalism, instrumentalism, and institutionalism. Finally, you considered artworks themselves: their content, context, style, and your personal criteria for what makes an artwork. Do any of the definitions and theories of art help you find a personal explanation for beauty and what is an artwork?

Chapter 8 What Are Value, Purpose, Meaning, and Truth in the Arts?

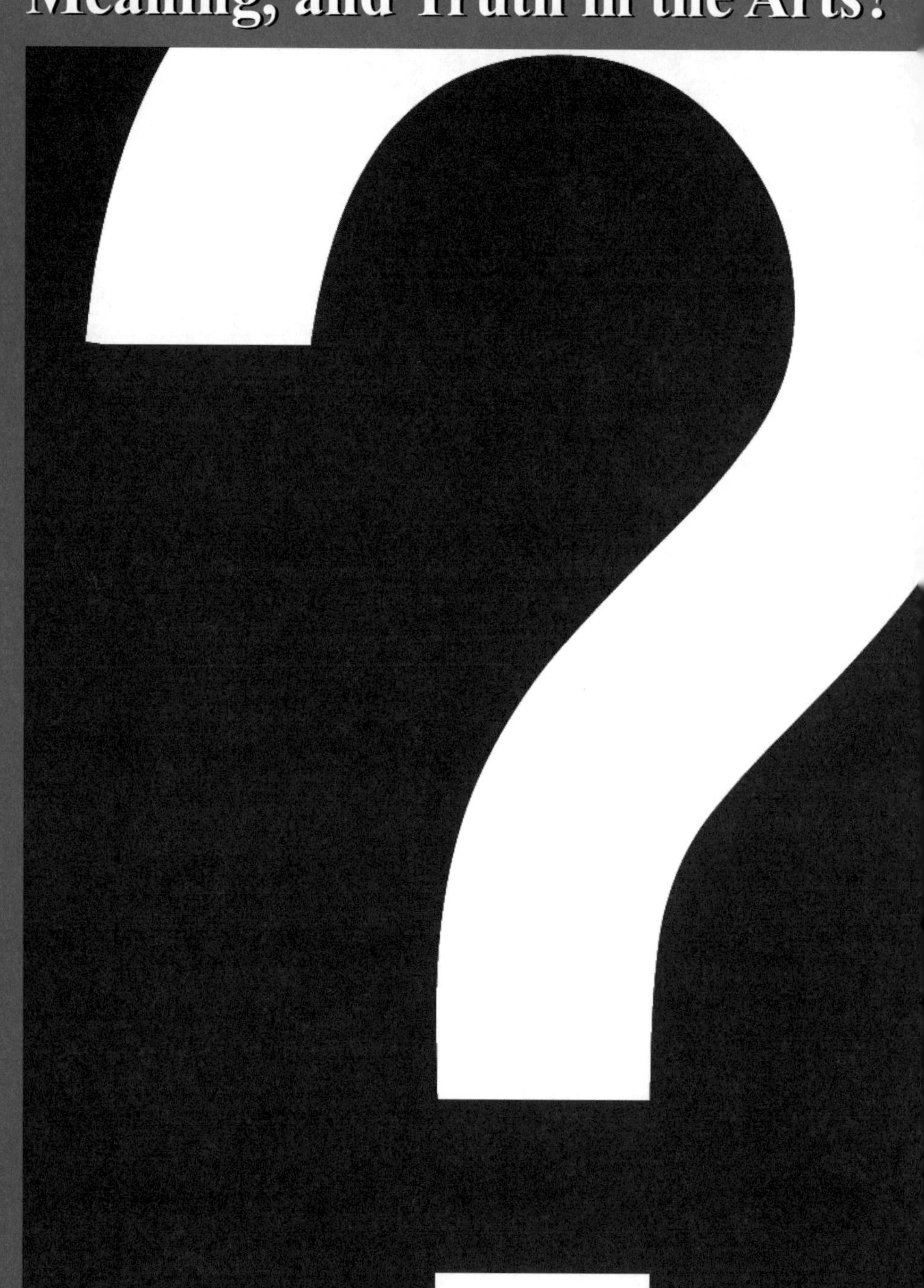

Key Words
Moral value
Utility value
Truth value
Aesthetic value
Entelechy
Instrumental value
Intrinsic value

Key People
Aristotle
John Dewey
Oscar Wilde
Cao Yu

Can Value, Purpose, Meaning, and Truth in Art Be Defined?

In Chapter 7, you considered how difficult it is to define and describe beauty and art. What about the value, purpose, meaning, and truth of art? Are these specific aspects of art any easier to define and describe? In this chapter, you will explore these four aspects in relation to beauty and the arts.

What do you think is the value of the arts?

We value objects, people, and events in a variety of ways depending on how much we like them, or think they are good or useful. The arts have all of these values, yet we value art in different ways as well. What is this special value?

What Is Value?

In philosophy, the word *value* has a range of meanings. There is the dollar value of a work of art, but it is not relevant to the ideas in this chapter. In general terms, value refers to the merit of an object or an idea. Because people always make value judgements, it is useful to distinguish between specific kinds of value. Here are three values with which people are most familiar:

- moral value
- utility value
- truth value

Moral value refers to goodness or ethical merit. Your opinion about your own character and behaviour and that of other people are examples. **Utility value** is an indication of how practical or useful an object is. A hammer has high utility value when it is used to hit a nail. **Truth value** means correct in the sense that information is correct or right. For example, the capital of Canada is Ottawa. This is a fact so it has high truth value.

What Is Aesthetic Value?

Specific to philosophy of the arts is **aesthetic value**. Remember that the word *aesthetic* refers to beauty and how you respond to it in the arts and nature. When you hold an opinion about the beauty of something or someone, you make an aesthetic value judgement. The degree of a thing's beauty, goodness, usefulness, or correctness determines its value. The aesthetic value

PHILOSOPHY IN MATH AND SCIENCE

Are Science and Math Beautiful?

Do you think it is possible that science and math can be beautiful? World-class mathematicians claim that their work produces an aesthetic experience. English mathematician G.H. Hardy (1877–1947) wrote, "A mathematician, like a painter or a poet, is a maker of patterns … The mathematician's patterns, like the painter's and the poet's must be beautiful; the ideas, like the colours and the words, must fit together in a harmonious way. Beauty is the first test; there is no permanent place in the world for ugly mathematics." Likewise, American inventor and engineer R. Buckminster Fuller (1895–1983) said, "When I am working on a problem, I never think about beauty. I only think of how to solve the problem. But when I am finished, if the solution is not beautiful, I know it is wrong."

The next time you work on a math or science problem, consider what Hardy and Fuller said. Do you agree with them? Is it possible to find beauty in the solution of a math or science problem? Does the satisfaction you feel in solving problems qualify as an aesthetic experience?

of an object corresponds to your aesthetic response to it. If you think an object or event is beautiful, then its aesthetic value is high for you. That is your subjective assessment because not everyone will share your opinion.

Do the Arts Combine Values?

Moral, utility, and truth values can co-exist with aesthetic value. Objects valued both aesthetically and morally include religious art. The stained glass windows that decorate gothic cathedrals are examples. Perhaps Ferraris are combinations of utility and aesthetic value. Ferraris look the way they do because they are designed to minimize air resistance so they will go faster and win more races. Perhaps the fact that their appearance is pleasing is a coincidence. For truth value, few will deny that knowing whether information is true or false is important. Some even suggest that things that are true, like answers to math or science problems, also have high aesthetic value.

Is Aesthetic Value Objective?

People have personal opinions about the beauty and value of things, but that does not rule out the possibility that aesthetic value is objective. Ancient Greek philosopher Aristotle's (384–322 BCE) theory of **entelechy** claims that the form of an object is inherent in an object. Inherent means existing in and inseparable from. For Aristotle, the form of an object, any object, exists in this world, not in the perfect, otherworldly realm that Plato described in his theory of ideal Forms. You read about Plato's theory in Chapter 2.

Take tables, for example. Aristotle believed that all tables show the form of tableness because the form is inherent or naturally present in the object. Certain objects are identified as tables because they look like tables and function like tables. It follows that form and function are the same thing and that function is also inherent in the object. From this, it follows that the purpose or value of that object is also inherent in its form. In other words, the purpose of a table exists within the form of a table. The table's basic form is a flat top with legs to hold it up. The table's purpose is to support things on the flat top.

Now think about entelechy in terms of the arts. Just as the purpose or value of an object is inherent in its form, Aristotle believed that aesthetic value is inherent in an artwork. In this view, art is objective and universal because the purpose is the same for all artworks. If an aesthetic value such as beauty is an objective property in all artworks, then the artwork will affect all attentive viewers. It is there for all to experience, although the experiences will not necessarily be the same.

> *"Art should be independent of all claptrap ... [such] as devotion, pity, love, patriotism and the like."*
>
> James Whistler

Is Aesthetic Value Subjective?

Some philosophers say that aesthetic value is subjective. They say that an aesthetic object, any work of art for example, is value-neutral—it has no aesthetic value in itself. It is called an aesthetic object because it has been identified as an artwork, but that does not mean that its aesthetic properties are objective. The subjective position is that the aesthetic value is in the mind of the perceiver. While it does enter the minds of all perceivers, each perceiver's value judgement is unique, individual, and subjective.

Where subjectivity is concerned, the question remains: Who can say you are wrong about your judgements of aesthetic value?

Does Art Have a Purpose?

What do you think are the purposes of a work of art?

Think about the purpose of everyday objects, such as hammers, chairs, and shoes. The purpose of a hammer is clear. However, because the uses of art are so varied, its purpose, if there is only one, is less clear. The following list is one way of identifying what is the purpose of an artwork. However, before reading further, brainstorm your own list of the purposes of art.

> *"The fundamental purpose of the artist is the same as that of a scientist: to state a fact."*
>
> Herbert Read

The following list identifies possible purposes of art. The purpose of a work of art is:

1. to impress your friends, clients
2. religious devotion
3. contemplation: statues of the Buddha, Japanese meditation gardens
4. decoration: colours of the painting match the upholstery
5. to provide an outlet for the artist's emotions, ideas or opinions
6. education: moral, cultural, political
7. propaganda

8. to convey meaning or truth that cannot be conveyed in any other way
9. to cause an authentic aesthetic emotional response

Which Purposes Apply to Philosophy and Aesthetics?

All of the purposes of art listed above, and more, are plausible. However, you can challenge some of the items on the list as being outside of the philosophy of the arts. Two examples are number 1, impressing your friends and clients and number 6, education. Check the other items on the list above and on your own list and decide which ones are within the areas of aesthetics and philosophy.

Do the Three Common Values Apply?

You can group the purposes of art from the list according to the three more common types of values: moral, utility, and truth. For each of the items, which of the types of values apply? For number 1, impressing your friends, utility is the likely value. In fact, utility seems to apply to them all. Make a list of which moral and truth values apply to the purposes of art. What about aesthetic value? Is there anything left on the list of purposes of art that is specifically aesthetic in its nature? You can argue that number 3 (contemplation: Japanese meditation gardens) has aesthetic value. Perhaps even number 8 (to convey meaning or truth that cannot be conveyed in any other way) has aesthetic value—depending on what truth means. Note that you can substitute the word *purpose* for the word *value*.

Is an Aesthetic Response the Only Purpose of an Artwork?

Many philosophers and artists believe that the only purpose of the arts is an aesthetic one, number 9—to cause an authentic aesthetic emotional response. According to this view, all other considerations, including utility, moral, and truth value are secondary purposes of the arts. They may be interesting and worthy of debate on their own but many philosophers say that these things are not as important as the authentic emotional response.

The point of creating a list of the purposes of artworks is to determine if a work of art has a single, clear purpose. What meets your personal requirements for an artwork's purpose will determine which item or items are important to you.

> *"The subject matter of art is life, life as it actually is; but the function of art is to make life better."*
>
> George Santayana

Is Art Its Own Purpose?

Do you think that the arts have no real-world value? Do you think that the only purpose of the arts is that they exist?

What Is Instrumental Value?

All non-art objects seem to have some utility, moral, or truth value that corresponds to the purpose for which they were designed. In this way, they are instruments of that purpose, like dance shoes, tools, movie cameras, and so on. They have **instrumental value**. Sometimes objects are used for purposes other than for what they were intended. You might use a sculpture as a doorstop because nothing else is at hand. While its new use may be arbitrary and temporary, its value for the time it keeps the door open is instrumental. However, this is an unintended, secondary function of the sculpture. Value is instrumental if the object is a means to an end. A hammer is a means-to-an-end, namely, to drive nails. But is there any such thing as an object that has no instrumental value? Can you think of one?

What Is Intrinsic Value?

If an object actually exists that has no instrumental value, it has **intrinsic value**. Its value is inherent, built-in—an inseparable part of itself. While you can say the same thing about tables and hammers, the sense of inherent is different here. An object that only has intrinsic value is not a means-to-an-end in the same way that tables and hammers are. Some philosophers and artists claim that artworks have intrinsic value, that they are ends-in-themselves, objects that have merit and worth in and of themselves alone. The value of all other types of non-art objects, from cheeseburgers to Ferraris, is instrumental. They are worth something because they are practical. In this sense, the arts can be called non-practical or useless, although these words should be used with caution.

POINT OF VIEW

Oscar Wilde

Do you think that art has intrinsic value, that it is an end in itself? The Irish playwright and philosopher Oscar Wilde (1854–1900) held this view. Wilde believed that beauty and art should be appreciated only for themselves. This doctrine is called "art for its own sake" and sometimes *L'art pour l'art*. According to this view, works of art are ends in themselves and exist in and of themselves—independent of anything else in the world. Wilde wrote, "Art never expresses anything but itself. It has an independent life … and develops purely on its own lines." Wilde thought that a finished artwork is so independent that it stops having anything to do with its creator—the artist.

Wilde said that any unintended, arbitrary use of an artwork is irrelevant. For example, using a sculpture as a doorstop would not qualify as a purpose of the sculpture for Wilde. While using the sculpture as a doorstop may be useful, it is only temporary and irrelevant to the purpose of the sculpture as an artwork—an end-in-itself.

Some philosophers and critics reject the idea of intrinsic value. American philosopher John Dewey (1859–1952) believed that only practical objects have value. In other words, Dewey held that utility value is the most important aspect of an object when you are determining its worth.

Note that if an object has no instrumental value, it does not necessarily follow that it has intrinsic value. It could have negative value. Environmental pollution is an example of negative value. Also, an object or event can have both instrumental and intrinsic value. An example is dancing, which has value in itself, or as a means of attracting a romantic partner, or as a form of exercise for physical fitness.

The concept of intrinsic value goes against everyday experience that defines objects by their intended purposes. It does not seem to make sense that an object can exist and not be purposeful. For example, if you are indifferent to an artwork, if you have no emotional response at all, it does not mean that it has no aesthetic value. It only means that it did not work for you. Can you think on an object that has no purpose?

> *"...when the [art]work is finished and becomes public—when the music, play or dance is performed, when the photograph is exhibited—it is no longer the property of the artist. It becomes a separate, independent object. The viewer can ignore it or take whatever meaning or purpose from it she or he wishes."*
>
> Oscar Wilde

What Is the Autonomy of an Artwork?

Autonomy, from the Greek word meaning self-governing, is a concept closely related to art for its own sake. According to this theory, an artwork is autonomous because it is independent of anything in the real, physical world. Put another way, art is an autonomous realm because the responses it evokes from us are independent. In this way, works of art do not conform to arbitrary community standards of taste. They do not correspond to anything that is external to themselves. Note also the close relationship between autonomy and the concept of disinterest. Can you think of any objects that are not artworks but that are autonomous?

Considering that the word truth is difficult to define, what kinds of truth do you think the arts convey? Consider a music concert at a sports arena, reading a novel, or looking at a Picasso exhibit. Do these three activities convey the same kind of meaning or truth? Is this a possible purpose of the arts?

PHILOSOPHY IN EVERYDAY LIFE

Are Artworks the Only Objects that Have Intrinsic Value?

Oscar Wilde suggested that art has intrinsic value. However, works of art, along with beauty, are needed for an aesthetic emotional response. Therefore, more than having intrinsic value, is causing an aesthetic response another purpose of art? Natural phenomena that you may consider beautiful, such as sunsets, coral, and storms also can give you an aesthetic emotional response. But do they have intrinsic value as art in the same way that artworks do? Philosophers like Wilde would probably say no. The aesthetic emotional response is secondary to the instrumental purpose that natural phenomena have in nature. In other words, if you think that flowers, sunsets, and storms are beautiful, your response is secondary to the practical purpose of these objects within nature. Are there any other things that have intrinsic value? For example, how would you describe the value of beauty? Is it intrinsic to art?

> *"There is only one valuable thing in art: the thing you cannot explain."*
>
> Georges Braque

POINT OF VIEW

Cao Yu

Many artists reject the concept of intrinsic value, or art-for-its-own-sake. They feel that this theory suggests that artworks are a luxury that only a privileged few can afford. They also reject the implication that education and sophistication are necessary to have an aesthetic experience.

An artist who felt this way was Chinese playwright Cao Yu (1910–1996). According to him, "Art for art's sake is a philosophy of the well-fed." He was concerned with how wealthy people treated their workers. His dramas examined corruption and the consequences that arise when privileged people do not honour their commitments to those who serve them. Cao believed that moral value is important in a work of art. He also believed that the arts are a powerful means of public education.

What Is Meaning in the Arts?

Most people assume that works of art convey a message or meaning of some kind. But there is no universal agreement about what that meaning is. Traditional art forms, such as the play *Hamlet*, or the ballet *Swan Lake*, convey meaning to the viewer. Their content is about something you can recognize, the characters and narrative of a story, for instance. In the case of a painting, you recognize the objects in a particular setting. However, much of the contemporary arts are nonrepresentational. This means that there is no recognizable content provided to the viewer. There is no connection to the real world. What kind of meaning does nonrepresentational art convey? Is it meaningless or does it convey meaning in a way that is unfamiliar to most people?

An example of language used in a nonrepresentational way is *Jabberwocky* by English poet and mathematician Lewis Carroll (1832–1898). These are the first four lines.

'Twas brillig and the slithy toves
Did gyre and gimble in the wabe:
All mimsy were the borogroves,
And the mome raths outgrabe.

Carroll follows the rules of grammar. The lines of the poem sound as if they should mean something, but it is hard to know what the words mean. They do not correspond to anything in the real world. The same is true with nonrepresentational visual art, theatre, and dance.

Where Is the Meaning of an Artwork Located?

Do you think the meaning of art is intrinsic to an artwork or is the meaning inside of you?

With both representational and nonrepresentational works of art, people wonder where the meaning of art is located. Is the meaning an intrinsic part of the artwork, an internal, inseparable part, or does the meaning come from within you? It is tempting to believe that whatever meaning you take from a work of art is an intrinsic part of that artwork. In other words, it is said that the location of the meaning is in the artwork, that something in the work of art triggers a response in you.

WEB CONNECTION

The Burghers of Calais

Search the Web for sites about Rodin's *The Burghers of Calais*. Try to find answers to these questions: Who were these men? Why were they so despairing? What happened to them? Why did Rodin sculpt them?

In the representational arts, the meaning is usually clear and closely related to or dependent upon content. An example is French sculptor Auguste Rodin's (1840–1917) *The Burghers of Calais*, which he finished in 1895. Six gaunt men with nooses around their necks look as if they have given up all hope. The large statues, made of dull, dark-coloured metal, are about one-and-a-half times life size. That description alone is not enough for you to grasp what Rodin was representing. To more fully appreciate and understand this piece, you must research the context and content.

> *"Everyone wants to understand painting. Why is there no attempt to understand the song of birds?"*
>
> Pablo Picasso

Is there Meaning in Non-Traditional Modern Art?

Have you ever seen a modern dance or heard a poem recited and said to yourself, "I have no idea what that means"? The non-traditional arts genres of the 20th century challenge older theories about meaning and its location. Nonrepresentational visual art, experimental and improvisational theatre, dance, poetry, and free-form instrumental music do not provide any of the usual references from personal experience. Their form and style may seem random, spontaneous, and accidental. Consequently, they do not mean anything that you might relate to personally in the way that the traditional arts do.

RESEARCH AND INQUIRY SKILLS

Comparing

Comparing is a valuable analytical tool to use in your research in all subjects, including the arts. But what is the best way to go about making comparisons? Imagine you are asked to find out what apples and oranges have in common. How will you do it? If you list the ways in which they are alike or similar, you are comparing. Your list will probably include physical properties and how they affect your senses: colour, aroma, flavour, texture and so on.

First, you identify the ways in which the two things are the same. Then, you estimate their similarities according to how much detail and precision is required. Apples and oranges are the same in that they are both fruit grown on trees. Their size, weight and shape are similar, but not the same. The similarities decrease by degree until you get to dissimilarities. This is where caution is needed because you might be tempted to see similarities where none exist. Identifying dissimilarities is called contrasting.

Practising Your Skill

In your favourite art form, select two items, one each by two different artists. Make a list of criteria to compare them. You will probably think of twenty or more right away. In the sense that apples and oranges are fruit that are grown on trees, how many true similarities are there? How many are on your list until you get to contrasts?

You may recognize the formal structures of non-traditional art, but not their content. For example, much current instrumental concert music does not follow the traditional rules regarding melody and harmony. As a result, it does not sound like what you may be used to. Two examples are the compositions of American Steve Reich (born 1936) and Canadian Alexina Louie (born 1949). Ask the music teacher or librarian in your school for recordings of their works. The same is true of some genres of modern painting. An example is the splatter painting of American visual artist Jackson Pollock (1912–1956). Standing above the canvas that was lying on the floor, Pollock dribbled paint onto it. When it comes to non-traditional art, perhaps ideas about meaning must be reconsidered and expanded.

THINKING LOGICALLY

Fallacy of the False Analogy

Analogies are used when it is necessary to describe something by comparing it with something that is similar, but not the same. If the number of similarities is high, then the analogy is strong. However, if the differences outnumber the similarities, or if differences are missed or concealed, the analogy can be misleading or false. At best, an analogy can only be based on similarities. For example, because baby chimpanzees seem to respond positively to being held and nurtured, it can be argued that human babies will respond the same way. This analogy is made about simian and human behaviour because it is known that about 98 percent of chimpanzee and human genetic material is the same. This counts as a strong analogy.

However, most analogies are not strong. Ninety-eight percent may sound good but it is not certainty and that is the problem with all analogies. You would think twice about jumping off a bridge if you knew that your bungee cord had a two percent failure rate. As Scottish philosopher David Hume (1711–1776) warned, similar does not mean the same and that is why analogies, even apparently strong ones, are never completely reliable.

Turn to the colour plates to see and read the comparison of three examples of non-traditional Canadian visual art by Michael Snow, Claude Tousignant, and Joane Cardinal-Schubert.

> *"Art is a human activity, whose purpose is the transmission of the highest and best feelings to which men have attained."*
>
> Leo Tolstoy

What Does Music Mean?

The matter of location of meaning is a controversial one, especially in the case of instrumental music. Instrumental music is a nonrepresentational art form. No matter what genre or century it was written in, the question of its meaning is problematic. Because it is sound only, its content is transmitted in a way that is not recognizable and translatable in the way words, gestures, and images are. The content of musical sounds is less concrete. They do not convey meaning in the same way that the word *tree* stands for that object.

Perhaps music does not mean anything. Maybe people take delight in the formal properties themselves when they satisfy a personal sense of order and structure on their own. Or perhaps any meaning taken from instrumental music is associative. This means that the particular combinations of notes and rhythms trigger connections with feelings that for those few moments trigger memories. Perhaps the location of music's meaning is in the formal structure alone. Can you enjoy an aesthetic experience from something whose content has no apparent meaning? Or is the meaning in the experience itself?

> *"Art is the only truth."*
>
> Auguste Rodin

Do you think that art and beauty express truth? Why?

Are the Arts and Beauty Connected to Truth?

Chapter 7 describes the close relationship between beauty and goodness since the time of Plato. The same is true for beauty and truth. Since the arts were considered to be the physical manifestation of beauty, what beauty looks like, it followed that the arts conveyed truth. This controversial view is still current today.

The problem with this theory is the difficulty in stating what truth means when it is applied to the content and value of an artwork. It seems to be a kind of truth that is different from mathematical expressions, such as $2 + 2 = 4$, or the definitions of statements about reality, such as "Pierre Trudeau was a Canadian prime minister." These types of truth are factual, objective, and they can be verified. Is there another kind of truth? If there is, how is it described, or can it be described?

Most philosophers and artists acknowledge the connection between truth and beauty, but their statements are not always helpful. Here are three of many examples. Iris Murdoch (born 1919), English novelist and philosopher, said: "Good art speaks truth, indeed is truth, perhaps the only truth." Alfred North Whitehead (1861–1947), English mathematician and philosopher, said: "The perfection of art has only one end, which is Truthful Beauty … In the absence of Beauty, Truth sinks to triviality. Truth matters because of Beauty." These are the last two lines of English poet John Keats's (1795–1821) *Ode On a Grecian Urn*. "Beauty is truth, truth beauty, that is all / Ye know on earth, and all ye need to know."

It has been said that the kind of truth that you find in beauty and the arts cannot be expressed in words. Because the tools that philosophers use are language and logic, this seems to put a possible answer outside of philosophy. This is a problem that you must solve yourself according to your own definitions of beauty, art, and truth.

Is Your Truth the Only Truth?

Here is a possible explanation of what truth means as it is applied to the arts. In his or her work, whatever the genre, content, context, or style, the artist sincerely expresses something about some aspect of human nature—the human condition. Whether you choose to experience it or not, it is still there. It exists independent of its maker, the perceiver, and the world. When you choose to experience it, to recognize and appreciate its aesthetic value, your authentic aesthetic response is what is true. It is a subjective truth because it is verifiable only by you. However, because you experience it, it is a fact. It is true for you. The artwork alone causes a profound, intense response. You cannot experience it in any other way. Your unique and subjective experience cannot be shared, so any attempt to describe it is meaningless. The essence of that experience, the truth of it, is yours alone. Something about your personhood is revealed or clarified in a way that is true and meaningful only to you.

Another possibility is that truth is used as a metaphor for something else, like simplicity, profundity, or integrity. Which is closest to your opinion?

As philosophers, you must work out the question of the arts, beauty, and truth to your personal satisfaction. Your healthy scepticism should not allow any statement or theory to go unquestioned.

What Do You Think?

It is safe to assume that the arts are meaningful or people would not make art, appreciate it, or talk about it. The arts have value and purpose although there is no agreement about what they are. Do you think that the possible meanings of artworks are as diverse as the art forms themselves? And what about the relationship among beauty, the arts, and truth? Perhaps you can take a cue from Carroll's poem *Jabberwocky* and make up the meanings as you go along.

Chapter 9 Is There Good and Bad Art?

Key Words

Taste
Subjective
Objective
Critic
Innate
Tabula rasa
Cultural relativism
Difficult art
Dangerous art
Aestheticized
Censorship
Propaganda

Key People

David Hume
Immanuel Kant
Leo Tolstoy
Karl Marx
Plato

Who Judges What Is Good and Bad Art?

You make judgements about what is good and bad all the time. Whether you are talking about food, music, or movies, you are expressing an opinion that is based on your taste. What is taste and how do you know yours is good? Is there a universal standard of taste?

In this chapter, you will see how the notion of good and bad relates to artworks. For example, the formal properties of an art object can be well or poorly made. The content of a work of art also can be difficult to understand or objectionable to the viewer. However, can a work of art be harmful or dangerous? This raises the question of censorship. Who, if anyone, decides what art you should be allowed to experience?

What Is Taste?

A dictionary definition of the word **taste** is a sense for what is good and the ability to identify the quality of something. The general definition can apply to anything you have an opinion about, from French fries to hockey sticks. Specifically, in the arts, taste is the ability to judge what is beautiful and what is artistically valuable. Although, something that has artistic value does not have to be beautiful.

You can measure the level of sophistication of your taste by the kinds of things you respond to aesthetically and the intensity of your response. One example is food. If your experience of food is limited to cheeseburgers, your knowledge of the great diversity of other kinds of food likely is limited as well. In other words, your judgement of food, or anything else, is limited by the scope of your experience.

Is Taste Subjective?

Scottish philosopher David Hume (1711–1776) said that standards of taste are established through disinterest. You examined the concept of disinterest in Chapter 7. Disinterest is the deliberate detachment from your everyday feelings and concerns that some say is necessary to have an authentic aesthetic response. Hume also said that, because your judgement of taste about something is subjective, it is actually an expression of your likes or dislikes. Therefore, your taste is neither right nor wrong. **Subjective** refers to an experience, thought, or belief that is particular to one person.

Just about everybody thinks they have good taste in certain areas. In what areas do you think your taste is good? How do you think you acquired it? Did you learn it or were you born with it?

> *"De gustibus non disputandem est."*
> *(Concerning taste, there is no dispute.)*
>
> Anonymous

German philosopher Immanuel Kant (1724–1804) related taste to disinterest. "Taste is the faculty of judging an object by an entirely disinterested satisfaction. . . ." He thought that people make judgements based on personal standards of taste—they are subjective judgements. However, Kant also believed that, because aesthetic judgements cannot be disputed, they are universally valid, or **objective**. Kant realized that this seems to be contradictory.

Whatever your level of expertise or experience, your judgement of taste must be accepted at face value because it is subjective. Someone can disagree with you but that does not make your opinion or theirs any less valid.

Does Taste Come from Experience?

In addition to disinterest, David Hume said that standards of taste are established through experience. Experience refers to the extent to which you have studied a particular subject or genre of art, or any subject. This includes your personal encounters with the subject over time and what you learn from experts. Education is one aspect of experience that contributes to raising your standard of judgement—your standard of taste. However, it takes time, motivation, and, often, money to do this. As an example, take the game of soccer. How much do you need to know about the sport and the players, and how many matches do you have to see before you can talk intelligently and make judgements about the game? This applies to any topic you pick. Although, just because you are an expert in soccer, it does not mean you will also be an expert in baseball or anything else.

Can Two Experts Be Right?

Despite receiving similar educations, many experts in one field of knowledge may not share the same opinions. Does this mean that one expert is right and the other is wrong? Take classical music, for example. Imagine that you and a friend hear two concert pianists perform the same Beethoven composition in two different ways. You may prefer one performance and your friend may prefer the other. However, if both of you are experts in classical music, then you may not be more correct in your judgement than your friend. Two experts with the same training and experience can disagree, but perhaps both opinions can be correct.

What is a critic? Do you think critics are necessary? Why?

Why Are Critics Needed?

The variety of styles in all the art forms makes it difficult for most people to gain wide-spread experience and understanding of these art forms. So people rely on the expertise of others to help them form their opinions. Generally, a **critic** is a person who reviews, analyzes, and judges the merits of something. A professional critic usually has a high degree of expertise in one field and writes for a newspaper, a magazine, or appears in the broadcast media.

However, a critic also can be anyone, including a friend, who knows more about something than you and is willing to share his or her judgement about it with you. Sometimes you are a critic, too. Critics are necessary because there is not enough time to develop your taste in all the subjects that interest you. You learn by comparing your judgement with that of the critic. Whether or not you agree with the critic, you still increase your experience and knowledge. This experience and knowledge helps you develop your personal standard of taste.

PHILOSOPHY IN EVERYDAY LIFE

Are You a Critic?

Critics help people to identify what is good and bad in a variety of subjects. Think about the different ways in which you act as a critic. List the areas in which you feel you are knowledgeable enough to advise somebody else. In what ways did you acquire your expertise? Who do you use as a critic when you need one?

Is Your Taste and Sense of Beauty Innate or Learned?

Most, if not all, people have a sense of beauty and taste. Philosophers debate where people's standards of judgement come from. Are you born with your sense of taste and beauty or is it learned throughout your life? To have **innate** abilities, capacities, or knowledge, means that you are born with them. These abilities and knowledge are said to be present in a person's mind at birth.

Philosophers such as Plato and Kant maintain that all or part of what you know and your ability to know it, is innate—including your knowledge of beauty. In contrast, empiricist philosophers, such as David Hume, hold that all or most of your knowledge is learned by everyday experience through your five senses, which begins in earliest childhood. Empiricists claim that, at birth, your mind is **tabula rasa**. This means your mind is a blank slate. Therefore, for empiricists, there is no universal standard of beauty or taste. Your judgements of beauty and taste are subjective and individual.

To support his theory of innateness, Plato tells this story in his dialogue *Meno*. Plato's written works are called dialogues because they explore ideas through the use of characters in conversation. In *Meno*, Socrates explains to a friend that all people possess certain kinds of innate knowledge—knowledge that each person is born with and is never taught. To prove his point, he has a young boy who has never studied mathematics solve a geometry problem. By asking simple questions and taking care not to show the boy any math operations, Socrates demonstrates that the human ability to perform logical operations is innate—that people are born with innate abilities. Plato believed that one of these innate abilities is discerning beauty.

> *"Art is made to disturb. Science reassures."*
> Georges Braques

What Is Cultural Relativism?

You have read that empiricist philosophers do not believe that any kind of human knowledge is innate. Empiricists use the idea of cultural relativism to challenge the idea of innate knowledge of beauty and taste. **Cultural relativism** refers to this fact: all societies or civilizations have cultures, yet each one is different from the others. These differences include artistic and intellectual activities as well as social customs.

Philosophers who hold this view point out that the art and customs of the world's cultures are diverse. This suggests that there are no commonalities that link all of the world's art or cultural practices. Even within a single culture, standards of aesthetic judgement change continuously. The dozens of styles of music, dance, written word, visual art, food, and dress seem to support the view that there is no universal standard of beauty. This seems to make sense because, if there is a universal standard of beauty, then everyone would agree about what are good and bad works of art. People would agree about what works are good and bad because everyone's taste would be the same as well. The fact remains, though, that all cultures make art and appreciate beauty. Perhaps these two commonalities support the idea of innateness.

What Do Good and Bad Mean in the Arts?

What is good and bad art may or may not change from culture to culture—you need to judge for yourself. To help you judge, it is useful to understand what the words good and bad mean in the context of the arts.

Generally, when you use the word *good*, you are referring to something you like. If something meets your standard of taste, you say that it is good. Good can also mean well-made in the sense that the object or performance is skillfully done. You may also say that the content of a work of art is good in the moral sense. To judge this type of good, you might ask if an artwork depicts or describes events or people of worthy character and behaviour in situations that demonstrate their goodness.

PHILOSOPHY IN WORLD CULTURE

Is Good Western Art Not Good in Other Cultures?

What is good and bad art tends to differ between Western and non-Western points of view. This may be because some non-Western conceptions of the arts, beauty, and taste are more like practices and beliefs compared to Western conceptions, which are based on philosophies that are meant to be argued. For example, some non-Western arts are more closely integrated into the religious teachings of a particular community.

In the Muslim tradition, for instance, the holy book the *Qur'an* forbids the pictorial representation of living things. In this context, the visual arts are limited to architecture and calligraphy—graphic design using the letters of the Arabic alphabet. Because of this, the decoration of buildings and objects, such as books, pottery, and fabrics take on great significance. These art forms have been raised to the highest level of sophistication. For example, calligraphy is important because it is visually beautiful. It is also meaningful because it is poetry or a verse from the *Qur'an*.

THEY DIDN'T WANT THE TOURISTS TO COMPLAIN!

Think about a person who is raised to believe in the teachings of the *Qur'an*. If this person looked at an example of good Western art, Michelangelo's *David*, for example, he or she might not think this sculpture is as good as a celebrated example of calligraphy. In fact, the viewer may be offended because *David* is unclothed. Do you think that what is considered good and bad art may change from culture to culture?

On the other hand, the word *bad* can refer to an artwork whose formal properties, the elements and principles of design, are poorly organized or put together. Bad can also refer to a well-made work whose content is difficult to understand, or if it is socially and morally repugnant. Some examples are depictions of pornography and obscenity, or the encouragement of hatred.

> *"One should never talk of a moral or an immoral poem–poems are either well written or badly written, that is all."*
> Oscar Wilde

What Is Difficult Art?

The content of **difficult** art confuses or disturbs the viewer such that it interferes with the understanding or appreciation of the artwork. Artworks that are difficult to understand are often called bad. Difficult art may shock its audience, causing them to question their commonly-held beliefs. One example of this is *Fountain*, by French visual artist Marcel Duchamp (1887—1968). Many people who reject *Fountain* as bad art at first, later understand and appreciate it.

However, just because a work of art shocks you or is difficult to understand, is it necessarily bad? Your emotional reaction may tell you it is bad, but is this a disinterested aesthetic response? If an artwork disturbs you and this reaction interferes with your disinterest, then your response may no longer be aesthetic.

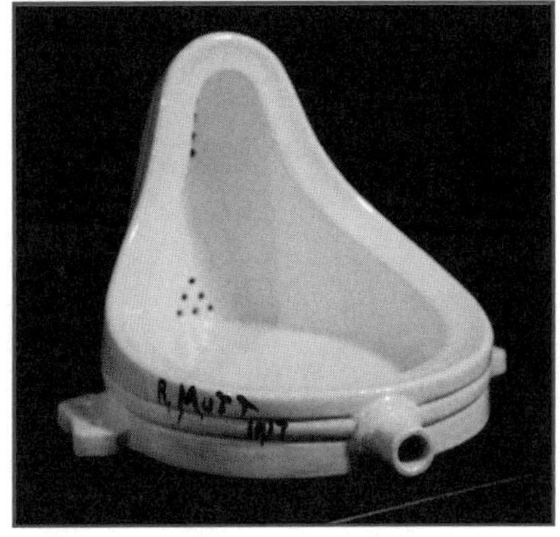

Marcel Duchamp created the work **Fountain** ***under the pseudonym R. Mutt in 1917. The sculpture was meant to shock its audience and mock the aesthetic value standards of the day. It succeeded, and on those grounds, might have been considered dangerous at the time. Now, the sculpture is considered a significant work of art. However, a urinal called a fountain seems trivial and harmless compared to the kinds of shocking images and depictions that are available today.***

> *"Art is difficult because contemporary culture is difficult. If art were not difficult, it would be less true to its times."*
>
> Leonard Diepeveen and Timothy Van Laar

Nearly everyone can identify something that they like now, but did not like when they first saw it. It is only in attempting to understand a difficult piece of art that you can eventually experience it with disinterest. Two examples of difficult forms of art are contemporary nonrepresentational painting and instrumental music. Recall that nonrepresentational artworks do not depict anything that is real or recognizable. Instrumental music, music with no lyrics, is also nonrepresentational. With these kinds of artworks, a certain amount of prior knowledge and open-mindedness is necessary to understand and appreciate them. The more you know about the genres, the more likely you can experience them aesthetically.

> *"Art is a human activity consisting in this, that one man ... hands on to others feelings he has lived through, and that other people are infected by these feelings and also experience them."*
>
> Leo Tolstoy

POINT OF VIEW

Leo Tolstoy

Do you have strong ideas of what is good and bad art? Leo Tolstoy (1828–1910) had strong views on the subject. Born into a wealthy, noble family in Russia, Tolstoy is famous for his novel *War and Peace*, which was published in 1866.

In his late forties, Tolstoy had a profound renewal of his Christian beliefs that deeply affected his views about art. Thereafter, he divided art into good and bad. According to Tolstoy, good art requires no special training or sophistication to fully appreciate it. It is the product of honesty, integrity, and simplicity. Its content has to be morally instructive and uplifting. Good art, in Tolstoy's words, is "Christian universal art." By universal, he meant that the Christian message should appeal to everyone.

Tolstoy also believed that good art transmits feelings. If someone creates a work of art that is good, then when another person experiences the art, he or she feels the same as the artist felt when the work was created. The degree to which someone experiences the same feelings as the artist determines how good the art is. However, the actual mechanism of the transmission of feelings is not clear.

One art form that does not meet Tolstoy's criteria for good art is instrumental music. He believed that instrumental music does not transmit the "highest religious feeling." However, religious hymns and chants qualify as good art because the lyrics are simple and devotional. The music is only the vehicle of their transmission.

> *"Beethoven's* Ninth Symphony *is considered a great work of art. To verify its claim ... I must first ask myself whether this work transmits the highest religious feeling. I reply in the negative, for music in itself cannot transmit those feelings. [Does it have] the quality of uniting all men in one common feeling: does it rank as Christian universal art? [Tolstoy says no.] ... therefore, whether I like it or not, I am compelled to conclude that this work belongs to the rank of bad art."*
>
> Leo Tolstoy

> *"Life, religion and art all converge in Bali. They have no word in their language for 'artist' or 'art.' Everyone is an artist."*
>
> Anaïs Nin

Is the Process of Making Art Good in Itself?

As with Tolstoy, and many other Western points of view, it is finished artworks that are judged good or bad. However, in some non-Western traditions good art does not just refer to the finished artwork. Making art is considered as important as the finished art object. If the artist is properly prepared, both mentally and physically, then the outcome of his or her efforts is likely to be good. For example, Japanese traditional artists carefully prepare themselves for their work. In a state of concentration that Zen Buddhists call *mindfulness*, the artist's energies and ideas are fully awake. Using physical exercises and meditation, the artists are able to concentrate their thoughts and actions to a high degree. This state of heightened awareness is sometimes referred to as being in the eternal present. This mental state may be similar to disinterest.

Can a Work of Art Be Dangerous?

> *"Real art has the capacity to make us nervous."*
>
> Susan Sontag

Sometimes people find the content of some art morally repugnant. It is believed by some people that this art has a negative effect on society. Because of this effect, they think it is harmful or **dangerous** art. The idea that the content of works of art can be dangerous to members of a community has been debated for over two thousand years. The nature of the content of an artwork and the purpose to which it is put determines whether or not it is dangerous. Whether you publish a book, make a music recording, or create visual art for display, many people think that an artwork that is available to the public should meet standards of public morality and decency.

PHILOSOPHY IN EVERYDAY LIFE

Is it Art or Is it Pornography?

Do you believe that the police should have the power to remove art from a gallery? This happened in December of 1993 to a Toronto art gallery called Mercer Union. The gallery opened a show of works by Canadian visual artist Eli Langer (born 1967). His drawings and paintings depicted children and young adults in poses with older men that suggested consenting sexuality. Acting on a public complaint, police used a warrant to seize several of Langer's paintings and drawings. Langer and the director of the gallery were charged with offences under the then-new child pornography laws. After much public debate, the charges were withdrawn in February 1994.

The problem with dangerous art is a conflict of values. If the values represented by the content of the artwork do not meet the community's minimum standards, the artwork is considered harmful and may be removed from public view. This is why access to certain artworks, including films and theatre, is sometimes restricted or forbidden, and some music recordings carry parent advisory labels. Some works of art are censored or banned outright because the risk of harm is considered too great. But who is at risk? It is usually thought that children and young people are most at risk, but, depending on the degree of potential harm, everybody may be.

Who Decides What Is Harmful?

If some art is considered dangerous to a community, who decides if it is dangerous? In most democratic societies, it is the public that decides what art is harmful. One citizen's complaint is all that is required to offend the public taste. If a person feels that the shock or insult to their sensibilities or morality is great enough, they file a complaint with the police. The police are required to respond. They can also remove the offending artworks and close the gallery until the court decides if the complaint is justified.

Should You View Obscene Art with Disinterest?

If public opinion considers a well-made work obscene or morally repugnant, should people view that work with disinterest? Should you even try? Are these types of works possible sources of an authentic aesthetic response?

POINT OF VIEW

Plato

Do you think that art can be dangerous? Plato thought that almost all art is dangerous. He made this claim based on his theory of ideal Forms. This theory holds that we inhabit a world of illusions. What you experience everyday with your five senses is not reality at all, but the subjective, imperfect, and ever-changing world of appearances. For Plato, the objective, perfect, and unchanging world of reality was found in the realm of Forms.

Think of a tree in a landscape, for example. A tree changes over time, as all things change. The tree is part of the ever-changing world of appearances. However, the tree exists for people to experience because the Form of the tree causes it. Forms are the perfect, objective, unchanging essence or idea of all the things that appear to people. The tree and everything else that you experience are only the appearances of reality, the perfect and eternal essences, the Forms that exist in Plato's otherworldly realm.

If humans only perceive the appearance of reality, then, according to Plato, when people experience art, they perceive the appearance of an appearance. A painting of a landscape, for example, is the appearance of the natural landscape that the artist was painting. But the natural landscape itself is the appearance of the ideal Form of the landscape. Therefore, art is even farther from Plato's true reality than the appearance of the world.

Plato thought that the power of the arts to create this false reality was so great that he condemned art as a dangerous illusion, an appearance of an appearance. With the exception of musicians who played military music, like marches and fanfares, he banished all artists and their work from the ideal society that he described in his book *Republic*.

Some philosophers and critics claim that when the technical skill and artistry of such an artwork is separated from its content, it is **aestheticized**. This means that obscenity and immorality are made beautiful, which elevates their status to that of an artwork. For example, German filmmaker Leni Riefenstahl (born 1902) was commissioned by Adolph Hitler to make a series of films about the rallies of the Nazi Party. In her memoirs, Riefenstahl states that she was not a member of the Nazi Party nor was she politically active. She says she accepted the commission because she was being well paid and she saw the work as an opportunity to expand her experience and reputation.

Of the three films she made, the most famous is *Triumph of the Will*, which portrayed the 1934 Nuremberg rally. The film was widely shown and won several prestigious international awards for its artistry and technique. After World War II ended, the film was condemned as an extreme form of Nazi propaganda and was—and still is by many—considered obscene for its glorification of the evils of Nazi nationalism and racism.

If you believe that *Triumph of the Will* is a well-made film but is obscene because it glorifies the Nazi party's beliefs, should you still try and find artistic merit in it?

> *"Art for me ... is a negation of society, an affirmation of the individual, outside of all the rules and all the demands of society."*
>
> Emile Zola

Is Censorship the Answer?

If there is such a thing as dangerous art, what should society do about it? Censorship has been one way that societies have dealt with dangerous art since the earliest times. **Censorship** is the restriction or banning of any materials that are considered harmful to the public. Society may censor any documents or images that may threaten its morals, beliefs, security, or well-being. Much of the ongoing debate about censorship is not about whether or not it is appropriate, but about how much censorship society needs.

Some people are against censorship. These people claim that education is the best censor. Those that support censorship cannot agree about how much is appropriate. Also, opinions about what should and should not be censored differ widely. An example of the problem is the recent attempt by a school board to ban J.D. Salinger's (born 1919) novel *The Catcher in the Rye* on the grounds that it encourages teenagers to rebel against the authority of adults. On the other hand, the book is included in the reading lists of hundreds of other school boards because of its realistic depiction of youthful rebellion and their search for meaning and personal identity.

Do you think that art can persuade people that something is true? How?

What Is Propaganda?

You have read how some people believe that the influence of some artworks is dangerous. Rulers of some countries take advantage of the persuasive power of the arts to spread particular ideas among their citizens. Using art in this way is often called propaganda. From the Latin word for *spread* or *multiply*, **propaganda** is defined as an organized publicity campaign using only selected information. However, a more negative meaning of the word is the deliberate use of selected information to promote misleading or dishonest ideas. It is in this sense that the word is most frequently used today.

Because of its power to stir human emotions, the arts have long been used as a propaganda tool. Several philosophers have recognized this persuasive power as a function or purpose of the arts. Propaganda is seen in varying degrees in all the media, for commercial as well as political purposes. For example, environmental activists claim that certain kinds of advertising are propagandistic. An example they cite is large industrial corporations who claim in their ads that they are protecting the environment.

How Is Propaganda Used?

History provides examples of using the arts as educational and propaganda tools. German philosopher Karl Marx (1818–1883), and most 20th century Marxist writers, recognized the power of the arts as an educational tool. Marx believed that the mass appeal and variety of art forms made them a good way to teach the public the goals and rewards of communism. The former Soviet Union embraced this view and included censorship as a key part of its arts education policy.

Through censorship, communism, especially Soviet-style communism, was shown in its best possible light. Government sanctioned works of art, in other words, good art, showed a society that was ideal, but that did not exist. In this way, the government tried to control public opinion by misrepresenting events at home and in other, non-communist countries. For example, films extolled the superiority of communism by showing thriving farms with modern equipment. However, the truth was that farming was backward and there were frequent food shortages. The content of the visual arts and literature included happy, healthy, and attractive families in a variety of community endeavours. However, corruption, alcoholism, and pollution were serious problems. Criticism of any aspect of communism's shortcomings was forbidden.

Non-government sanctioned art, in other words, bad art, was usually critical of the government or entirely non-political in style and content. This art was produced and experienced in secret. Viewers or readers of this art did so at risk to their personal freedom. Similar censorship practices are in place today in countries with communist and theocratic regimes. Theocracy is the rule by the clergy of one religious group. Two modern examples are Iran and the Afghanistan regime of the Taliban, which lost power in 2001. Prior to losing power, the Taliban ordered the destruction of priceless Buddhist statues because they claimed that these artworks were not permitted by their religion.

> *"Creative work in literature and art must be permeated with the spirit of the struggle for Communism."*
>
> Nikita Khrushchev

Democratically elected governments also use propaganda. One example is using advertisements in the media that claim that government policies are working. In these countries, censorship is limited and public criticism of government policy is legal.

> *"Art is a direct challenge [to communist totalitarianism]. One true artist is more dangerous to a totalitarian regime than any political adversary."*
>
> Mihajlo Mihajlov

WEB CONNECTION

Film Censorship in Ontario

Go to the Web site of the Ontario Film Review Board: www.ofrb.gov.on.ca. Read about the Board's review policy and answer these questions.

1. What are the Ontario Film Review Board's criteria for ordering a film to be edited?
2. How many films are screened each year by the OFRB?
3. What percentage of the films that they screen are edited?
4. What is the average length of an edit?
5. What is the ratio of appeals won to appeals lost?
6. Does the OFRB perform a useful service? Justify your yes or no answer.

"Every artist and poet is an anti-social being."
Pablo Picasso

What Do You Think?

Your senses are bombarded every day with information in the form of sounds and images. How do you separate the good from the bad, and the beauty and the art in them? Your taste helps you decide what is good and bad art. Some philosophers think people are born with an innate sense of taste, while others believe that taste is learned throughout life. Your taste may determine that certain artworks are dangerous or harmful, but should this type of art be censored? Some governments have used censorship and propaganda to limit what types of art their citizens can make or experience. Do you think this is a good thing to do and does it make good or bad art?

Unit 4

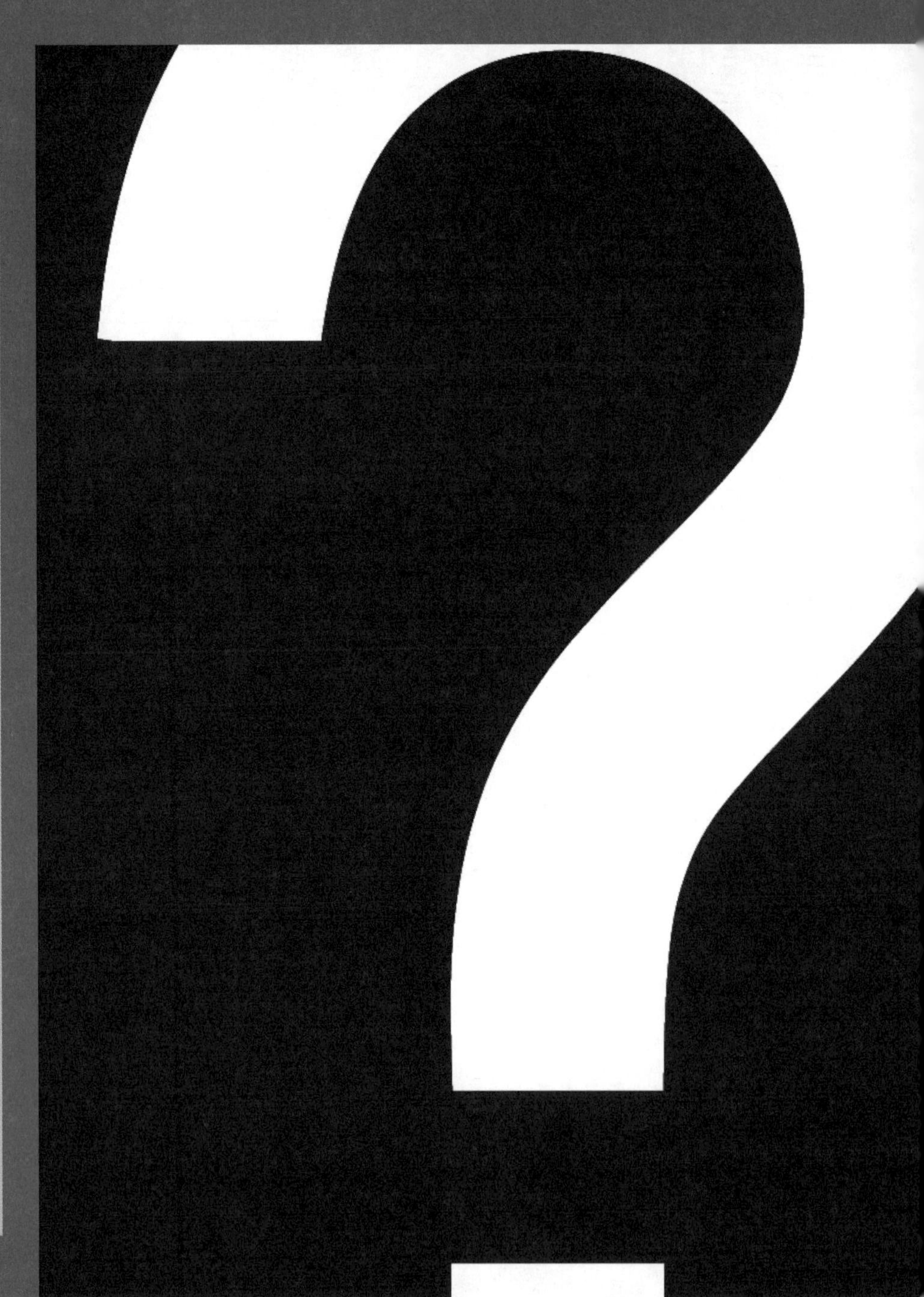

What Are Good and Evil?

Some concepts are so important to people that they are part of the very essence of each individual. Morality is such a concept. Think of whether your moral beliefs are important to you. Do you conclude that morality plays an important role in your life and in the operation of your society?

Can you explain why you hold the moral beliefs that you do? Where do your beliefs originate? How sure are you of the correctness of your answers to the above questions? No matter how confident you may be in your answers to these questions, not all philosophers would agree with your answers. Philosophers have never been in complete agreement about the concept of morality. Do you think people will ever agree about morality? In this unit, you will explore philosophical questions concerning morality that have endured for centuries.

Chapter 10 Where Do Good and Evil Come From?

Key Words
Divine command theory
Self-evident truth
Atheist
Theist
Moral rationalism
Natural law theory
Best reasons approach
Categorical imperative
Innate
Moral relativism
Universal law
Moral scepticism

Key People
Plato
William of Ockham
St. Thomas Aquinas
Martin Luther King, Jr.
Bertrand Russell
Immanuel Kant
Thomas Hobbes

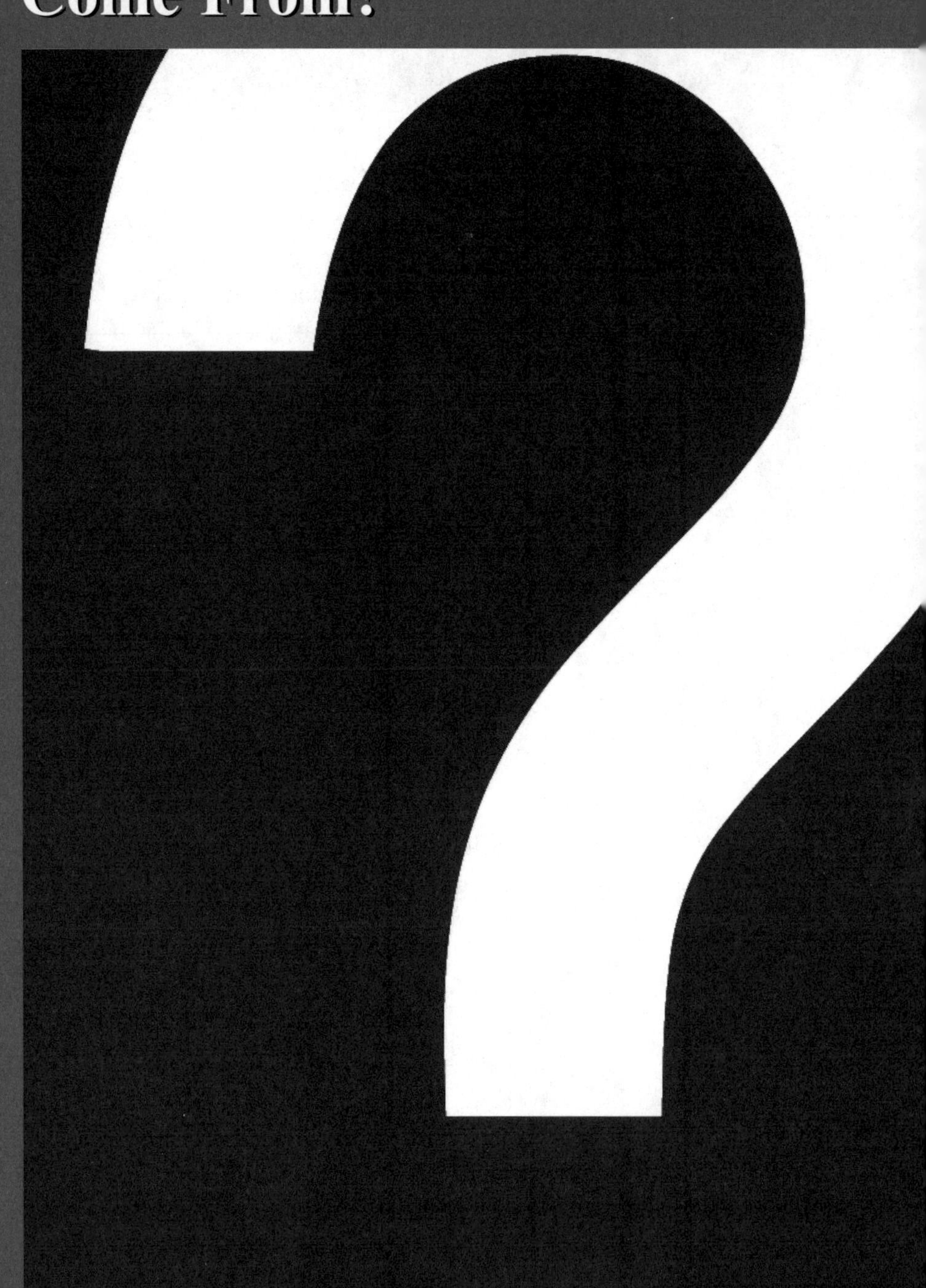

Where Do Morals Come From?

Do you believe it is wrong to kill another person? Where do you think this belief and all of your moral beliefs came from?

> *"And what is good, Phaedrus, and what is not good—need we ask anyone to tell us these things?"*
>
> from the book *Zen and the Art of Motorcycle Maintenance*, by Robert Pirsig

Morality refers to what is right and what is wrong. You probably have a good idea of what is considered right and wrong in your society, school, home, and among your friends. But have you ever thought about where your morals come from—what is their origin? Perhaps someone invented these rules. On the other hand, maybe morals are like laws of nature. Maybe God made rules for people to live by. Maybe people construct moral beliefs, just like they construct homes, music, art, and culture. Do you think that a moral code is an essential part of every human being—something you are born with, that no other animal on Earth has? There are many answers to how morality originated, some of which you will explore in this chapter.

Can You Explain the Origin of Your Morals?

Imagine that you have constructed a time machine, which you can use to travel to any time or place in the past. On one occasion, you decide to visit an ancient society. Their culture is sophisticated, but also different from yours. Naturally, they are interested in the things that you have brought with you and the stories that you have to tell them.

One of the things that you have with you is a pocket flashlight. Your new friends are used to seeing artificial light from oil lamps, but they have never before seen light generated from a light bulb. They are curious, and so they ask, "Where did that come from?" You explain that you purchased it at a hardware store, but that does not really explain the ultimate origin of the bulb, so they ask you more. At that point, you would probably explain that Thomas Alva Edison invented the light bulb in 1879, and, if you wanted to, you might describe how important electricity is in your society.

The people of this ancient society find you fascinating and so they want to know about some of your beliefs. For example, take your belief that people should try their best never to kill another human being. Your new friends have the same belief as well, but they want to know about the origins of this belief in your society. Would that be as easy to explain as the origin of the light bulb?

> *"The liberty of discussion is the great safeguard of all other liberties."*
>
> Thomas Macaulay

Do Right and Wrong Come from God?

Some philosophers link moral principles to God, saying that being morally good is to obey God's will. It makes sense, these philosophers argue, that God is the one who has given people the ultimate standard to live by because God is said to be all-powerful, all-knowing, and all-good.

The belief that there is a relationship between God and morality goes back at least as far as people have written down their ideas. It has been such an influential belief that it is found embedded in the laws, customs, and language of our society.

Do you believe that moral rules were created by God or by something outside of God's power?

RESEARCH AND INQUIRY SKILLS

Discussing and Explaining

Do you say what you mean and mean what you say? Being able to discuss complex and controversial issues is essential for active citizenship. Being able to explain yourself in a clear, compelling, and meaningful way is a valuable skill with many rewards. Good discussion and explanation skills will help to strengthen your relationships, help you reach your goals, and get better grades. Here are some tips for discussing and explaining:

- Think of the main point you want to make, and clearly communicate it.
- Be succinct. Avoid extraneous material that does not support your main point.
- Be logical. Break down complex material into smaller parts, and plan how to best communicate your material in a step-by-step process.
- Make clear transitions. As you move from one point to another, do so in a clear and organized manner. Conclude and sum up your arguments logically.
- Be a good listener. Be sensitive to others. Chances are, a person will be more open to listening to you if they know that you are listening to them.
- Ask questions. If you are not sure of another person's point of view or meaning, ask for clarification.
- Manage your discussions. If one individual is dominating, request that they step back. If others are not being expressive, ask their opinion.
- Be assertive. Being assertive does not mean being aggressive. It means being sure that you are communicating your ideas and being heard.
- Disagree in agreeable ways. Philosophical minds will always find areas of disagreement. Avoid put-downs and show respect for other points of view. No one has a monopoly on the truth.

Practising Your Skill

Have you ever noticed the similarity between children and philosophers? They always seem to be asking the question "Why?" Imagine that you are walking with a four-year-old child, and the issue of being good enters the conversation. You tell the child that it is important to be good and not to hurt others. He or she asks you, "Why?"

Write the dialogue that would occur between you and the child, one which incorporates each of the discussion and explanation skills listed above.

Are Right and Wrong Separate from God?

In ancient Greece, philosophers often wondered about morality and the nature of the relationship between morality and the ancient Greek gods. The ancient Greek philosopher Plato (427–347 BCE) wrote a dialogue, *The Euthyphro*, that addressed the issue of morality and the gods. Plato's written works are called dialogues because they explore ideas through the use of characters who speak together. In *The Euthyphro*, Socrates asks Euthyphro whether the gods love what is good because it actually is good, or whether things are called good simply because the gods love them? The important implication of his question is that it sets up an "either/or" situation, only one of which may be true. In other words, morality is either something that exists independently of the gods and discovered by them, or it is created by the gods. Both things cannot be true at the same time, because they are contradictory. In Plato's dialogue, the dilemma is whether the ancient Greek gods invented morality, or if these gods had to follow a set of universal moral truths that existed outside of their control.

Although European philosophers of the Middle Ages, such as St. Thomas Aquinas (c. 1225–1274) and William of Ockham (c. 1285–1349), did not believe in ancient Greek gods, they believed in God of the *Bible*. However, the Euthyphro Dilemma was still important to them and still debated. For example, Aquinas believed that God endorsed a moral standard that God "discovered." This morality existed independently, outside of God. Later, Aquinas believed that God instilled this moral standard into human beings when God created them. On the other hand, William of Ockham argued that God actually invented the standards of what is good and what is evil, and that people should obey them. Ultimately, however, Ockham said that people choose to obey or not to obey these standards of their own free will. Ockham's notion is now called the **divine command theory**.

Logically, however, both sides of the Euthyphro Dilemma present further problems. For example, if God is the creator of morality, and then decided to change the rules at whim, God could allow murder or theft on some days, but not on others. If this happened, would murder or theft still truly not be wrong? If, on the other hand, morality does exist somewhere outside of God, then there must be rules that God must obey. God is said to be all-powerful, but if God had to obey rules, God's power would be lessened.

POINT OF VIEW

Martin Luther King, Jr.

Martin Luther King, Jr. (1929–1968), a Christian, strongly believed that all good is found in God's will. King believed that this good was a much greater good than any single individual's self interest. So much so that King was willing to risk his life and go to jail for his beliefs. Would you be willing to go to jail for your beliefs?

King believed that the laws of the United States discriminated against blacks, and were morally wrong. For example, in some restaurants in the southern United States, blacks had to sit in a separate section. In some schools, they even had separate water fountains and washrooms. This is called segregation. King argued that segregation and discriminatory laws were wrong because they were against God's will. They could be proven wrong using what philosophers, including King, have labelled self-evident truths. A **self-evident truth** is one that is so pure and simple that any reasonable human being can see and understand it. In this case, for King, the self-evident truth was that all humans are created equal. King's answer to end discrimination was his strategy of using non-violent civil disobedience, inspired by Mohandas Gandhi.

King felt that people have a duty to do what is good and to obey the truth, and he worked to convince all of society to do this as well. If this meant breaking the written law, and even going to jail as a consequence, then so be it. It was a person's duty as a free and responsible moral agent to bring good into the world and to obey the truth.

In 1963, King was arrested and put in jail as a result of his protests. While in jail, he composed his now famous *Letter from Birmingham Jail*. The quote in the margin is an excerpt from his letter. King thought that the suffering he had to endure to achieve the greater good was compensated by redemption. He was struck dead by an assassin's bullet, soon after his famous "I Have Been to the Mountaintop" speech, on the balcony of the Lorraine Motel in 1968.

WEB CONNECTION

Taking a Moral Stand

Martin Luther King, Jr. was willing to go to prison and risk his life for his beliefs. Go to a search engine and look up *civil disobedience* and *nonviolent resistance*. Compile information on other people who have risked their lives and personal freedom for what they believed.

> *"A just law is a man-made code that squares with the moral law or the law of God. An unjust law is a code that is out of harmony with the moral law. To put it in the terms of St. Thomas Aquinas: An unjust law is a human law that is not rooted in eternal law and natural law. Any law that uplifts human personality is just. Any law that degrades human personality is unjust. All segregation statutes are unjust because segregation distorts the soul and damages the personality. It gives the segregator a false sense of superiority and the segregated a false sense of inferiority."*
>
> Martin Luther King, Jr.
> *excerpt from* Letter from Birmingham Jail

If God Exists, Why Is There Evil?

> *"A line which I often thought was a very plausible one, that as a matter of fact this world that we know was made by the devil at a moment when God was not looking. There is a good deal to be said for that, and I am not concerned to refute it."*
>
> Bertrand Russell

One question philosophers ask those who believe that God created morality is this: If God is all-powerful and all-good, and if God witnesses evil, does

God have an obligation to stop evil? Imagine that a good person witnesses the suffering of another. It is in that person's power to end the other person's suffering without bringing any harm to him or herself. You may think that a good person would stop the other person's suffering. It is evil to allow this suffering to continue, is it not? Then why does God allow evil to exist?

An answer that is often given to this problem is that human beings have the free will to make choices. God does not intervene because that would be to interfere with personal decision making. However, people must live with the consequences of their choices and actions. If a person is to be called truly good, it must be because that person has made a choice to be so. In this view, good and evil are connected to the concept of free will. The concept of morality can only apply to rational beings that make choices.

Some philosophers, such as Bertrand Russell (1872–1970), do not find this answer satisfactory. Russell spoke of the fact that many victims of diseases, such as cancer, must at times endure months of agony. How could an all-good, all-powerful God have created such a world? Russell concluded that it must mean that either God permits evil, or that God does not exist. Russell was an **atheist**, which means he did not believe that God exists.

Does Being Good Just Come Naturally?

Do people need to be taught to be good? If your parents did not teach you to be good, would you be an evil person?

Most **theists** believe that God would not blindly dictate rules to people. Both theists and atheists require alternative ideas toward the origins of morality. Their ideas centre more on human rather than divine origin of morals. Although they have different opinions in many areas, these thinkers all seem to agree that the capability of human reason is a special thing. They contend that it has played an important role in constructing human moral codes and behaviours. **Moral rationalism** is the term that describes moral theories emphasizing the use of human reason to discover moral truths. Two such theories are:

- natural law theory
- best reasons approach

Does Morality Come from Reason?

The **natural law theory** maintains that the standards that govern human behaviour are derived from the very nature of human beings. Human thinking processes, by their very nature, produce moral beliefs and judgements. For instance, because you know what it is like to feel pain, you easily reason that inflicting pain upon others is a bad thing to do. St. Thomas Aquinas argued that human reason is central to humanity, and that it is natural for a moral code to come from this ability to reason.

Some philosophers note that all human beings undergo this process of reason in a similar way. They believe that, even though people are different individually, human reason seems to produce just about the same results for everyone. It seems to these philosophers that there is a similarity of moral codes within various religions, individuals, and cultures. This means that the great moral truths that people perceive, such as not killing another human being, are objective truths (factual) as opposed to subjective truths (personal opinion).

Does Logic Produce Perfect Morality?

Like natural law theory, the **best reasons approach** maintains that human reason can lead people to moral behaviour. According to best reasons, moral actions are the consequence of people thinking about questions, such as, "What shall I do in this situation?" In the end, people act according to what they see as the most rational thing to do, in other words, the best reasons. Philosophers who believe in the best reasons argument suggest that it is because human reason is imperfect that moral errors occur. Moral errors could be either the result of faulty reasoning, or of having insufficient facts to make the best decision in the first place. For example, a person may steal because they see the short-term benefit from such an action. However, another person may reason that stealing is wrong. The problem is that now both people believe that they have followed the best reasons—that they are correct. How can both people be correct?

> *"When the question is of moral worth, it is not with the actions which we see that we are concerned, but with those inward principles of them which we do not see."*
>
> Immanuel Kant

POINT OF VIEW

Immanuel Kant

If you do something good for another person, does it matter why you did it—what your motive was? The philosopher Immanuel Kant (1724–1804) thought not. For him, the moral worth of people depends entirely on their doing their moral duty. On Kant's view, you do not need to know someone's motives to know whether they are doing this duty. All you need to know is whether they are acting in accord with the moral rule that he called **the categorical imperative**.

Kant's categorical imperative states: "Act as though the maxim of your action were by your will to become a universal law of nature." This rule is "categorical" because it allows for no exceptions. It is an "imperative" in being a command that Kant thought a moral person must give to him or herself.

PHILOSOPHY IN EVERYDAY LIFE

What if Everyone Acted this Way?

Kant thought that morality is a product of a person's thought and free will. If this is true, then this is another example of how reason may help guide people to proper moral behaviour. So take a moment and use your reason similar to the way Immanuel Kant thought. For Kant, one way of measuring if something was the right thing to do was to determine what the result would be if the action were to become a universal law. In other words, people should ask themselves "What would the result be for all of humanity if everyone acted in this way?" Think of what society would be like if everyone lied and no one told the truth. Could society still function? Think of a decision (big or small) you made recently. Ask yourself what would happen if everyone in the world made the same type of decision.

Is It Human Instinct to Be Good?

The theory of evolution maintains that animals must possess behaviours that benefit their species in order for the species to be fit and to survive. Destructive, or what scientists call *maladaptive*, behaviours may lead to species extinction. As human beings appear to be successful as a species, it may simply be human instinct to possess behaviours that are good and helpful to other members of the human species. If people were not good to one another, perhaps humans would have become extinct long ago. This would mean that beliefs about morality are **innate**—that is, ideas we are born with. Do you believe that people are born with moral knowledge, or is it learned throughout life?

Is it really human instinct to be good? Some philosophers, such as Thomas Hobbes (1588—1679), say no. Hobbes believed that human beings are basically selfish creatures, and that people's lives are an ongoing struggle to fulfil selfish desires. Strong laws and enforcement are needed, Hobbes argued, to prevent conflict among selfish people from destroying society.

Can What Is Good or Evil Ever Change?

Do you think that there are certain moral values that are true for all time and in all places? For example, does everyone in the world, at any time or place, believe that murder is wrong, or that people should care for children, or that people should not lie?

Plato held that certain things, such as mathematics, are timeless concepts—that is, they never change and they apply absolutely everywhere in the universe. For instance, the fact that 2+2=4 will be true forever and always. It does not matter that others may use a different language to express the concept. In any language, the concept is universal and unchanging. Humans did not invent, and cannot alter, numbers. Numbers are a truth, which people have discovered. Plato believed that numbers are abstract entities that exist apart from the human mind.

Are there moral truths, such as a person should not inflict pain on another person, which exist forever and all time, similar to the way that numbers do? If something is true forever and always, it is called a universal. If something is a custom that can change over time or from place to place, it is called

PHILOSOPHY IN SCIENCE

Are Animals Moral?

Philosophers wonder about the origin of human morality, but what about animals? Do you think that animals have a sense of morality that is more than just instinct? Philosophers have tended to believe that animals are not moral creatures because they do not reason and think at the same level as humans. This is why animals are not considered to be morally responsible for their actions, and why it is not an evil for an animal to pursue and kill its prey.

Scientists have demonstrated, however, that certain creatures undertake some activities that are helpful to each other. An interesting example of this is the behaviour of a species of vampire bat that lives in Costa Rica. Vampire bats feed on blood. They obtain this blood at night, mostly from cattle and horses. Not all bats are successful in finding blood each and every night, but the ones that do sometimes obtain even more than they need. These bats live in groups, usually in hollow trees. Scientists have discovered that, back in the nest, the bats that obtain a surplus of blood share it with those who obtain no blood. They do this by regurgitation. Scientists call this phenomenon *reciprocal altruism*. Simply put, the bats give away some blood to other bats to keep open the possibility of receiving the same favour later themselves. Is this activity an act of kindness, which would be a moral behaviour, or is it simply an instinct? Similarly, is it possible that humans are good to one another only in the hope that they will be treated well themselves?

relative. Some philosophers believe that morality is universal, while others, such as the ancient Greek Protagoras (c. 490–420 BCE), believe that it is relative.

The philosopher James Rachels believes that morality is universal. He argues that there is a core set of values that are common to all societies, and that they are necessary for any society to exist. He says there are three main universal moral values:

- care for your children
- tell the truth
- do not murder

PHILOSOPHY IN EVERDAY LIFE

Should Morals Be Relative or Universal?

Do you think it is acceptable for morals to change with time and place, or do you think that the same moral rules should apply to all people in all times? It may help to examine a moral situation toward which different societies have held different opinions. For example, is it morally wrong to have more than one husband or wife? In Canada, many people believe it is, so much so that it is even against the law to be married to more than one person. There have been other societies, however, where it was common to have more than one husband or wife. The practice of having one partner is called monogamy, and more than one partner is called polygamy. There have been a number of societies where the practice was for women to have more than one husband, which is called polyandry. More common, however, has been the practice of men having more than one wife, called polygyny. Many societies have had combinations of monogamy and polygamy. Are societies that practise polygamy doing something morally wrong if that is their custom? Today, in Canada, if someone wanted to have more than one husband or wife, should it be allowed?

If you believe it is not wrong for other societies to practice polygamy, but that people should not do so in your society, then you are a moral relativist. **Moral relativism** is the view that morality can change depending upon the time or place. If you believe that all of the people in the world should not practice polygamy—in other words, you think the same moral rules should apply to everyone all the time, no matter where or when—then you believe in morality as a **universal law**.

> *"Man is the measure of all things."*
>
> Protagoras

Does Morality Come from an Obligation to Be Good to Others?

> *"All who are not lunatics are agreed about certain things: That it is better to be alive than dead, better to be adequately fed than starved, better to be free than a slave. Many people desire those things only for themselves and their friends; they are quite content that their enemies should suffer."*
>
> Bertrand Russell

Do you believe that society forces you to be morally good? Why?

Some philosophers believe that morality originates in intelligent or enlightened self-interest. These philosophers argue that, even if people are completely selfish, they will see it is in their interests to act in a cooperative way. Knowing that you could be robbed or murdered while you sleep, these philosophers maintain that society agrees to live by basic rules so as not to live in perpetual fear. Pure selfishness—to protect your life and property—motivates each individual to live by a basic set of rules that allows for a civil society. This is an important part of the theory behind what philosophers of politics call the social contract.

How Does the Contract Work?

An important aspect of the social contract is the need to enforce society's basic set of rules. If everyone in society is to live in this agreed-upon social arrangement, it is necessary to have a neutral third party to enforce the rules and punish transgressors. Hence, there is the need for police and a system of justice. Without organized and agreed-upon laws and law enforcement, justice cannot occur. Punishments for crimes would then consist of vigilantism, which would defeat the purpose of the contract. Vigilantism is when a person, or group of people, punish criminals as they see fit when there is no official law, or go beyond existing laws to punish people as they choose.

Does Being Good Come from the Human Conscience?

Some philosophers suggest that morality comes from the human conscience. Most people appear to have a sense of moral awareness, that is, a sense of what they believe to be right and wrong. Your ability to reflect morally upon your actions is often called having a conscience. Many people agree that the purpose of the conscience is to ensure that there is a relationship between doing good and feeling good, and doing something bad and feeling guilt. In other words, if you do something good, you will feel good, and if you do something bad, you will feel badly. However, philosophers hold various opinions as to where the conscience actually comes from.

What Is a Conscience?

The conscience is explained by some as being the will of a divine power appearing in people's decisions. Others believe that it is an innate sense of right and wrong, which exists in each person when he or she is born. Does this mean that it is passed on to you genetically from your parents? Some religions teach that conscience is an inner sanctuary of laws inscribed by God.

Others believe that conscience is something you learn. To others, conscience is wholly a product of personal experiences. To some, an absence of conscience is an indication of a deeply disturbed, even insane, individual.

Can People Really Know the Answers to These Questions?

Why is there so much disagreement about the origins of morality? Perhaps it is because the answers are beyond the intellectual capacity of human beings. This is the position held by the moral sceptics. **Moral scepticism** suggests that there are limits upon human understanding and that people do not have the knowledge or justification for believing in objective moral truths.

The sceptics do not necessarily argue that people should not be good, nor do they say that society does not need rules. But they do believe that there is no real evidence that morality is objective, that is, outside of human opinion. Such an understanding may require knowledge beyond human experiences and capabilities. Perhaps you have a pet dog. No matter how smart your dog is, it cannot perform higher mathematics. Similarly, are the questions concerning the origins of morality simply beyond human capability to answer?

What Do You Think?

This chapter asked you to think about the origins of your morals. Where do your beliefs in right and wrong come from? Some argue that God created morality. Others suggest that morality exists outside of God so that even God must obey these rules. This suggests that morality is universal—the same in every time and place. However, others believe that morality is relative, that it changes in each time and place. There are those who say that morality is constructed by human reason alone, while some say that morality is instinctive—that you are born with knowledge of right and wrong. If this is true, why were laws invented to enforce good behaviour? Some philosophers say that this is because humans are selfish by nature and require strictly enforced laws to be good. What do you think? Do any of these ideas correspond with your notion of where your morals came from?

Chapter 11 Why Be Good?

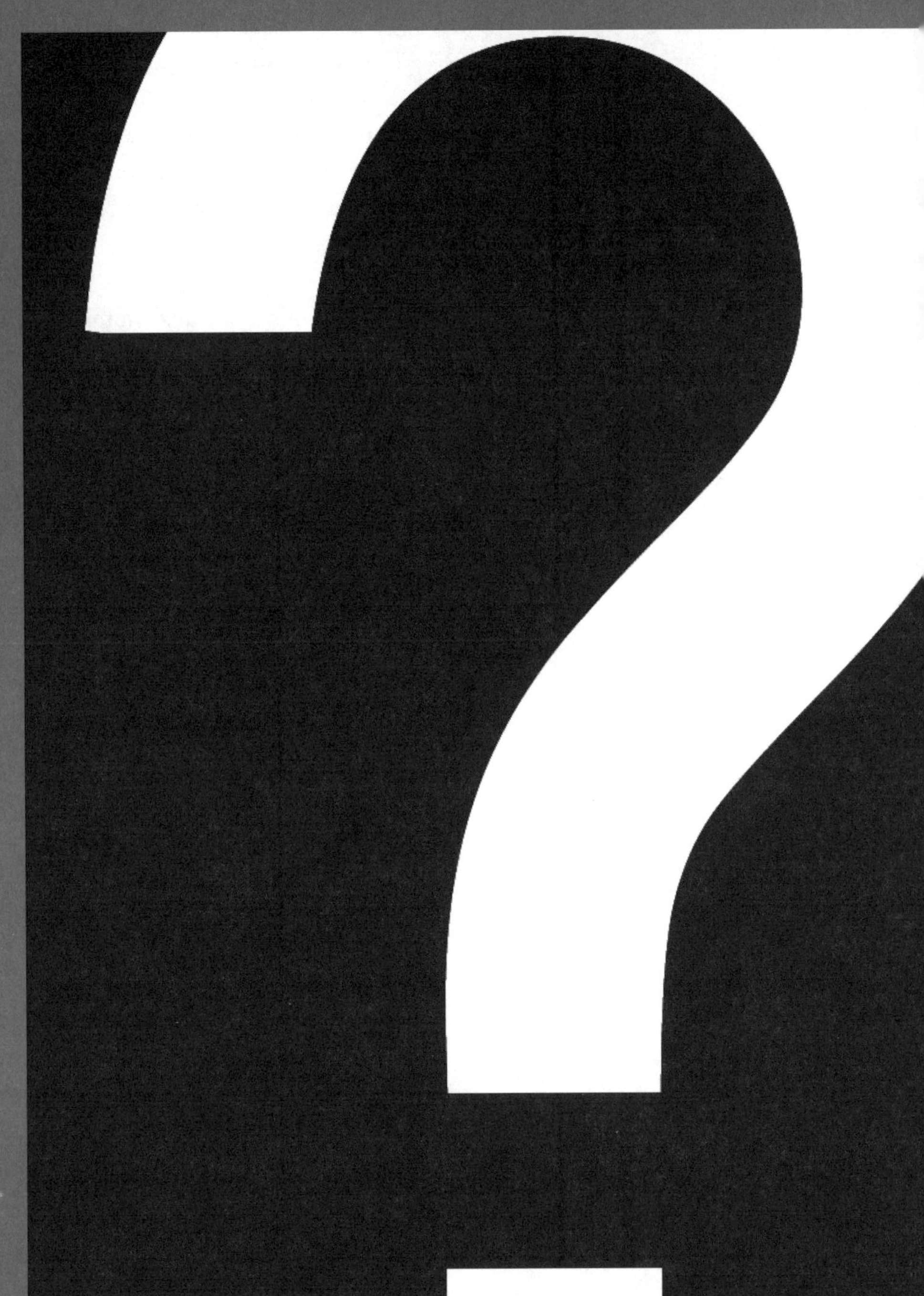

Key Words

Intrinsic qualities
Ecocentrism
Environmental anthropocentrism
Animal rights view

Key People

Aristotle
Saint Augustine
Thomas Hobbes
Marcus Tullius Cicero
Immanuel Kant
Hippias
John Donne
Stanley Milgram
St. Thomas Aquinas
René Descartes
Peter Singer
Tibor Machan
Aldo Leopold
Michael LaBossiere

Why Should a Person Be Good?

Why do you think people should be good? For example, what reasons would you give to a child to explain why they should not steal?

Are there any clear and compelling reasons why people should be good? If you made a list of the qualities that you would most like to see in your friends, chances are, lying to you and stealing from you are not going to be at the top. It is likely you would say that the way your friends treat you is important. What about strangers, animals, and the environment—should people be good to them as well? Does it really matter if you were to lie to or steal from a stranger? The material gain from theft is obvious. Are the reasons not to steal as obvious? Saying "it is just not right" is not a good enough answer to satisfy philosophers. They demand to know the underlying reasons for things. In this chapter, you will explore different reasons why a person should be good.

"Do unto others as you would have them do unto you."
Luke 6:31, *The Bible*

"Hurt not others in that you yourself would find hurtful."
Udana–varga 5:18

"No one of you is a believer until he desires for his brother that which he desires for himself."
Sunnah

"What you don't want, don't do to others."
Confucius, *Analects* 15:23

Are People Good to Avoid Punishment?

Most people perform acts that are thought to be bad and they often suffer consequences for these acts. Parents discipline their children, schools impose penalties upon students, and the state imposes punishment upon those guilty of crime. An individual's own conscience may make him or her feel bad. However, the fear of punishment is usually thought of as one of the most basic reasons why people perform good acts. It does not involve the complexity of higher moral reasoning.

The idea that people who do bad things will be punished is very old. Ancient Greek philosopher Aristotle (384–322 BCE) argued that, if a person makes bad decisions about how to live life, then these mistakes must be the result of irrationality. The desire for pleasure or power, for example, may have overcome the desire to act ethically. Aristotle argued that parents have a duty to teach proper habits and behaviour to children. Adults have a duty to be an example in reflecting intelligently on their aims and actions. Even virtuous people have the potential for irrational thinking, Aristotle believed. Therefore, laws and the threat of punishment are necessary in a community.

Saint Augustine (354–430) believed that most people are evil and will suffer eternal punishment by an omnipotent God. Only a small minority, according to Augustine, are saved and go to heaven.

Thomas Hobbes believed that it was the duty of the state to impose punishments upon transgressors. Without strong governments that have the power to impose harsh penalties, Hobbes believed that society would be a "war of all against all" and life would be "solitary, poor, nasty, brutish and short." His recommendation for those who break society's rules included capital punishment by decapitation.

> *"People seem not to see that their opinion of the world is also a confession of character."*
>
> Ralph Waldo Emerson

How Is Punishment Justified?

Do you think people should be punished for committing crimes? Why?

WEB CONNECTION

Wrongful Conviction

Search the Web for information about Guy Paul Morin and David Milgaard. How does the fact that these innocent men spent time in jail influence your opinion on the death penalty?

A crime generally refers to breaking one of society's laws. A person is usually punished for committing a crime. However, if the punishment brings harm to another, and if doing harm to another is wrong, then how is punishment justified? In answering this question, it is useful to distinguish between the different circumstances in which individuals are punished. For example, parents may discipline a child, but that does not mean necessarily that the child has committed a crime. The same may be true of a student in school who is disciplined by a teacher or the school administration. Aristotle said that the threat of punishment is necessary for parents to teach children proper behaviour. Do you think this kind of punishment is justified?

There are circumstances where punishment is not justified, such as if a person is falsely accused and convicted of a crime. There are some famous cases of people who have been found guilty in a trial, put in jail, and later found to have not committed the crime. There are examples of this in Canada. One is Guy Paul Morin, who was found guilty of murdering a child and sentenced to prison with no chance of parole for twenty-five years. He was later proven innocent. Another example is David Milgaard. He spent twenty-three years in jail for a murder that he did not commit.

What if Someone Really Is Guilty?

How is punishment justified if a person is truly guilty of a crime? For many philosophers, punishment is justified if the crime affects the community. If an act is truly to be called a crime, then that act must be one that concerns the entire community. For example, if some harm came to one of your friends, this would affect you. It would also affect your friend's parents, relatives, and other friends. This implies that some kind of public response from the community is suitable through the justice system. However, this also means that, if justice is to be fair, there needs to be general public awareness of its process. In other words, everyone needs to know the rules.

> *"[It] is of fundamental importance, that justice should not only be done, but should manifestly and undoubtedly be seen to be done."*
>
> Lord Hewart from *Rex v Sussex Justices; Ex parte McCarthy*

Is the Justice System Just?

Punishment is imposed for two main reasons: to bring about justice, and to help prevent bad acts from occurring. This may sound reasonable, but to justify punishment may not be enough in itself. Many philosophers believe that if society is to justify punishment, society must justify its entire system of justice and the manner in which laws are enforced. The British legal philosopher Herbert Hart (born 1907) wrote that there are at least three significant questions that must be resolved if punishment is to be justified.

1. *What is the motive behind a system of punishment?* Is it to bring about justice, or for some other selfish reason? Some governments for example have been known to imprison people for unjust reasons because of their political beliefs.
2. *Who may properly be punished and upon what principles?*
3. *How is the appropriate amount of punishment determined, and by whom?* For instance, in Canadian society, the idea of precedence is important. This means that, to be fair, punishments

should be as consistent as possible with those imposed for similar crimes in the past.

What Acts Should Be Punished?

Can you know what is a truly good or bad act?

To say that the main reason to be good is to avoid punishment has deep philosophical implications that make the position hard to maintain. For example, punishment is something that occurs after the crime itself. Moreover, to punish someone, you need to know what factors determine the rightness or wrongness of the action to be punished. For if all that makes something wrong is the fact that you will be punished for it, then is it really a bad act? Could you ever know what acts should be punishable in the first place? In other words, how do you know what is a truly good or bad act?

Different ideas will always exist about what is right and wrong. However, it seems to make sense to many that, if something is truly good or bad, then, there must be something within actions themselves that is good or bad. In Chapter 8, it was stated that philosophers often call qualities that exist within things intrinsic qualities. It follows that one compelling reason to be good is that there is an **intrinsic goodness** in being good. It follows as well that punishment is only justified when it is imposed upon an individual for an act that is intrinsically bad.

Do you think the state has the right to kill convicted criminals?

> *"If you pursue evil with pleasure, the pleasure passes away and the evil remains; if you pursue good with labour, the labour passes away but the good remains."*
>
> Cicero

POINT OF VIEW

Marcus Tullius Cicero

Most people probably agree that it is better to be happy than to be sad, but does being good make you happy? Marcus Tullius Cicero (106–43 BCE), an ancient Roman statesman and philosopher, argued that being good is an essential part of being happy and having a good life.

When his son, Marcus, was in his late teens, studying philosophy in Athens, Cicero wrote a work on moral duties and dedicated it to him. In this book, Cicero explains that a good person never does harm to another. The reason is that any advantage that may be gained from doing a bad deed, such as stealing, is only a short-term gain. In the long term, doing the right thing is always equal to doing the best thing. Doing what is best leads to a happy and prosperous life. In other words, one clear reason for being good is that you will find inner happiness and have a better life.

Do You Have a Duty to Be Good?

Whether or not being good makes you happy, some philosophers, such as Immanuel Kant, have argued that people have a duty to be good. Kant explained that morality is based upon existing laws and codes with a long-standing history. While it is the individual who must choose his or her actions toward these codes, the individual does have an obligation to be moral.

Why Should Anyone Be Good to Others?

> *"How far that little candle throws its beams! So shines a good deed in a naughty world."*
>
> From the play *Merchant of Venice*,
> by William Shakespeare

Hippias (5th century BCE) believed that there is a good, common within the laws of all countries, which constitutes their essential basis. Good and wise people of all countries are by nature similar, and therefore should regard all the citizens of the world as citizens of a single state. Being good to your neighbour extends to strangers with this type of thinking, as the notion that all human beings are interconnected underlies it. The ancient Romans used this type of thought as a model. This helped them to justify their imperial expansion and the imposition of ancient Roman law on other societies. The Romans argued that, in conquering their neighbours, they were merely bringing Roman goodness to them. They used this type of philosophical argument to justify their actions on moral grounds. However, some people may argue that the ancient Romans were exploiting and oppressing other cultures.

Are People of Equal Value?

Hippias' view that there is a common good among people of the world may suggest that goodness interconnects people of the world. John Donne (1572–1631), an English poet, shared a similar view. His poetry often contained philosophical messages. He too believed that people have an obligation to be good to others. An unconventional thinker for his time, his faith in the conventional order of his society was influenced by the political, scientific, and philosophic scepticism of his era. In one of his poems, entitled *No Man is an Island*, he wrote:

> No man is an island, entire of itself;
> every man is a piece of the continent, a part of the main …
> any man's death diminishes me,
> for I am involved in mankind,
> and therefore never send to know for whom the bell tolls;
> it tolls for thee.

Donne meant that, as members of a community, anything that affects one member is of importance to another member. If fate puts an individual in a certain position, then anyone could conceivably be in the same position. Natural human empathy, by way of reason, suggests that people should treat each other as they would want to be treated. Donne's idea extends to the law and system of justice. All people are subject to its rules. An injustice toward an individual within that system could conceivably be perpetrated against any individual within that system. Since all members of a community

PHILOSOPHY IN PSYCHOLOGY

Would You Intentionally Harm a Stranger?

Why do you think people cause other people to suffer? Stanley Milgram (1933–1984) was a social psychologist who was interested in events such as the Holocaust. He wondered why people who were otherwise good would inflict suffering on others. Milgram hypothesized that it is because people are overly obedient to authority.

He set up an experiment in which subjects were told that they were participating in a teaching and learning experiment. In fact, what was actually being tested was obedience to authority. It was set up so that a subject "teacher" would appear to give an electric shock to a "student" who was in another room. The student was shocked every time he or she made an error in answering a question asked by the teacher. Milgram constructed a machine with switches clearly labelled "Danger Extreme Shock." The machine started with a low voltage and went to 450 volts. Every time the student made an error, the teacher was to punish him or her with a shock, and then increase the voltage, ready for the next error. The teacher was told that the experiment was attempting to see if punishment improved learning. In fact Milgram wanted to see how many people, and at what point, would disobey authority and refuse to continue to administer shocks. At a certain voltage, the student even started screaming, and pleaded with the teacher to stop the experiment.

However, the teacher did not know that the student was not hooked up to the shock machine. The student was an actor who was part of the experiment, which turned out to be a good thing for the students. Sixty percent of the teachers obeyed orders to continue punishing the learner to the very end of the 450-volt scale. No subject stopped punishing the learner before reaching 300 volts!

The teachers were upset while they thought they were harming the student. Some teachers even pleaded with the authority figure to call off the experiment, but then continued. For the majority of the teachers, their desire to please, or at least not upset, the authority figure overcame their compassion for the student.

are interconnected, all members of that community must be concerned with other members. In the 20th century, the ideas of John Donne were one influence on Martin Luther King, Jr. and the civil rights movement.

People, such as Donne, would argue that people should be good because every human being is of value and deserves to be treated well. To not treat

THINKING LOGICALLY

Appeal to Authority (Argumentum ad Verecundiam)

Why do you choose to perform good and bad acts? Is it because someone in authority tells you it is good or bad? Would you kill someone just because a person in authority said it was good? Perhaps you have heard someone making a point that begins "experts say that …"? While it is true that experts or people in authority are often correct, it is also true that they are not always correct. No matter what expert, scientist, politician, or philosopher is making an argument, the argument must be weighed and tested upon its own merits, not because of who said it.

Here is an example of the fallacy of appealing to authority. During the 15th century, people with religious authority held a great deal of power. In 1486, two Dominican Monks, Heinrich Kramer and James Sprenger, wrote a book called the *Malleus Maleficarum*, which means "Hammer the Witches." Essentially, this book was a handbook for the torture and prosecution of witches during the Inquisition. The Inquisition was the organized, state sponsored persecution of innocents, mostly women. While the arguments made in *Malleus Maleficarum* are clearly illogical, it was widely believed to be true when it was written. This was largely because of the perceived authority of the authors.

An example follows of the fallacious thinking shown in *Malleus Maleficarum*. The authors make clear that they are talking about all women, not just witches. They write: "she [all women] is a liar by nature, so in her voice she stings while she delights us. Wherefore her voice is like the song of the Sirens, who with their sweet melody entice the passers-by and kill them." Today, it is known that hundreds of innocent people were tortured, and many executed, as a result of this book.

When you evaluate an argument, then, be sure to examine closely what is said, not just who says it.

another person well is equal to not treating yourself well because you are also a human being.

> *"The only thing necessary for the triumph of evil is for good men to do nothing."*
>
> Edmund Burke

Are People Obliged to Be Good to Animals?

Do you think that people should be good to animals? Why?

Traditional arguments answering the question "Why be good?" tend to focus on people's treatment of other people. However, in the 20th century, and continuing today, there has been a growing philosophical movement that addresses the issue of the treatment of animals.

People use animals in many ways: for food, as pets, and sometimes in animal testing and experiments. For example, manufacturers of products used by human beings have a legal and moral responsibility to ensure that their products do not injure the consumer. They need to ensure that the chemicals used in products, say a new type of shampoo, do not cause blindness if the shampoo gets in your eyes. For many years, animals were used to test products to ensure their safety. To test shampoo, it was poured into an animal's eyes, such as a rabbit. Scientists documented whether or not eyesight damage occurred and how much of a particular chemical could be poured into the rabbit's eyes before it went blind. Proponents of animal testing argued that the suffering endured by animal test subjects was necessary to prevent the greater evil of human suffering. While animal testing is not as common now as in the past, animals are still used in experiments and tests by scientists.

In the past, philosophers such as St. Thomas Aquinas, René Descartes (1596–1650), and Immanuel Kant all argued that people do not have any direct moral obligation to animals. They believed that the morality of people's actions was determined by how those actions affected human beings, not the animals directly. Aquinas argued that it is wrong to hurt an animal if that animal is the property of another person—it is an injustice toward the owner. Descartes maintained that, because animals lack reason, they are the same as mechanical things. For this reason, people have the right to use animals as they wish. While Kant conceded that people should not torture animals, this was only because it may cause a person to be less sensitive to human suffering.

Do Animals Suffer?

Peter Singer is a modern philosopher who opposes the views of Aquinas, Descartes, and Kant. Singer believes that people do have a direct moral obligation to animals. In 1975, Singer wrote the book *Animal Liberation*.

In this book, Singer argues that many animals do feel pleasure and pain. Since traditional moral values state that people should not cause suffering, and because many animals are observed to experience suffering, it is logical to conclude that people should not cause animals to suffer.

However, not all modern philosophers believe that animals are entitled to the same rights as people. For instance, Tibor Machan (born 1939) wrote an essay called "Do Animals Have Rights?" In this essay, Machan argues that, since people cannot demand that animals behave morally, animals are not moral creatures. For example, you cannot demand that an animal not kill a human being. Try telling a Kodiak bear to stop killing a person and it will not listen to you! You can only tell people not to kill people. This is because, for Machan, morality is a purely human phenomenon. Since morality applies only to humans, and because animals are not human, people are not obliged to treat animals with moral consideration.

Are People Obliged to Be Good to the Environment?

Do you have moral obligations to future generations or only to people alive today? For instance, do people have an obligation to leave natural resources for future generations?

A relatively new branch of philosophy, environmental ethics, addresses the question of whether people have a moral obligation to the environment. Many people today have concerns about the environment. Given the environment's importance to human survival, it is not surprising that some philosophers have devoted themselves to this topic.

Most philosophers who have written on the topic of environmental ethics agree that people have an obligation to be good to the environment. There are three main schools of thought on this. They are: ecocentrism, environmental anthropocentrism, and the animal rights view.

What Is Ecocentrism?

Ecocentrism is the view that environmental concerns should be central to human actions and decision-making. Aldo Leopold (1887–1948) was a defender of ecocentrism. In 1949, after his death, an essay Leopold wrote called "The Land Ethic" was published. In this essay, Leopold suggests that morality evolved over time. In the beginning, he says, morality was based on religion. Later, morality was based on the golden rule and the social contract. Society is now in transition, he argues, entering into what he calls the land ethic. When society fully advances into the land ethic, the social contract will extend beyond people and also include the environment. This means that people will include effects upon the environment as a factor in moral decision-making.

What Is Environmental Anthropocentrism?

Environmental anthropocentrism, unlike ecocentrism, focuses on human interests. This view relies on traditional moral concepts, such as the social contract and individual rights. Since every human life has value, and since humans cannot live without the environment, it follows that people have a responsibility toward the environment because it is necessary for human survival. Rather than grant the environment special rights, this position is based purely on human interests.

What Is the Animal Rights View?

The third environmental ethics position is the **animal rights view**. One question asked in Chapter 3 was if animals should be considered persons. The animal rights view maintains that it is persons that are of value and worthy of rights. As at least some animals, and all human beings, are persons, humans have an obligation to be good to the environment in order to support animals' existence.

Should Nature Take Its Course?

Some dissenting philosophers have argued that environmental and animal rights ethicists are too idealist. They say that their goals are unrealistic. For example, in a provocative essay called "Letting Species Die," Michael LaBossiere argues that people should not be concerned with saving all endangered species. One reason for his argument is the premise that animal extinction is a natural occurrence. Extinctions have occurred many times throughout history. LaBossiere also states that, because human beings are not all-powerful and have limited abilities, it is not possible for people to come to the rescue of every creature in every circumstance.

What Do You Think?

Philosophers throughout the ages have directed many thoughts toward the question, Why be good? Some philosophers say that people are good only to avoid punishment. To others, people are good in order to obey God's will. Some philosophers believe that a person's good behaviour comes from the ability to reason. They say that it just makes sense to be good. Some philosophers also say that part of being good is to be good to animals and the environment. What do you think are the reasons that people are good?

Chapter 12 What Is Good?

Key Words

Noncognitivism
Epicureanism
Hedonism
Cynic
Virtue theory
Stoic
Anachronistic fallacy
Utilitarianism
Greatest happiness principle
Consequentialism
Ethical egoism
Just war theory
Nihilism

Key People

G.E. Moore
Epicurus
Erasmus
Diogenes
Aristotle
St. Thomas Aquinas
Marcus Aurelius
Jeremy Bentham
John Stuart Mill
Elisabeth Anscombe
Ayn Rand
Henry David Thoreau
Friedrich Nietzsche

What Does It Mean to Be Good?

Of anything in the world, what do you think is the greatest good?

Philosophers of all time periods have suggested many answers to the question "What does it mean to be good?" or, more simply, "What is good?" For example, some philosophers say that pleasure is good, and therefore one should seek pleasure in life as the ultimate goal. Another point of view is that the pursuit of pleasure is selfish, and that, to be good, a person has to take others into consideration. In ancient times, some philosophers believed that to be virtuous is good. However, the concept of virtue may have been different to these ancient philosophers than your own concept of virtue. For example, is it really important to you how well you perform in a military battle? To some ancient philosophers, this was one way to be virtuous. Today, this type of virtue may or may not be important. Nevertheless, many philosophers today address issues concerning conflict and morality. They ask, for example, if a good or moral war is possible.

People's concepts of what is good have an impact on how they live and treat others. Society's attitudes toward what is good affect current events and shape the future. In this chapter, you will consider many philosophical viewpoints that try to answer the question "What is good?"

> *"Every belief, every considering something-true is Necessarily false because there is simply no true world."*
> Friedrich Nietzsche

Can Anyone Know What Is Good?

Philosophers may not agree on what is good, but they would all probably agree that it is a complex and difficult question to answer. One philosopher, G.E. Moore (1873–1958), believed that moral goodness cannot be defined. Moore meant that the idea of goodness is so basic a property that it cannot be analysed any further than just calling it good. Another example of such a basic property is the colour red. What more about red can you say other than it is the colour red? Think of things that are red. Can you say why they are red? They just are red. Now, think of something that is good. Can you say why it is good? Moore says, no, you can only recognize it as good, you cannot say why it is good. Unless you are colour blind, you do not have any trouble distinguishing the colour red. Goodness is a similar thing because good things are as easy to recognize as is a colour. Goodness is a thing so basic that people intuitively recognize it

Can Moral Statements Be True or False?

Moore suggested that you can know what is good intuitively. Some say that, if you know something is morally good, then that is a truth—at least, it is true for you. However, there are some philosophers who propose that moral statements are neither true nor false. This is called noncognitivism. To understand what this means, it is helpful to first understand two different types of statements. The first, called a propositional statement, can be proven right or wrong. The second, called a nonpropositional statement, cannot. Here is an example of a propositional statement:

Elvis was in my favourite donut shop this morning.

The propositional statement that Elvis was in the donut shop this morning can be proven true or false. You could do this by observation and analysis, which are forms of thinking. Another word for this type of understanding is cognition.

On the other hand, think about the following statement. Can it be proven right or wrong?

Turn down your music!

Notice that terms like right and wrong or true and false do not apply to the above nonpropositional statement. It does not make sense to ask if the statement "Turn down your music!" is true or false. Since the statement cannot be proven true or false by cognition, it is called a noncognitive statement.

Noncognitivism asserts that moral statements, such as "murder is wrong," are also nonpropostional statements. That is, they cannot be true or false. The statement, "murder is wrong" is easily reworded, "do not murder," and is then the same type of statement as "Turn down your music!" It is neither true nor false. The terms true or false do not apply to the statement. In this view, to say that something is good is a noncognitive statement.

Is Pleasure Good?

Do you consider your pleasures to be truly good? Why?

> *"We recognize pleasure as the first good innate in us, and from pleasure we begin every act of choice and avoidance, and to pleasure we return again, using the feeling as the standard by which we judge every good."*
>
> Epicurus

As you have read, G.E. Moore believed that you can say something is good, but you cannot say why it is good. This may or may not be true, but you can explore some of the things that philosophers have called good. Take pleasure, for example. There are probably many things in life that give you pleasure. Do you often seek out the things that give you pleasure rather than pain? If you do, you are not alone. There are some philosophers who believe that the greatest good is pleasure. Some in ancient times held this position. In particular, the ancient Greek philosopher Epicurus (c. 341–270 BCE) is associated with this idea. Epicurus was the founder of a school of philosophy called Epicureanism.

How Should You Seek Pleasure?

Epicureanism is a complex philosophy, part of which maintains that people should seek pleasure in life. Say you were to ask Epicurus the question, "What is good?" He would probably reply to the effect that good is found by maximizing your pleasure and minimizing your pain. Epicurus also suggested that if you have fewer desires, you would find happiness easier to attain. According to Epicurus, then, rather than just greedily seeking pleasure, you should determine the few most important things that will bring you pleasure, and pursue them.

Many Epicureans say that pleasure is found in the highest forms of human achievement, such as art, music, fine cuisine, and other forms of culture. Epicurus argued that good is found in kindness and friendship. There was more to Epicureanism than devotion to self-gratification. The pursuit of pleasure alone is often called **hedonism**.

Is It Wrong to Seek Pleasure?

For some Christian philosophers in the Middle Ages, Epicureanism and hedonism became associated with more basic physical forms of pleasure. These philosophers denounced Epicurus, not only for the pleasure-seeking element in his philosophy, but also because he denied the value of God. They further disagreed with Epicurus because he did not believe in an afterlife. Epicurus also taught that, because there is no immortality, people should live only for today.

Still, Epicureanism did not die out. During the Renaissance, philosophers such as Erasmus (1466–1536) used some Epicurean ideas. They argued that, because God wants human beings to be happy, and because pleasure brings happiness, God wants human beings to pursue pleasure.

Is Poverty Good?

How good is money? What would you do to become rich?

You have read that there are people who believe that pleasure is the highest good. Some people also believe that the greatest pleasure lies in what money can buy them. However, a group of ancient philosophers believed that wealth is not good. These philosophers were known as the **Cynics**, a word which is derived from the Greek word for "dog." Some say that this name comes from the fact that they lived life as simply as dogs. The ancient Cynics attacked the values of their ancient world. Some Cynics went so far as to dress in rags, live a wandering homeless life, and have few or no possessions. One ancient Greek Cynic Diogenes (404–323 BCE) is said to have owned only a cup, a knapsack, and a cloak, but upon witnessing a boy drink water from his hands, threw away the cup.

The Cynics became well-known in the ancient world. One legend has Diogenes meeting Alexander the Great. Alexander was interested in philosophy and had sought out Diogenes to speak with him. Upon seeing his poor condition, Alexander asked if there was anything that he could do to help. Diogenes, who apparently was lying on the ground dressed in his rags, said, "Yes, you can move, you are blocking my light."

The Cynics believed that it was good to live in poverty, and had little faith in humanity. They did not believe that people could behave morally or altruistically. Diogenes is said to have wandered with a lantern in daylight and when asked why, replied, "I am searching for an honest man."

Is Virtue the Most Important Good?

What virtues do you think are possessed by a person who is perfectly good?

Not all philosophers believe that good is to be found exclusively in the pursuit of pleasure and wealth. Some philosophers suggest that good comes from increasing your good character traits and decreasing the bad ones. Good character traits are called virtues, and bad character traits are called vices. **Virtue theory** suggests that good is found in developing good character traits, or virtues. Philosophers who accept this view say that good is found in a person who has many virtues and few or no vices. Virtues include such things as truthfulness, generosity, courage, justice, discretion, conviction, friendliness, and modesty. Vices include such things as cowardice, cruelty, injustice, and conceit.

Virtue theorists recognize the complex nature of human personalities and see virtues as things that regulate extreme emotions, desires, and behaviours. For example, fear is a natural human emotion. To be overly fearful could be an impediment to a good life. People should therefore develop the virtue of courage. Yet, being courageous without careful thought is to be foolish, rather than brave. Foolishness is a vice. Virtues are traits that regulate behaviours and help to make people good.

Are Virtues Learned?

Some virtue theorists maintain that virtues are learned. In other words, people are not born good but can be taught to be good. If a person is not taught well by his or her parents or school, then this person may develop vices and become a bad person. For a virtue theorist, moral education is essential for a good society, and these character traits are best learned in one's youth. Adults, then, have a moral responsibility to teach the young well.

Is Reason the Highest Virtue?

Another group of philosophers who taught that one should live a virtuous life were the ancient Greek and Roman **Stoics**. While they listed many virtues, they thought the most important virtue was to live life according to reason. However, the Stoics believed people should live by universal reason rather than individual reason. That is, there are some common universal virtues that exist outside of all people for all time, such as intelligence, modesty, and bravery. Stoics believed that a person should follow this universal reason, and not just follow his or her own individual whims and wishes for an immediate personal gain.

Does Practice Make You Virtuous?

Aristotle was also a virtue theorist. In his writings on ethics, he explained that one should live life according to certain virtues—courage, temperance, justice, and wisdom. Aristotle's views on virtue were so respected, that it was still one of the most important moral theories through much of the Middle Ages (500–1450). During the Middle Ages, these virtues became known as the cardinal virtues.

Christian philosophers, such as St. Thomas Aquinas, adopted Aristotle's work, and added to it the theological virtues of faith, hope, and charity. Aristotle's ideas of virtue, and the additional theological virtues, focus on a person's need to practice these virtues to remain virtuous.

Later, during the Enlightenment (18th century Europe), moral philosophy expanded, and the focus of the question "What is good?" became centred not so much upon the individual as the individual's role and duties in society.

THINKING LOGICALLY

The Anachronistic Fallacy

Many ancient philosophers were concerned with the concept of virtue. Many philosophers today are also concerned with the concept of virtue. It is important to remember, however, that ancient values were different than modern ones. Things change over time: fashion, technology, values, and culture are very different today than a century ago, and vastly different than a millennium ago. It is possible to incorrectly place an item or idea in the wrong time period than the one in which it actually belongs. To do so is called an anachronism.

Sometimes placing something in the wrong time period is done for entertainment purposes, for example, cartoons that show cave dwellers driving cars or using microwave ovens made out of stone. To do so in a scholarly sense, however, is to commit a fallacy. Slavery, for instance, was widely practised and accepted by the ancients. People would also watch others fight to the death for entertainment in ancient times. Modern values say that these things are wrong. This raises a question about whether, as most philosophers of ethics think, slavery and brutality have always been wrong, or whether, as some claim, this conclusion is an anachronism.

> *"And thou wilt give thyself relief, if thou doest every act of thy life as if it were the last."*
>
> Marcus Aurelius

PHILOSOPHY IN HISTORY

Marcus Aurelius

Marcus Aurelius (121–180) was a Roman emperor who was also known as a philosopher. From the time of his youth, Marcus was a devout Stoic. He believed strongly in the concepts of temperance and virtue.

During his reign, Rome faced increasing difficulties with tribes along the frontiers of the empire who were waging war with the Romans. He spent much of his time fighting battles against these tribes. Later in life, Marcus wrote a book of Stoic philosophy called *The Meditations*. It is still widely read, and serves as a valuable insight into the Stoic philosophy of his time. Aurelius died in a military campaign on the frontier in 180.

His son, Commodus, who became more famous for his vices than his good deeds, succeeded him. One of the unusual things that made Commodus famous was the fact that he actually fought in the arena as a gladiator.

Is It Good to Be Good to Others in Society?

Which is best: to be good only to yourself or only to your society?

Perhaps you agree with virtue theorists and think being virtuous is the highest good. While being virtuous may be good, virtue focuses mostly upon individual conduct and behaviour. For this reason, some philosophers argue that it does not adequately explain what good is for society as a whole. One important philosophical idea that addresses this question is called utilitarianism. The word *utility*, from which the term "utilitarianism" is derived, refers to the usefulness of something. Jeremy Bentham (1748–1832) and John Stuart Mill (1806–1873) are famous proponents of this philosophy.

Utilitarianism maintains that the proper course of action for individuals in their moral decision-making is this: evaluate the possible consequences of their choices, and undertake actions that produce the greatest good for society. Human actions that are useful to society as a whole have the highest value.

POINT OF VIEW

Elisabeth Anscombe

Imagine you live in a utilitarian society and every decision you make has to be for the greatest good of the whole society. What if murdering one person could somehow save two lives? Is it good to kill one person to save two lives? The philosopher, Elisabeth Anscombe (1919–2001) said no. Anscombe wrote that, while all moral actions have consequences, some actions, such as murder, are wrong no matter what the consequences. She coined the term **consequentialism** for the utilitarian ethical theories she opposed.

Utilitarians are less concerned with moral codes and religious doctrines than with the practical results of individual choices and actions. They believe that the moral value of an action is measured by its result. These philosophers, then, say that the greatest good is what is most useful and valuable for all of humanity.

Does Pleasure Help Society?

Similar to ancient Epicureans, utilitarians believe that pleasure is important for happiness. However, rather than individual, selfish pleasure, utilitarians are concerned with undertaking actions that maximize pleasure or happiness, and well-being in society. Bentham called this the **greatest happiness principle**. For example, think of the occupation that you want to pursue when you finish school. On Bentham's principle, you should choose an occupation that will usefully contribute to society and not just benefit you personally. This does not mean that you should completely sacrifice your own happiness, because if you are happy in your work, you will do it well, and you will make people around you happy at the same time.

Moral actions are further divided into consequentialist categories. If the consequences of an action are meant just to be favourable to the person performing the action, this is called egoism. When a person's aim is to produce consequences favourable to others, this is called altruism. For example, if a large corporation donates to a charity mainly to publicize their name, this could be called egoism. On the other hand, if someone risks their life, with no thought of reward, to save the life of a stranger, this could be called altruism.

Most philosophers of ethics think that altruism is, in general, a good thing and egoism a bad thing. However, some, such as the Russian-born American screenwriter and political philosopher Ayn Rand (1905–1982), claim that egoism is morally good. This view, called **ethical egoism**, is the position that people's first moral obligation is to themselves. The title of Rand's main book on this subject, *The Virtue of Selfishness,* well expresses the idea of ethical egoism. Critics of this view maintain that, on closer examination, it does not literally maintain that selfish behaviour is morally good. Rather, they say that the ethical egoists actually argue for the different conclusions: (1) that people are, in fact, selfish by nature, so any alternative to egoism is unrealistic; or (2) that altruism is bad for society as a whole, because it makes people too dependent on one another.

1. Do you think it is possible for people to act altruistically?

2. If it is possible to act altruistically,* should *people try to be altruistic, or should they look out only for themselves?

3. If people are selfish by nature, does it automatically follow that they should only act selfishly?

> *"All good things are wild and free."*
> Henry David Thoreau

Is It Good to Obey the Law?

Should you break a law if you think the law is morally wrong?

Utilitarians believe that what is good for society is the highest good. Some people may argue that a country's laws help provide what is good for society. Take Canada's laws, for example. These are based upon history and tradition, and are deeply rooted in the moral beliefs and codes held by many Canadians. However, do you believe that all of Canada's laws are morally just? What would you do if you felt that one of Canada's laws advocated behaviour that you felt was not moral? In this case, would breaking the law be good—good on any level—for an individual or for society? These are the sorts of questions that were faced by American philosopher Henry David Thoreau (1817–1862) when he contemplated the existence of slavery.

Thoreau decided it was wrong to obey a morally unjust law. He refused to pay a state poll tax used to enforce the Fugitive Slave Law. For this, he went to jail. Thoreau then wrote an essay entitled "Civil Disobedience," which explained his actions. In the essay, he argued that a person was morally compelled to obey a higher moral authority than an unjust law.

Thoreau and his ideas of civil disobedience provided inspiration for Mohandas K. Gandhi, in India. Gandhi led a non-violent movement to free India of British colonial rule. It was also used during the civil rights movement of the 1960s. Proponents of civil disobedience almost always argue that it must be a non-violent, public action, meaning that it not be done in secret. Further, the person must be willing to face the consequences of his or her actions rather than become a fugitive.

What Is the Right Choice?

You have considered many things that may be good, such as pleasure or being virtuous. But have you ever been faced with a situation for which no good choice can be made? In this kind of situation, making the right choice is not easy. Philosophers have tried to tackle the question of knowing that, no matter what the decision, the outcome would be bad. Plato gave this example:

Imagine that a person borrows a weapon from a neighbour, and promises to return it when asked. Later, the neighbour comes back, extremely angry and agitated, and asks for the weapon back. It is clear that he wants to kill someone with it. What should the borrower do? Break the promise, or be an accessory to a crime? A moral dilemma exists when there are two or more choices available to someone, each of which has a moral consequence. Philosophers have wondered whether it is possible to resolve such issues, and if so, how.

A utilitarian resolves a moral dilemma by saying that the proper course of action is the one that brings the greatest amount of good to society. Failing that, one should undertake whatever action brings the least amount of damage.

Others may look to their religious beliefs in such instances, or, choose actions that are the greatest demonstration of virtues.

Can War Ever Be Good?

War is another kind of moral dilemma. Even if there are some beneficial outcomes for one country, some people of that country may die in the war. For a leader, taking a country to war may be the hardest choice of all. Despite this, countries go to war all the time. Does this mean that war can be good? Many philosophers say that war is never good, but that it is sometimes justified. The question "What is a just war?" has been studied seriously. It is difficult to imagine any human activity with potentially more devastating and damaging aspects than the consequences of war.

Philosophers who examine this question are concerned with what is called **just war theory**. Philosophers examine wars either historically, such as World War II, or hypothetically, that is, a fictional situation given as an example. Philosophers who try to understand if a particular war is just may look to some existing guidelines for help. For example, historical traditions exist toward combat, and rules have been set out in documents, such as the Geneva and Hague conventions. These rules limit certain kinds of warfare and specify the treatment of prisoners of war. For example, the Geneva and Hague conventions outlaw germ warfare and bioterrorism. These conventions also state that, if a nation takes prisoners, it must provide them with the basic necessities of life, and not undertake actions against them that could be deemed cruel or inhumane, such as torture.

These rules of war deal with moral considerations. However, some say that codes of moral behaviour (such as laid out in the Geneva and Hague conventions) are practical as well as moral. History shows that, when warfare is over, nations very often survive, and then continue to interact and trade. These people argue that it is simply in a nation's best interest to minimize damages before, during, and after conflict. This enables countries to get back to the business of manufacturing and trading goods and services, upon which countries thrive.

While a number of different positions are held on this topic, philosophers who examine the ethics of war are concerned with specific things. They ask questions such as:

- Does the war have a just cause?
- How was the war declared and by whom?

POINT OF VIEW

Friedrich Nietzsche

Friedrich Nietzsche (1844–1900) was a Prussian-born student of classic languages and literatures. He subjected the philosophical, moral, and religious ideas of his time to radical criticism. He believed that beneath the surface of ordinary morality and rationality is a passionate will to power. Most people fear this will and, with the help of religion and ordinary morality, they try to deny it in themselves and others. Against this denial, Nietzsche hoped for a future of "supermen" who would proudly recognize and exert their powers as creative individualists, not hindered by the constraints of the "animal-herd mentality" that he thought dominated most of humanity.

In a book called *Beyond Good and Evil*, Nietzsche distinguished between moral systems that reflected the timidity, resentment, and petty vengefulness of followers or "slaves," and the morality of the "masters," which is marked by independence and self-affirmation. Some see in Nietzsche's views a refreshing criticism of complacency and assertion of creativity. Others think that by his relentless criticisms of religion and traditional morality he contributed to the very nihilism that he thought his supermen would overcome.

- Was the degree of force used appropriate under the circumstances?
- Are the goals of the combatants justifiable?
- Are the methods of warfare appropriate?
- Was the treatment of prisoners reasonably humane?

Others argue that war is never justified. It is hypocritical, they say, that murder is immoral in society but permissible in war. Those who refuse to participate in war because of religious or philosophical views are called conscientious objectors.

Are good and evil just figments of human imagination?

Is There No Good?

Many ideas discussed in this chapter identify what has positive or negative value: to say that pleasure is good is to give a positive value to pleasure; to say war is bad is to give a negative value to war; to say a murderer is evil is to place a negative value on the murderer. There is a branch of philosophy that maintains that all values are without meaning—nothing can be known that is true with regards to moral or ethical questions. This is called **nihilism**, from the Latin *nihil*, meaning nothing, or, that which does not exist. The word *annihilate* comes from the same root. Some nihilist philosophers go so far as to advocate the annihilation of all established beliefs, morals, and religious convictions. This is because, to them, these beliefs are untrue, and, therefore should not be followed.

Nietzsche believed that society would face the greatest historical crisis ever as a result of the corrosion of faith in predominant values, brought about by nihilism. Faced with a meaningless life in a meaningless universe, nihilism is an extreme form of pessimism that finds little comfort in conventional wisdom or commonly held beliefs.

Nihilism therefore represents a basic challenge to philosophers of ethics. Nietzsche's own reaction to the decay of the traditional values of his times (especially of Christian values) was to *celebrate* this. Traditional values, he argued, hold back individuals and make societies weak. Philosophers who disagree with Nietzsche on this point, still see it as an important job of philosophy either: (1) to defend traditional values, thus putting them on a secure footing to withstand nihilism; or (2) to explain and defend alternative values by reference to which people can judge positive and negative values in themselves and others.

What Do You Think?

In this chapter, you have learned that it is difficult to find principles of what is good. While some philosophers say that individual pleasure is the highest good, others believe that there are more worthy pursuits, such as serving others in society or living virtuously. As rational beings with the ability to make choices, people's decision-making often has a moral component. The decisions that you make on a daily basis affect your life and other lives. Do you think, as some philosophers do, that people should make those decisions based on what brings the greatest good to society?

Unit 5

What Is a Just Society?

What is a good and just society? If you were going to set up a new state, what kind of a political society would you create? You would have to decide on the form of government and you would have to decide how the leader(s) would be chosen.

Another job in this new state would be to decide how things should be divided among its citizens—things such as goods, services, work, leisure time, money, and so on. How would you divide things? For example, would all the citizens receive an equal share of everything, or would you divide things based upon what each person contributes to the society?

What rights should people have in this new society? And what role should the state play to ensure that people's rights are met? Should the government take a more hands-on or hands-off approach to rights? Once the state lays out its citizens' rights—perhaps both individual and group rights—these rights may conflict. How can you resolve conflicting rights? Do some rights take precedence over others?

As you read this unit, you will consider and respond to many philosophical viewpoints that explore the questions of what makes a just society.

Chapter 13 What Is Justice?

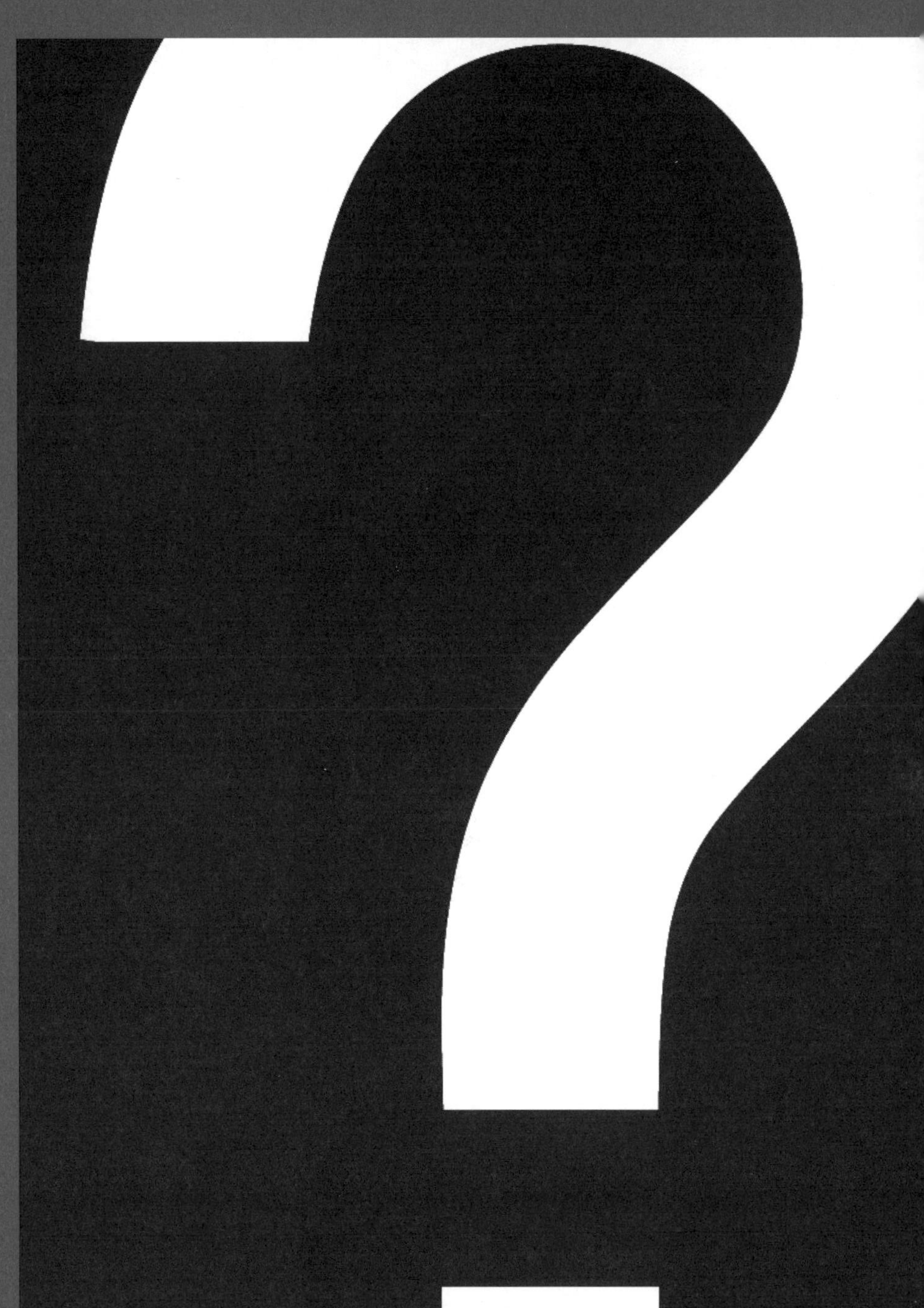

Key Words

Distributive justice
Restorative justice
Compensatory justice
Retributive justice
Egalitarianism (simple equality)
Equity
Meritorians
Legalists
Valid Argument
Sound Argument
Libertarianism
Natural law
Social contract

Key People

Han Fei
Iris Marion Young
Plato
John Locke
St. Thomas Aquinas
Jean-Jacques Rousseau
Thomas Hobbes
John Rawls

What Is Distributive Justice?

Almost everyone can give examples of times that he or she has been treated unfairly, whether at home, in school, or in society as a whole. Is it fair that some people work hard but make little money, while others are born rich? Is it fair when people who make important contributions to society gain the same or fewer rewards in life as those who make no contributions at all? If some people have disabilities, through no fault of their own (for instance, due to an accident or a birth defect), is it fair that they must bear this burden without help from the rest of society?

These are questions that concern philosophers of **distributive justice**. They ask whether such examples are unfair, why they are unfair, and how a just society would deal with them. In this chapter, you will investigate different philosophies of distributive justice. You will also learn about philosophers who proposed these theories.

Kinds of Justice

There are kinds of justice studied by philosophers other than distributive justice. Theories of **restorative** or **compensatory justice** address questions, such as: Should people who have been disadvantaged due to bad treatment in the past be compensated? What is fair compensation? Compensatory justice is discussed in Chapter 14. Theories of **retributive justice** address questions, such as: What is fair punishment? This topic was discussed in Chapter 11.

Bases for Distributive Justice

The key question of distributive justice is this: What is the basis for a just distribution of benefits and burdens in a society? A society is a country, a city, a workplace, a school, a family, or even the world itself. In any society, everyone enjoys at least some *benefits* and endures at least some *burdens*. Benefits include consumer goods (or the money necessary to buy them), access to education, health care, interesting and enjoyable work, and free time for personal relaxation or development. Burdens include hard or unpleasant work, doing without benefits, or devoting time and energy to taking care of dependents.

What do you think is the fairest way to divide work and money among people in society?

How Should Things Be Divided?

There are three main notions about the basis of just distribution defended by philosophers of justice: **simple equality**, **equity,** and **merit**. The example that follows illustrates the differences among these three notions of just distribution.

Imagine that Grandma has brought a cake to the table and put it in front of Simone to divide among her and her cousins. Simone proposes to cut it into equal pieces, but not everyone agrees. Len points out that he is the biggest person at the table and therefore needs a larger piece than the others. Laura objects that Len did not help Grandma either in making the cake or by doing chores around the house. She suggests that the people who are the most helpful should get the bigger pieces.

Simone's idea is one version of the philosophical theory of **egalitarianism**. This is the view that nobody deserves more or fewer benefits or burdens than others. For many, like Simone, this is achieved by simply dividing benefits (like the cake) or burdens (like household chores) equally. This version of egalitarianism is also referred to as **simple equality**.

Or do you agree with Len? He reasons that, because he is biggest, he needs more cake. Len's argument is a more complex version of egalitarianism, which is called **equity**. An equitable distribution is one that takes account of special needs. Of course, the special needs that society must consider are sometimes much more important than Len's. An example of equity is when tax dollars are used to provide public buildings with wheelchair ramps—the special needs of some are provided for by taxing everyone. Provision of special education classes is another example.

> *"It's very hard in military or personal life to assure complete equality. Life is unfair."*
>
> John F. Kennedy

When Laura suggests that larger pieces of the cake should be given to those who deserve them, she is using a third basis for distribution, namely **merit**. This is the principle defended by philosophical **meritorians**. In many

POINT OF VIEW

Han Fei

One philosopher who would agree with Laura is the ancient Chinese philosopher Han Fei (280–233 BCE). He was a member of a school called the **legalists**. They argued that the laws of the land should ensure that "those who have merit should be rewarded."

times and places, it was thought that some people deserved more of the worlds benefits and less of its burdens simply because of their birth: people born of noble families deserved more than ordinary people; people born as boys deserved more than girls; people born into under classes or as slaves were thought to deserve their burdensome lives. Though some people still hold such views, no modern philosopher does.

Like Laura, modern meritorians think that some people deserve to come out ahead in the distribution of benefits and burdens, but they have different ideas about why they deserve this. Laura argued that those who helped Grandma with chores deserved more of the cake. However, suppose that she worked hard in performing chores, but was not very good at doing them. Meanwhile, Anna, who is more talented than Laura, was much more help to Grandma, even though she needed to exert less effort. A question that meritorian philosophers ask is whether the effort people exert or their actual contributions make them especially deserving.

THINKING LOGICALLY

Arguments

In philosophy, an argument is not a shouting match. It is an attempt to persuade others to agree with a conclusion by giving good reasons to believe it. This means that the conclusion must actually follow from the reasons given. Suppose, for example that Len said that the others ought to give in to him, since, being the biggest, he can simply take as much of the cake as he wants.

This so-called argument might get Len a large piece of cake, but it is not a good reason to believe that he *ought* to get it. By contrast, when Len argued earlier that he should have the biggest piece because he needed it, he was making an appropriate argument, which can be spelled out as follows:

Premise 1: People should receive shares of things depending on how badly they need them.
Premise 2: Larger people need larger portions of food than do smaller people.
Premise 3: Len is the largest person at Grandma's table.
Conclusion: Therefore, Len should receive a larger portion of the cake than the others.

This is a **valid argument** because *if* its premises are true, so is its conclusion. Of course, to prove that the conclusion really *is* true, the premises must also be true so it is not enough for it just to be valid. For an argument to be what philosophers of logic call a **sound argument**, its conclusion must follow from its premises (that is, it must be valid), *and* these premises must also be true. An argument may therefore be valid without being sound. An example is: All humans are three-legged (premise one); Fred is a human (premise two): therefore Fred has three legs (conclusion). This argument is valid because its conclusion follows from its premises in accord with rules of logic even though one premise is false.

Philosophers of logic are mainly concerned only to discover rules of valid arguments. Other philosophers, however, are looking for true conclusions and therefore want their arguments to be valid and their premises to be true. The famous example used by the ancient Greek philosopher Aristotle (384–322 BCE) is: All persons are mortal; Socrates is a person; therefore Socrates is mortal.

Even if Simone and Laura granted that Len's argument is valid, they may still not think that it gives them a good reason to give him the largest piece of cake, because they disagree with the truth of Premise 1. In fact, they could also challenge the truth of Premise 2, by maintaining that it is not physical size but degree of activity that determines how much food someone needs. With this premise, Len should only get the largest piece if he has been the most active of the cousins.

Make up your own valid arguments for the other conclusions about how to divide Grandma's cake by giving reasons, which, if true, would mean that the conclusion is also true. Then evaluate the soundness of these arguments by deciding whether the premises are true.

Egalitarianism

An argument for egalitarianism—whether the simple form of strictly equal division or the more complex, equity version—is that humans are born into a world not of their own, personal making. Therefore, it is just a matter of blind luck that some people have more of the riches the world has to offer or suffer more of its pains. In most parts of Canada, if you are born into a family that can afford to provide you with adequate care and education, you will probably lead a much better life than someone born, for instance, in a poor country marked by famine or war. So the egalitarian argues that there is no basis for claiming that the resulting difference in quality of life is fair. They say that active measures should be taken to see that a just distribution is achieved.

> *"Let us exert every ounce of man's energy and everything produced by him to ensure that everywhere the common people of the world get their due from life."*
>
> Madame Sun Yat-Sen

Meritorians versus Egalitarians

Against the egalitarians, meritorians argue that people may be born with certain advantages or disadvantages. However, it is a person's abilities and work that determine whether he or she earns the right to retain the advantages or to overcome the disadvantages. Egalitarians grant this, but maintain that the abilities people have or whether they are prepared to work hard are also matters of luck.

A slogan of egalitarians faced with people who are especially disadvantaged is "there but for fortune go you or I." Is this a good argument for sharing wealth with people less well off?

> *"I wasn't lucky, I deserved it."*
>
> Margaret Thatcher

Equity

Philosophers who support an equity view insist that there is a difference between treating people justly and treating them equally, where equality means "exactly the same." Sometimes, they say, it is just to treat people unequally. For instance, it is just to provide people with physical handicaps with such things as wheelchairs or seeing-eye dogs, even though people without handicaps are not provided with such things.

Critics of the equity version of egalitarianism sometimes retort that this principle of distribution leads to unfair results. For instance, Anna (who was, recall, another person at Grandma's table) might have an uncontrollable sweet tooth. On this basis, Anna claims that her need for cake is greater than the others, so she should get more of it. Egalitarian defenders of equity claim that not all needs should get special treatment, but then they must produce reasons to show when special treatment is justified and when not.

Three More Theories about Distributive Justice

Supposing the cake dividers were philosophically educated, they would come up with variations on simple equality, equity, and merit, as well as some new ones. The main examples follow.

Plato's Theory

Another version of Laura's meritorian position is that of the ancient Greek philosopher Plato (427–347 BCE). He designed an ideal society around a theory of justice based on people's special talents. These talents, he thought, are different from person to person and are natural to them. A just society is one in which each office or job is performed by a person who is especially qualified for it. For example, if a father is a business person, it does not necessarily mean that his son or daughter should also be one. Nor does it

POINT OF VIEW

Iris Marion Young

Iris Marion Young (born 1949) is an American philosopher who, in a book called *Justice and the Politics of Difference*, applies the equity interpretation of justice to groups of people. For example, as long as women have the main responsibility of early child care, different employment and promotion standards should be applied to them than to men. Women should not be disadvantaged because they have less time to devote to their early working lives than do men due to having child care responsibilities.

matter that someone badly wants or needs a particular job. All that should count is whether people have the required abilities.

Once people's positions in society are determined in accord with their special abilities, the rewards of the position are also determined according to what is needed to perform jobs well. For example, assuming that Len is best suited for manual labour, this means that he would probably merit the largest piece of cake, since he needs the energy to do his physical work. It should be noted, however, that Plato was an anti-democrat who thought that whoever is best suited to political leadership should make important decisions for the society without input from others. That person also would be entitled to make such decisions as whether Grandma's cake should be offered to the table at all.

Libertarianism

Noting that Grandma has placed the cake before her, Simone might be tempted to abandon the egalitarian position imagined for her before. Instead, she might argue that, since Grandma gave the cake to her, it is her private property. If anyone else wants a piece, they can pay her for it or trade with her something they own for a piece of the cake. This view is one expression of **libertarianism**. According to this theory, the cake originally could only belong to Grandma, since she made it ("mixed her labour with it" as philosopher John Locke put it); though, subsequently, it could belong to whomever had acquired it in a legitimate way, such as by buying it or being given it by its original owner.

POINT OF VIEW

John Locke

John Locke (1632–1704) was an important English philosopher who defended a doctrine that individuals have rights that limit the powers of governments. In his time, Great Britain was ruled by monarchs, who were losing their ability to rule without constraints. Locke welcomed this change. He argued that the main political power in a society should be an elected parliament. Locke also insisted that people had rights that neither monarchs nor parliaments could violate. In addition to life and liberty, he considered private property an important value to which people had rights. In fact, he limited the right to vote or hold office to people who owned property (and to males). At the same time, Locke maintained that in acquiring their property, people had an obligation to leave enough behind for others to make use of if they were able to.

© Bettmann/CORBIS/MAGMA

For what purposes should private property rights be overruled?

Natural Law

Anna might think that there is something immoral about Simone or anyone else hogging the cake for herself, even if it is technically her property. For Anna there is a higher moral law than the laws of private property, which require people to use their property to help others if necessary. One philosophical tradition that takes this view is **natural law**. Natural law theorists do not reject the idea of private property, but they do insist that people have an obligation to help those who are less fortunate and to put their wealth to good use even if this means violating a right to use their private property any way they please.

POINT OF VIEW

St. Thomas Aquinas

The most famous defender of natural law was St. Thomas Aquinas (1225–1274). In his view, God ordained "natural," moral laws, which take precedence over laws invented by humans. Though derived from God, these laws do not need divine revelation to be known, but can be discovered by human reason alone. While natural law theory is central to Roman Catholic political thought, it may be found in Protestant, Jewish, Islamic, and secular traditions as well.

© Bettmann/CORBIS/MAGMA

Should there Be Private Property?

Suppose Grandma hears the debate between Simone and Laura over whether people have a duty to use their property for the benefit of others. Grandma might say that she does not like the idea of private property at all, at least if it just means that people can exclude others from the use of what is owned. She says that she gave the cake to Simone to take care of and to distribute the pieces justly. Grandma thought of Simone as the custodian of the cake, not as its private owner. This egalitarian viewpoint was one held by the philosopher Jean-Jacques Rousseau. It is also typical of a **socialist** perspective on justice (discussed in Chapter 15).

PHILOSOPHY IN THE ARTS

How Would You Distribute the Money?

An Arts Radio broadcast featured spokespeople from local organizations, each arguing for a different way of dividing some money granted to the arts. *The United Arts Council's* view was that the money should be given to it to be equally divided. *Breakthrough*, a professional artists' association, argued that their work brought in tourist dollars for everyone, so they should get the most funding. *Expressing Ourselves*, a disability arts group, wanted extra funds to help artists with disabilities. *Artists for Social Responsibility* maintained that arts money should be distributed so that artists with lower incomes should receive more. A wealthy local artist said that, if artists were producing good art that people wanted, they would be able to support themselves by selling it and should not need grants. Think about the above example in relation to theories of distributive justice and answer these questions.

1. Identify the basis for distribution employed by each of these spokespeople.
2. Which solution do you favour? Give reasons for your preference.

POINT OF VIEW

Jean-Jacques Rousseau

Jean-Jacques Rousseau (1712–1778), a Swiss philosopher, maintained that inequalities are not natural and are avoidable. He was one of the few philosophers of his time who did not think of Aboriginal peoples as inferior. In fact, he thought that their communal lifestyles and closeness to nature made them superior to so-called civilized Europeans. Central to this communal life was an attitude that the benefits of the world belong to everyone in it. As he put it "the fruits of the earth belong to us all, and the earth itself to nobody." As a result, benefits, and also burdens, should be equitably divided.

Is It Natural to Want to Own Things?

Libertarians and egalitarians have a basic disagreement about whether it is human nature to want private property. Most libertarians think that it is natural, while some egalitarians think not. Living in a society where private property is considered important is what makes people want it, egalitarians in the tradition of Rousseau believe. The following (true) story illustrates the egalitarian point of view on this subject.

PHILOSOPHY IN EVERDAY LIFE

The Influence of Society

A few years ago a woman who lived with her five-year-old son, Stanley, on a Native reservation in northern Alberta was visiting some friends in Toronto. Stanley was playing in a park and saw a boy get off his tricycle and leave it to play on the swings, so Stanley rode the tricycle. The boy's mother came over, took the tricycle from Stanley, and scolded him for taking it. Stanley was confused and bewildered. His mother explained to her Toronto friends that Stanley did not understand what was going on. On the reservation, children had toys that belonged to them in the sense that, when they wanted to play with them, they could. But when they did not want to play with their toys, anyone else could. As Stanley had been raised, keeping other children from using a toy even when he did not want to play with it was a foreign idea to him.

Use arguments and examples to support your agreement or disagreement with the following statement: Every person has the potential to develop a sharing attitude like that of Stanley if he or she is raised to think this way, and everyone should be so raised.

Social Contracts

In defending their opinions about distributive justice, philosophers employ various methods. One of the most popular, from ancient times to the present, is to appeal to a real or imagined **social contract**. The cake-dividing example helps illustrate what a social contract is and the method of reasoning behind it.

Suppose that Simone, Len, Laura, and Anna had met earlier—before Grandma's cake appeared, and were not even certain that she was going to bake one. At this meeting, they decide to figure out what rule to follow in the event that in the future she should give them a cake, or if any other occasion should arise where they would have to decide how to distribute something, for instance household chores. They will try to reach agreement among themselves about how to make these decisions in the future. The result of this agreement, or social contract, will be binding on all of them, and none can complain about the result, since they will all have agreed to it. Many political philosophers think that imagining such a contract is the best way to justify ideas about justice. However, they disagree about how people making a contract would reason, and hence, about the conclusions of the contract.

Locke's Contract

In the cake-dividing example, Laura might think that making the contract is a good occasion to guarantee that, when specific decisions must be made, they are guided by moral principles. For her, these are the principles that people are entitled to their own property provided they leave enough behind for others. She would therefore see the contract as endorsing the libertarian principles of John Locke, whose views were summarized earlier.

Hobbes' Contract

Len might reason that morality has nothing to do with how the cake should be divided. He would have no hesitation to take what he could by force, if necessary, but he recognizes that the fight would likely get ugly. For instance, Laura, Simone, and Anna might first form an alliance against him and then turn on each other. In the process, the cake itself might even get destroyed. To avoid such warfare, Len decides that only one of them should be empowered to make decisions about the cake or any other decision. Len would prefer that he be this dictator, but he and the others must all agree on what rules to follow and therefore who should get to make the decisions. They might flip a coin, or perhaps agree that Grandma should be the dictator.

Rawls' Contract

Simone calculates that it is best to play it safe. She will support rules that would work to her advantage, even if she finds herself in a weak position when the cake is divided. She might reason that many weeks could elapse

POINT OF VIEW

Thomas Hobbes

Len is reasoning like philosopher Thomas Hobbes (1588–1679). Hobbes wrote a famous book about the origin and nature of government, called *Leviathan* (or "monster," which is what he thought government is relative to individual citizens). In this book, Hobbes claimed that people are mainly interested in preserving their own lives and advancing themselves. People will take whatever means are required to do this, including threatening or killing other people. In a world without government to enforce rules for keeping the peace, the result would be a "war of all against all" and life would be "nasty, brutish, and short."

Though self-interested, the people in this "state of nature" (before there is any government) are rational. They realize that it is in each person's interest to make a social contract in which everyone agrees to give up all their powers to some form of government. This government will have the ability to make and enforce major social policies. The two possible forms of government Hobbes considered are: democracy, where a majority rules and an autocracy, governed by a single dictator. Of these, he thought that only an autocracy could keep the peace, since the members of a majority in a democracy would start the war of all against all among themselves.

between the time the contract is made and when Grandma makes a cake. During this time, she might lose a job that gives her spending money. So when the time came to divide the cake, she could not buy pieces of it from the others if the libertarian decision-making rule had been adopted (unless, of course, Grandma gave the cake to her, but since she is playing it safe, Simone must reckon that she would not be the lucky owner).

If Simone was reasoning well, and if all the others reasoned the same way, then this social contract would probably eliminate the libertarian option. What cake-dividing rule they would choose (or even whether they would reject the libertarian option) is a matter of debate among social contract political philosophers.

POINT OF VIEW

John Rawls

Simone's way of reasoning is the one defended by the American philosopher, John Rawls (1921–2002). In an influential book, *A Theory of Justice* (written in 1971), he supposed that rational people playing it safe would want to live under two general rules. First, they would want each person to have as much personal liberty as is compatible with everyone else having the same liberties. Second, like Simone, they would want to ensure that they are not penalized if they find themselves in a disadvantaged position. So they would want this rule: any unequal treatment of people must work to the advantage of the least advantaged person.

PHILOSOPHY IN EVERYDAY LIFE

Do You Agree with Progressive Taxation?

Rawls did not say what unequal treatments would benefit disadvantaged people. Rather, he left this for people using his theory to interpret. This led Rawls' followers into a debate about the justice of a "progressive taxation system." This is a system where, the more money someone makes, the higher percentage of it is taxed by the government. Progressive taxation treats people unequally, but some think it is justified because it works to the advantage of the poor. Others argue that, in the long run, progressive taxation works to the *disadvantage* of the poor. They argue that, unless there is incentive for people to try to get rich, nobody will work hard, the economy will decline, and everyone, including the poor, will suffer. But when there is such incentive the economy flourishes, and the poor end up ahead.

Defend a view of your own about this question.

WEB CONNECTION

Social Contracts throughout History

Go to the *Internet Encyclopedia of Philosophy* (www.iep.utm.edu) and read the article on social contract theory. Using the information on this Web page, and the life dates given for philosophers who are (1) mentioned on the Web page and (2) also mentioned in this text, develop a timeline for social contract theory.

Rousseau's Contract

Another variation on the social contract theory is Rousseau's. Hobbes thought that people are self-interested by nature, both before and after they make a social contract. Rousseau agreed that people begin to calculate a social contract from entirely self-interested motives. However, as they discuss and negotiate together about what sort of contract to strike, they begin to take each other's interests into account and their natures change to be more cooperative. The result is that, by the time they are through deliberating together, the original fear either that there would be an unending war of all against all, or that each person might find him or herself in a disadvantaged position would have gone away. People now would be able to trust one another to make decisions on the basis of what is best for all of them as a society of friends.

What would be the result if this basic change in human nature took place in the cake-dividing example? One possibility is that when Grandma finally brought the cake, people would reach a friendly consensus that it be divided equitably, and they would take each other's interests into account in figuring out their different needs.

An imaginary social contract is supposed to say what is a just principle for distributing benefits and burdens, and also to suggest what is the best form of government. For example, Hobbes thought that an anti-democratic monarchy was the best government, while Locke, Rawls, and Rousseau favoured different versions of democracy.

What Do You Think?

When distributing the benefits and burdens of society, there are those who suggest that things should be divided equally and those who say that distribution should take account of special needs. But what special needs do you think deserve to get more? Others say that the distribution should be based upon merit—that some people deserve more or less based upon their contributions to society. However, if you put in effort but are unable to contribute much due to inability, should you bc penalized or rewarded in a meritorian society? Libertarians say distribution should be determined just by how people privately exchange things in an economic market. Then there is the matter of the social contract. How do you think people would reason out the contract? What type of just society would they negotiate?

Chapter 14 What Are Rights?

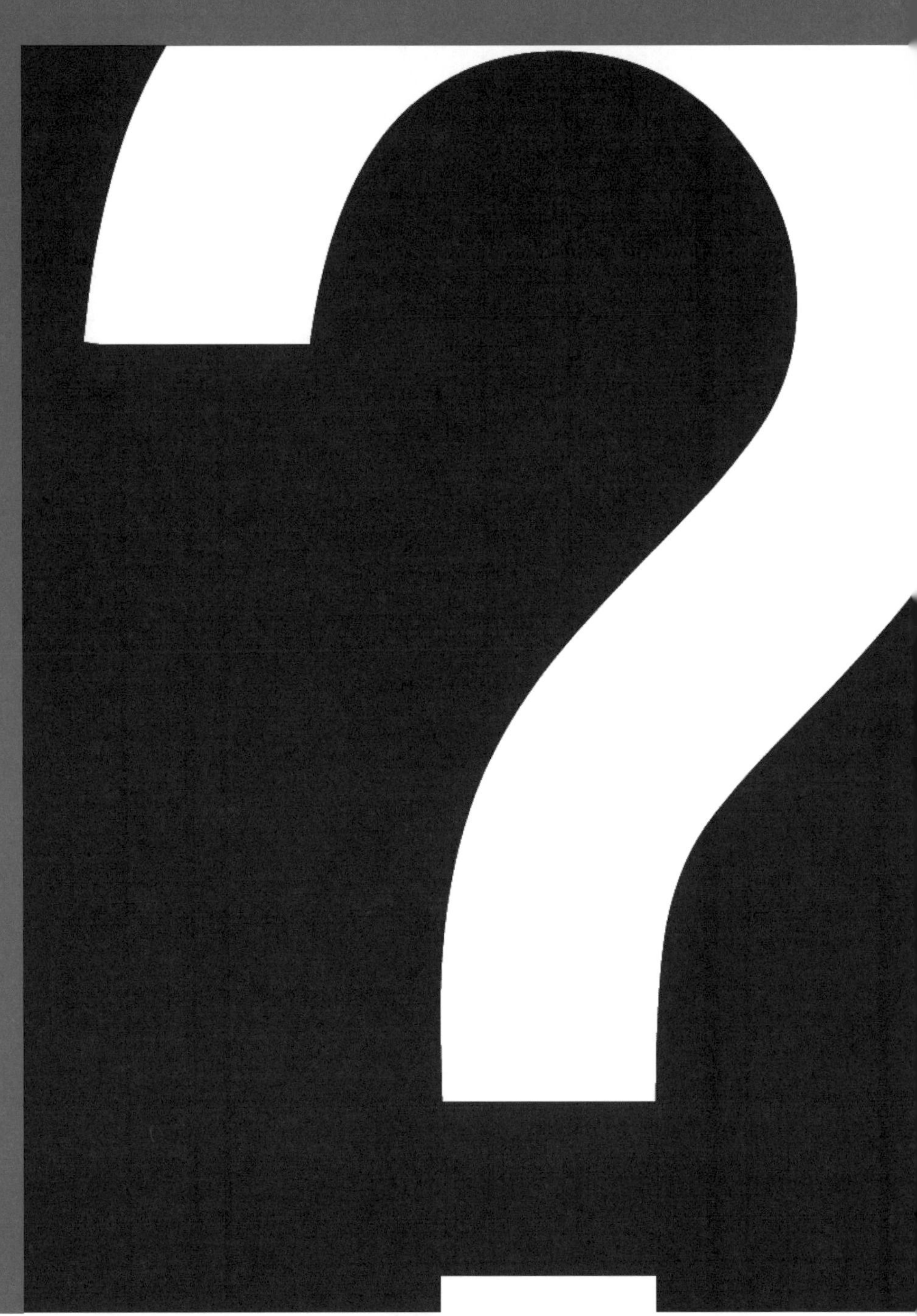

Key Words

Right
Negative right
Positive right
Individual rights
Group rights
Restorative justice
Marxism
Feminism
Autonomous

Key People

Robert Nozick
Ronald Dworkin
Kai Nielsen
Mary Wollstonecraft
Michel Foucault
Karl Marx
John Stuart Mill
Jeremy Bentham
Carol Gilligan
Immanuel Kant

What Questions Do Philosophers Ask About Rights?

Canadians enjoy many rights: to worship as we please, not to be arrested without cause, freedom of speech, and many other things. In this chapter, you will explore some basic questions that political philosophers ask:

1. What are rights?
2. Who or what ought to have rights?
3. When rights conflict, how do you decide which is more important?
4. How are claims about what rights people have justified?

What rights do you wish students at your school had that you do not now have?

Understanding the Philosophy of Rights

If there were never conflicts among people about what rights they have, there would be little need for philosophy. But, in fact, people often disagree about what rights they should have. Here is an example.

Central High School decides to start a soccer team, but there are different opinions about who can play on it. Coach Fred feels there should be tryouts to determine who are the best soccer players. Any student in the school may try out, but only those who meet high athletic standards will be accepted. Anil, the student council president, disagrees. He thinks that anyone who wants to play soccer should be allowed on a team, and if there are very many such students, there can be more than one team.

What Is a Right?

Despite the difference between the coach's and Anil's views, there are some general things on which they agree:

- *Rights are* ***guarantees****.* The coach and Anil agree that certain interests of students should be guaranteed—either to try out for a team or to play on one.

- *People are **entitled** to rights.* They agree that this guarantee is not a favour students must request, or that authorities in the school can give or take away whenever they wish. Rather, students can claim these rights as legitimately theirs.
- *People have duties to **respect** the rights of others.* Possession of rights by students means that people in the school, such as other students, teachers, or the administration must respect the rights. In the case of the rights Coach Fred supports, people have an obligation not to prevent students from trying out for the team. On Anil's view, the school must provide facilities for everyone who wants to play.
- *Rights are general **rules**.* Finally, each thinks that the students' rights should be endorsed for everyone by setting them down in school rules, or at the very least by informal agreement on an unwritten rule about what is fair.

The points above help provide this standard definition of the term **right**: an advantage conferred on someone by a law or rule, to which people have a legitimate claim, and which places duties on others to respect it. Like almost all the central concepts of political philosophy—justice, freedom, equality, democracy, and so on—definitions of the term "right" are contested. This means that there are debates about how to interpret the term, so not all political philosophers agree with all parts of the above definition.

What Are Negative and Positive Rights?

The conflict between the coach and Anil over the school's soccer team policy illustrates an important philosophical point: the difference between *positive* and *negative* rights.

For the coach, the main duty of the school is not to prevent anyone from trying out for the team. A right that carries with it such a duty is called a **negative right,** because the core duty is simply not to interfere with the exercise of the right.

If, however, all students have a right to be on a soccer team, as Anil wants, and very many of them wish to take advantage of this right, the school must do more than just ensure people are not kept from trying out. It must provide things for several teams: playing-field time for everyone, equipment, a coaching staff, and so on. This is called a **positive right**, since the duties it carries call for actively providing resources beyond those needed just to prevent interference with exercising a right.

Another example is a right set down in the *United Nations Declaration of Human Rights:* "everyone has the right to a standard of living adequate for the health and well-being of himself and of his family, including food, clothing, housing and medical care." Taken as a positive right, this places a duty on rich countries to help poor ones. But if the right is considered negative, the only duty of the rich countries is not to interfere with the attempts of poor countries to try bettering their standard of living.

What duties do rich countries owe poor ones? To help them? To stay out of their way? None at all?

Are Positive Rights Justified?

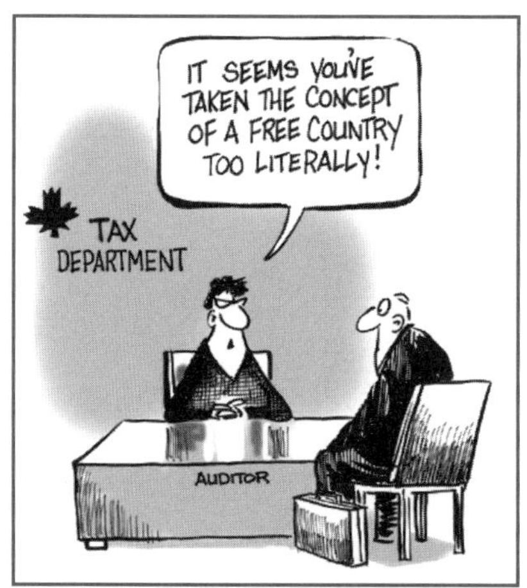

Libertarian philosophers maintain that positive rights threaten what they view as the most important right: individual liberty. For instance, the liberty of individuals to dispose of their income as they wish is infringed upon if governments tax them to provide funds for aid to poor countries.

Those who disagree with this idea sometimes argue that provision of aid to disadvantaged people is necessary for these people to enjoy personal liberty. For example, freedom from discrimination on the grounds of gender or race when applying for jobs is not worth much to people in a society where most jobs require a level of education that most people cannot afford. Therefore, it is argued, provision of aid is consistent with highly valuing liberty.

Others agree with the libertarians that individual liberty is an important right, but claim that sometimes justice as interpreted by egalitarians is more important. So if providing quality universal education means that employed people will have to pay taxes, the freedom of the employed ought to be limited for the sake of equality in education.

Are Positive Rights Realistic?

It is sometimes argued that duties like those of the U.N. Charter are unrealistic to enforce, and therefore large-scale positive rights should be considered only recommendations about goals to work toward. Critics from poor parts of the world see this as a cop-out. They say that rich countries can give small amounts of aid to the poor ones, and declare that this counts as "working toward" the goal of respecting people's rights.

Conflict of Individual Rights and Group Rights

The following example illustrates another kind of rights conflict.

Tanya is dissatisfied with the low pay and harsh conditions at the fast-food restaurant where she works. She joins with other employees who want to form a union with the right to strike if necessary. Marvin does not want to be in a union, especially if this means that he could not work if it went on strike. Tanya claims a right of employees to unionize and to strike—their **group rights**. Marvin maintains that this violates his right to work when and how he wishes—his **individual rights**. The philosophical difference between Tanya and Marvin is whether group rights should override individual rights.

Generally, **group rights** apply to anyone in a group. Typically, they are only exercized by an entire group. Tanya, and the other employees who agree with her, seek group rights in the form of union rights, most importantly, the right to strike. Other group rights on this meaning are: the right of self-government claimed by Aboriginal peoples in Canada, and the right to form their own nation-state (national self-determination) appealed to by those who want Quebec to be a separate country.

Group rights sometimes conflict with individual rights. If Marvin and others at the restaurant can opt out of the union, or refuse to join in a strike, the union could not be effective. So Tanya insists that the right to strike should limit Marvin's ability to work when he wants. Marvin, however, claims that his right to work when he wishes is more important than union rights.

POINT OF VIEW

Robert Nozick

Robert Nozick (1926–2002) was a professor of philosophy from the United States who defended the libertarian position. On his view, individuals use whatever talents and possessions they have to pursue goals they choose for themselves. They may wish to help others, but to force them to do so constitutes removal of their talents and possessions from their control. This, he says, is an illegitimate interference, which is a form of theft.

POINT OF VIEW

Ronald Dworkin

Ronald Dworkin (born 1931) is another American political philosopher. He supports a form of egalitarianism against Nozick. A crucial part of his theory is that people do not have an exclusive right to use their talents or assets just as they please. For one thing, how well off people are is to a large extent a matter of luck. This is obvious in the case of inherited wealth. However, it is also true of special talents, which people are born with, or are in fortunate circumstances conducive to their development—a supportive family, enough to eat, good educational facilities, among other things.

POINT OF VIEW

Kai Nielsen

Kai Nielsen (born 1926) is a Canadian philosopher who shares Dworkin's view but pushes it in a socialistic direction. He also argues against the view held by libertarians and others that freedom and equality are conflicting values. If someone sincerely values freedom, then, Nielsen claims, they should value it for everyone equally and, therefore, also value everyone having thc rcsources necessary to exercise freedom.

PHILOSOPHY IN HISTORY

Restorative Justice

Many claims have been made in recent years that people in a group are entitled to payment for wrongs committed against their ancestors. These are called claims for **restorative justice**. Here are examples of claims for restorative justice:

- by Native peoples for wrongs done by the European colonizers
- by Canadians of Japanese descent for imprisonment and confiscation of property during World War II
- by Canadians of Chinese descent for the head tax and other hardships imposed in the early part of the 20th century
- by African Americans in the United States for the enslavement of their ancestors

Research the details on one example cited above. Decide if the claim for restorative justice is valid and explain your view.

> *"A trade unionist—of course I am. ... How else to grapple with the complex problems of employment, over employment, and underemployment alike, resulting in discouraged, undernourished bodies, too tired to resist the onslaughts of disease and crime?"*
>
> Maud Younger

> *"Government cannot make us equal; it can only recognize, respect, and protect us as equal before the law. ... America was founded on a philosophy of individual rights, not group rights."*
>
> Clarence Thomas

Conflict Over Restorative Justice

Like all rights claims, there are conflicting views about claims of restorative justice. Opponents of compensation maintain that it makes no sense to say that one group as a whole has any claim on another group as a whole. On their view, only individual descendents of original victims who are currently badly off as a result of the treatment of their ancestors have a just claim for compensation. What is more, they deny that any Canadians living in the present have obligations that come from wrongs committed by Canadians in the past.

A response to compensating only descendants who are poorly off is that there are more harms than economic ones. For example, forcing Native people off their lands has made it difficult or impossible for them to lead their lives according to their own traditions. Government discrimination against Chinese immigrants was an affront to the dignity and self-respect of everyone in their communities, extending to present times.

Some political philosophers point out that the question of who causes a wrong and who has an obligation to compensate for it are different matters. For instance, when a country provides funds for flood relief, it is using the tax dollars of people who did not cause the flood to help other people who were affected by it. Also, people sometimes profit from wrongs even if they are not guilty of perpetrating them.

For example, the majority of Canadians—both those descended from the original European colonizers and those from more recent immigrant communities—owe their relatively high standard of living to the expropriation of land from the original, Native inhabitants of the land. As another example, valuable farmland, homes, fishing boats and other possessions of Japanese Canadians in British Columbia were, as the Government of Canada admitted in 1988, unjustly taken from them and sold to others during World War II (proceeds from the sales were used to pay for the Japanese-Canadians' relocation to prison camps). Descendents of those who acquired these possessions still have the benefit of them or have profited from selling them.

Take a viewpoint on one of the examples of debates over restorative justice and defend it with arguments.

POINT OF VIEW

Mary Wollstonecraft

Though the campaign for women's rights only began to achieve successes in the 20th century, there were demands for equality earlier, for instance by John Stuart Mill and his partner Harriet Taylor in the 19th century. Even earlier, Englishwoman Mary Wollstonecraft (1759–1797) wrote *Vindication of the Rights of Women*, in which she argued that women possessed the same intellectual abilities as men. Therefore, they should have the same rights. One of the philosophers she criticized was Jean-Jacques Rousseau. Although an egalitarian in other ways, Rousseau shared an attitude common at the time (and even held by some today) that women cannot reason as well as men and are only suited to such things as childcare.

Who Has Rights?

In one sense all rights are group rights because they belong to individuals insofar as they are members of some group. For example, the right of individuals to vote in a country's elections is one they have because they are citizens of the country.

It may seem obvious that the most important group for determining who has rights is the group of all human beings, but this has not been obvious through most of human history. For example, in Canada, women secured the right to vote and hold office only in the 20th century.

Similar campaigns have been conducted to expand the rights of other groups, and there are continuing debates over who should have what rights. Some examples are:

- Should people have the right to vote at age 18 or even younger?
- Should same-sex couples have the same rights as heterosexual couples (for instance, to marry)?
- Should prisoners have the right to vote?
- Do foetuses have rights?
- Should animals have rights?

PHILOSOPHY IN EVERYDAY LIFE

Charter of Rights and Freedoms

Here are some of the rights of Canadians with respect to federal and provincial governments as set out in the *Charter*:

- *Freedom Rights* of thought, religion, association, and expression (including of the press and other media or communication), among other things
- *Democratic Rights* to vote or be eligible to hold public office
- *Legal Rights* to life, liberty, security of the person, and due process of law
- *Equality Rights* of freedom from discrimination on the basis of race, national or ethnic origin, colour, religion, sex, age, or mental or physical disability

The *Charter* cannot be appealed to in any simple way to resolve actual conflicts over rights. Three examples follow:

1. Controversies over violent rap lyrics and over pornography are examples of one conflict of rights that makes straightforward appeal to the *Charter* difficult. Freedom to produce and distribute rap music or pornography is held by some to be a matter of freedom of expression. Others maintain that the expression of violence in some rap music and pornography, especially when it is directed toward women or children, is a threat to personal security and contributes to discrimination on the basis of sex.
2. Freedom of religion is guaranteed in the *Charter*, but it is not specified how far this can go. When a religious group forbids its members from providing their children with professional medical treatment or sanctions physical punishment of them, does this constitute an infringement on the children's right to life or security?
3. There are differences over whether the inclusion of security rights (such as to welfare or adequate old age support) in the *Charter* means that Canadians have a positive right to these things, in which case governments have an obligation to provide them.

When Rights Conflict

A challenging task for political philosophers is deciding which rights should take precedence when they conflict. There have been three main approaches to this challenge: appeal to **law**, to **power**, and to **ethics**.

Appeal to Law

When there are conflicts among rights, as between Coach Fred and Anil, or between Tanya and Marvin, the simplest way to make a decision is to appeal to a rule or law.

Labour legislation (made by provinces in Canada) specifies the conditions under which workers may form a legal union and when they can strike. So if the legislation in the province where Tanya lives supports her cause, Marvin's only option is to try to have the province's laws changed.

One problem with appealing to the law is that sometimes there are no laws to which to appeal. For example, the dispute between Coach Fred and Anil does not fall under statutory law. If their school has no rule about who may play on a team, it cannot be decided by appeal to a school law either. Rather, the dispute would be about what rule the school *ought* to have.

Another problem is that sometimes the laws themselves conflict. Even the *Charter of Rights and Freedoms*, which came into force as part of Canada's *Constitution* in 1982, and is supposed to list basic rights of all Canadians, is subject to conflicting interpretations.

Discuss one or more of the examples described in the feature above. Make a list of reasons you can think of to justify positions taken on them.

Appeal to Power

Some political philosophers maintain that conflicts among rights cannot be resolved by reasoned argument at all. Instead, they think that such conflicts are decided by whoever has the most power.

Versions of this view have been around since ancient times. For instance, an opponent of Plato named Thrasymachus defined justice as "the interest of the stronger." German philosopher Friedrich Nietzsche (1844–1900) also supported this view. The French philosopher Michel Foucault argued that any claim of universal truth—even medical or social-scientific claims—are in fact ways that people exert power over others.

WEB CONNECTION

Conflicting Freedoms

Read the *Canadian Charter of Rights and Freedoms* online at laws.justice.gc.ca/en/charter. Conduct research into possible conflicts between the listed rights and freedoms.

POINT OF VIEW

Michel Foucault

French philosopher Michel Foucault (1926–1984) made historical studies of such things as sexuality, crime, and medical practices, especially relating to insanity. His studies led him to conclude that all human institutions and customary practices are filled with power relations, most often oppressive. This is evident in prisons and insane asylums. Additionally, in these places, but also everywhere else in society, power is exerted by making people complicit in their own oppression. For instance, by instilling habits of orderly, disciplined behaviour in hospitals, prisons, the military, workplaces, and schools, people unthinkingly regiment themselves in the interests of those who have authority over them. By encouraging images of a single, true human nature, people come to think of such things as homosexuality as perversions. Thus, as part of his exposure of power relations, Foucault challenged the traditional view that (1) there is a fixed and normal human nature, and (2) that anyone who deviates from the traditional view of human nature requires punishment or cure.

Marxism

The most famous version of the power interpretation of rights is by followers of Karl Marx. **Marxism** maintains that the mainstream view of rights is biased toward individual and negative rights and against group and positive rights. Marxists claim that the reasons for this are found in the history of class conflicts: first between capitalists and the feudal order of kings, and now between workers and capitalists.

In feudal systems, the kinds of work people could do were legally fixed and inherited. Capitalists wanted the freedom for themselves to engage in whatever trade or manufacturing activities would bring in the most profit. They also wanted freedom for peasants to leave farms to become employees in the new factories. Modern, individual freedom rights helped this end. At the same time, capitalists did not want workers to organize against them. Capitalists encouraged the individualistic attitude, like Marvin's, against group rights of the kind Tanya wanted in the earlier example.

Similarly, capitalists championed democratic rights against the anti-democratic feudal order. This was so they could gain control of state institutions, such as the military, the courts, and the civil service, and make laws that serve their own economic interests. However, this posed a problem for them since the majority of citizens are not capitalists but are in the workforce.

In the early days of capitalism, capitalists solved this problem by making it a legal condition of having democratic rights that someone own property. This was successfully challenged by reformers, and by workers as they organized and demanded political rights. However, according to Marxists, capitalists have achieved the same aim by financing the campaigns of politicians friendly to them. At the same time, capitalists ensure that democratic rights are mainly negative rights to *try* to affect government policy by voting. However, these negative rights do not provide most people with money and other resources to mount successful political campaigns.

Feminism

Feminism advocates equality of the sexes. Feminist philosophers agree with Marxists that societies and politics consist of conflict between dominant and subordinated groups, and that rights help to maintain the power of a dominant group.

However, feminists differ with Marxists on this point: they do not see economic class domination as the only or as the most important form of power. Most of human history, according to feminists, is marked by patriarchy, or the rule of men over women.

Feminists are divided about how to deal with this problem. Some feminists combat patriarchy by insisting that women have the same rights as men. Other feminists believe that the emphasis on rights itself is an example of patriarchy. They believe that women naturally follow an ethic of care as opposed to an ethic of rights. Carol Gilligan provides an example of this view.

POINT OF VIEW

Karl Marx

Karl Marx (1818–1883) was a German philosopher of economics and history. He defended a materialist theory that human history has been shaped by irreconcilable conflicts between economic classes—in modern times, capitalists and workers. States are not independent of class struggle but always serve a dominant class, and philosophical, religious, and political ideas are expressions of class interests.

In the dynamics (or "dialectics") of class struggles, Marx thought that capitalism was "its own grave digger." He thought that capitalism unwittingly paved the way first for a state that serves working-class interests. This would then be replaced by a thoroughly cooperative society. Marx referred to these as two phases of communism, but many later Marxists called the first phase "socialism," reserving the term "communism" for the second, fully cooperative, phase.

Marx predicted that socialist revolutions would occur in the developed countries of Europe and North America. Instead, they took place in the underdeveloped world, beginning with the Russian Revolution in 1917. The resulting socialist societies violated Marx's democratic values and self-destructed in the former Soviet Union and Eastern Europe beginning in 1989.

POINT OF VIEW

Carol Gilligan

Carol Gilligan (born 1936), an American feminist thinker, believes men and women relate to others differently. This difference is especially important during conflicts. Men, according to Gilligan, follow an "ethic of rights." Men see conflicts and the resulting competition as unavoidable. They appeal to rights to settle them. The rights are much like the rules of a game. Appealing to them is like appealing to a referee. Gilligan believes that women, by contrast, follow an "ethics of care." They place the highest priority on empathy and cooperation.

> *"It is not a question of 'can we live in the same world and cooperate' but 'we must live in the same world and learn to cooperate'."*
>
> Eleanor Roosevelt

Some feminists do not agree with Gilligan that an ethics of care is more natural to women than men. They argue that women have been confined to caregiver roles. Therefore, it is hardly surprising that they play these roles effectively. However, both types of feminist philosophers agree on one thing: the rights expressed in a patriarchal society function mainly in the interests of men.

> *"Men have laid down the rules and definitions by which the world is run, and one of the objects of their definitions is woman."*
>
> Sally Kempton

Justifying Rights

If power were all there is to rights, there would be no need for political philosophy. People would just figure out what rights serve what interests and pick a side. But most people reject this extreme position. For example, the students at Central High would be unhappy if either the coach or Anil won just because he was more powerful.

In fact, Foucault, Marxists, and feminists themselves think that some rights are justified and others not. The highest social value for Foucault is freedom from domination. Most Marxists and feminists endorse positive rights and group rights.

Ethical Foundations for Rights

Most philosophers use ethics to determine what rights people have and how to decide among conflicting rights. Therefore, philosophers with different theories of ethics have different theories about rights.

Natural Law

St. Thomas Aquinas argued in favour of a natural law based ultimately in religious truths, but not requiring religious belief to be known. Appeals to natural law, rather than to the laws of a state, are the final authority on what is right for him. In this way, he justified a right to property (provided it is not used to violate other natural laws), and a right to life, among other things.

Justice

Ronald Dworkin thought that what is important about rights is that everyone holds them equally. So recognizing and protecting rights is a way of ensuring that people receive equal respect.

Utilitarianism

John Stuart Mill thought that actions or policies should be valued in accord with how far they promote the greatest happiness for the greatest number of people. This stance leads him and other utilitarian philosophers to recommend that sometimes it is justified to set rights aside. For example, you cannot shout "fire" in a crowded movie theatre even though this violates your freedom of speech, since this could lead to a panic rush to the doors in which many would be injured or killed.

> *"Natural rights is simple nonsense, natural and imprescriptible rights [that is, rights that cannot be changed by law], rhetorical nonsense, nonsense upon stilts."*
>
> Jeremy Bentham

Some utilitarians, such as Mill's predecessor Jeremy Bentham (1748–1832), thought that because rights should always be capable of being changed, the only meaningful sense of rights is as laws of the state. The idea that there are natural or moral rights, that may or may not be reflected in laws, is meaningless. Mill was more sympathetic to the idea of there being moral rights that may or may not be official laws. The feature of rights Mill focussed on is that they are general rules of action. This is because it is not possible always to make calculations about what would provide the greatest amount of happiness. Instead, it is best to act in accord with general rules that are most likely to have this result.

For instance, in extraordinary circumstances, it may be justified to do something that would take another person's life (as in self-defense). However, the world will be a better place if everyone adopts a general rule that all people have a right to life. Or, while it may sometimes be justified to limit freedom of speech, it is best for a society to promote a general rule protecting this freedom. Free discussion and debate is essential to advancing knowledge, which, in turn, is important for general human well-being.

Are there times that you think it is justified to violate someone's rights? Give an example.

Respect for Individual Autonomy

For many political philosophers, rights are supposed to provide strict limits to how governments can relate to citizens, or to how citizens can relate to one another. Unlike the defenders of utilitarianism, they think that the whole point of defending rights is to remove them from the realm of practical calculations about what is good in the long run for individuals, for particular societies, or even for humanity as a whole.

The alternative most often appealed to is Immanuel Kant's ethical theory. On this theory, the most important ability shared by all individuals is that each can set goals for him or herself and strive to achieve them. That is, every human seeks to be **autonomous**. Since all humans equally have this ability, they should be equally respected. Kant put it that everyone should be treated as an end, and nobody should be treated as a means to someone else's ends. Rights ensure that people are respected in this way.

To deny people a right to freedom of speech is disrespectful because it determines in advance that the views they may express are not worthy of being heard. In setting down a rule that citizens have equal rights to vote, a country insures that there are not first- and second-class citizens. By defending a person's right to life, a society affirms that it cannot be sacrificed for someone else's benefit.

Ethical Theories as Guidelines

Ethical theories cannot directly settle conflicts among rights, but they do provide guidelines. For a utilitarian, the crucial question to ask in the soccer team conflict is: Which right—to try out for a team or to play on a team if someone wants to—is best for the school as a whole? Anil's position may be the strongest here, because more people will be able to play.

However, Coach Fred can counter that his policy would help to build a winning soccer team that would bring glory to the school. This would create pride and satisfaction for everyone that outweighs the disappointment of students who tried out for but did not make the team. This is an example of how the utilitarian ethical theory would not automatically decide between these two rights. However, it would focus debate in a way that helps to make a decision.

The same point applies to an ethics of respect for individual autonomy. Here is a possible debate between two philosophers (A and B) who share Kant's perspective but disagree about how it apply it:

A: It is important to respect students who want to play on the soccer team by not discriminating against any of them. This does not require that anyone can play on a team but only that anyone can try out.

B: By limiting soccer playing to those who pass the tryouts, the coach is using students as means to putting together a winning team, rather than respecting their interest in playing soccer.

A: An important part of respecting people is recognizing them when they do something well. If standards are set aside, the game of soccer will be cheapened in the school, and students will not be respected or be able to respect themselves in playing it.

B: This may be true of students whose aims are to be very good soccer players. However, it does not apply to students whose aims are to develop their soccer skills, or simply to have fun by playing on a school team.

Who, between philosopher A and B, do you think wins the debate? Construct another debate on this topic between two utilitarian philosophers, C and D, where C takes the coach's side and D takes Anil's.

What Do You Think?

There are many kinds of rights: positive, negative, individual, group, and claims for restorative justice. Should society provide resources to enable positive rights—those that might help the less fortunate in society, such as through progressive taxation—as egalitarians want? On the other hand, should society take a more hands-off approach, such as lessening taxation, as required by negative rights? Do the rights of the individual outweigh the rights of the group or vice versa? Or when it comes to claims for restorative justice, should Canadians living today pay for wrongs committed in the past against particular groups? And when rights between groups or individuals conflict, which rights should take precedence? Philosophers have suggested that these problems should be resolved either through the law, through power, or through ethical considerations. What do you think is the best method for solving rights conflicts?

Chapter 15 What Is a Good Political Society?

Key Words

Socialism
Capitalism
Neoliberal capitalism
Welfare capitalism
Social democracy
Social choice theory
Taoism
Argumentum ad hominem
Theocracy
Democracy
Direct or participatory democracy
Representative democracy
Possessive individualists
Liberal democracy
Pluralism
Civic virtue
Communitarians

Key People

Mencius
Lao Tzu
Joseph Schumpeter
C.B. Macpherson
Peter Kropotkin
Murray Bookchin
Jürgen Habermas
Charles Taylor
Will Kymlicka

> *"Every state is a community of some kind, and every community is established with a view to some good."*
> Aristotle

How Should a Society Distribute Talents and Possessions?

Imagine that you could design any kind of society you wished. You get to decide what kind of government it has, what rights people enjoy, and how its benefits and burdens are distributed. What would you do? Maybe you would take advantage of this situation to design a society that is advantageous just to yourself and your friends. Philosophers from ancient times have the different aim of asking what is a *good* society.

As you read this chapter, you may find that philosopher's theories give you ideas, but since the theories differ, you will still have to think through this question for yourself. To begin, consider the following imaginary story about how a good society might distribute things.

Thirty people from Central High take a trip to Japan to perform in an international music festival. However, their airplane crashes in the middle of the Pacific Ocean. Luckily, everyone gets safely to a remote island. Not knowing when or even whether they will be rescued, these people have to make some serious decisions to survive.

Each person on the island—the survivors—has unique talents, such as camping skills, farming or hunting abilities, organizational skills, and medical knowledge. Each has salvaged from the plane some possession that will prove useful—for example, a knife, strong cord, a jug for holding water, matches, and so on. So one decision they must make is whether or how to pool their talents and possessions. Another is how to coordinate their activities.

Some of the survivors had taken a philosophy course and had studied the theories of justice described in

Chapter 13. They use the arguments of their studies to defend different positions about what to do.

Silvana takes the egalitarian view that possessions should be pooled, and each individual should put his or her talents at the disposal of the entire group. At an opposite extreme is the libertarian position taken by Marvin. He thinks that the possessions and talents each brings to the island are their personal property. They may do what they want with them, including trading the possessions or striking deals for skills exchanges.

The Socialist Position

In actual politics, Silvana's egalitarian position, in its fullest form, corresponds to **socialism**. In a political state that embraces socialism, the government ensures that factories, banks, raw materials, and other major sources of wealth are used to further the goals of equality and social cooperation. This makes socialism incompatible with capitalism. **Capitalism** is a system where major sources of wealth are privately owned by individuals or by groups of shareholders. Their freedom to use these sources of wealth to gain profit for themselves is largely protected by the state.

The Libertarian Capitalist Position

Marvin's libertarian opinion corresponds in politics to advocacy of **neoliberal capitalism**. On this view, individuals should be free to make use of their property and to negotiate with one another in a free market. The role of government should be limited to enforcing contracts and maintaining police forces.

Intermediate Positions

Many of those marooned on the island think that each of the socialist and the libertarian views is too extreme and look for other positions. In between neoliberal capitalism and thoroughgoing socialism are welfare capitalism and social democracy. **Welfare capitalism** allows room for government to regulate the conduct and fruits of the economy while still leaving major private ownership in place. **Social democracy** shares the egalitarian goals of socialism but takes a less confrontational view toward capitalism.

Some social democrats think capitalism can accommodate equality, while others believe capitalism should be gradually phased out. Social democrats of both varieties are criticized by socialists for being too soft on capitalism and by procapitalists for being socialists in disguise. Meanwhile, welfare capitalism is thought of by socialists as nothing but profit-motivated capitalism in disguise and by neoliberals as a dangerous step toward socialism.

Can Self-Interested People Make the Best Decisions?

In trying to decide what decisions people *should* make on the island, attention needs to be given to what decisions they are *capable* of making. There are philosophers who think that in making rational decisions people are always motivated by individual self-interest. These philosophers see a dilemma.

Suppose that the survivors have been working away at fishing, gathering building materials, harvesting plants, bringing in water, and so on. Each can decide whether to put what he or she has acquired in common storage for general use or to hoard it for personal use. Being intelligent, each person realizes that it is in everyone's long-range best interests to pool the resources. Then the resources can be distributed without waste, providing critical masses of such things as roof thatching or firewood. But at the same time, none of them can avoid the conclusion that the most rational thing for him or her to do is not to share but to hoard.

John reasons that either the others will hoard or they will not hoard. If they hoard and he does not, John will have given away his things for nothing. If the others do not hoard, John will enjoy the advantages of the large pool of resources, plus what he has hoarded for himself; so either way, he should hoard. But here is the problem: if all the survivors calculate this way, they will all hoard; so self-interest guided by rational calculation will lead to a result they all know falls short of the best interests of everyone.

The Hobbesian Tradition

Of course, if the survivors are friends or if they think it is immoral to hoard, they will act cooperatively, thus promoting their self-interest as well

The Prisoners' Dilemma

This problem is a version of the **prisoners' dilemma**. It has dominated the thinking of political philosophers called **social choice theorists** who think that rational human action is just making calculations about what is in an individual's self-interest.

Two prisoners charged with committing a crime together are separately offered a deal:

- if both confess each will receive a one-year sentence;
- if neither confesses, they will both get six months;
- if one confesses and the other does not, the one that confesses will get off, while the one that does not confess will get two years.

According to the social choice theorists, each prisoner will calculate that it is rational to confess, which means that they will both get heavier sentences than if neither confessed.

The prisoner's dilemma presupposes that rational people always look just to their self-interest. Some of the major traditions in political philosophy agree with this view of human nature; others do not.

as being friendly and moral. Philosophers in the social choice tradition grant that this often happens. However, they insist then that the survivors are not acting rationally, since things such as friendship and morality fall *outside* of rational action. In holding this view, they place themselves in the tradition of Thomas Hobbes. They are therefore called **Hobbesians**.

The Rousseauean Tradition

Against the Hobbesians are philosophers who prefer the theories of Jean-Jacques Rousseau, or **Rousseaueans**. They do not see rational calculation to further self-interest as the core of human nature. Instead, they believe that cooperation is an important part of human nature and the desire to cooperate is no less rational than a desire to serve self-interest.

THINKING LOGICALLY

***Arguing to the Person (*Argumentum ad Hominem)**

Silvana favours a Rousseauean view that things on the island should be equally distributed and, therefore, disagrees with John's Hobbesian opinion. She argues that, back at the school, John was well known for his selfish behaviour, so why should people believe him when he defends hoarding and claims that people are self-interested by nature?

Silvana is committing the fallacy of "arguing to the person" (*argumentum ad hominem* in Latin). She may well be right that John is a selfish person. Moreover, her observation about his selfishness might help to explain why Hobbesian theories seem right to John. But these things do not mean that the Hobbesian theories are wrong or that her Rousseauean theories are right. She has not given arguments relevant to John's *conclusion* but to qualities of his *person*.

East Asian Philosophical Traditions

Also opposed to the Hobbesians are most classical East Asian philosophers. Mencius (371–289 BCE), a philosopher in the tradition of Confucius, maintained that wishing to exercise power over others was not part of human nature. He believed that a politics based on the realization of human nature would avoid selfish conflicts. Another East Asian philosopher, Lao Tzu (c. 6th century BCE), who was the founder of Taoism, urged that all individual actions be seen from a universal or cosmic perspective, rather than in terms of narrowly individual aims. A politics based on this perspective would be free of domination and conflict.

If you and your three closest friends were stuck on the island, which tradition best expresses how you would reason about cooperation?

What Form of Government Is Best?

Another decision the survivors confront is how they are to be governed in order to coordinate their affairs. Marvin has been reading the views of the libertarian philosopher, Robert Nozick, and claims that no government is needed at all. Social coordination will be achieved automatically as people make individual deals with one another for the exchange of their possessions and the use of their talents.

For instance, some think it is advantageous to set up a hospital tent, and everyone, or at least everyone who thinks ahead, will save up things to trade for access to it if they get sick. Marvin proposes the same solution for the provision of child care, education, and other things the survivors will need if they remain on the island for a long time.

Some reject Marvin's proposal. They think that having a hospital tent is too important to leave it to chance that someone will see enough profit in setting one up to do so. Others object that, if people get sick, there should be provision for their care even if they cannot exchange anything for it. Silvana points out that even Marvin's scheme requires a minimal government to make and enforce laws, such as prohibiting theft or breech of contract.

If these arguments persuade the survivors that some form of government is required, the problem remains of which is the best one. They see only two general possibilities: that the survivors govern themselves democratically, or that some govern the others undemocratically or, to use another word for the same thing, **autocratically**.

Government by Tradition

One of the students on the island, Mei-Yu, holds the view that the pilot of the airplane should make the major decisions. It is traditional that pilots of planes have final authority and the island can be seen as an extension of the plane. Several others object to this choice since the pilot, depressed over the crash, has become withdrawn and morose, and could not be trusted to make good decisions or to have the respect of people he governs.

Moreover, it happens that accompanying students on the plane were Ms. Jenkins, the principal of the school, and its spiritual counselor, Father O'Connor. Some maintain that if traditions of leadership are to be followed, Ms. Jenkins should be selected; while others point out that the most important tradition is religious tradition, so the leader should be Father O'Connor.

The debates among the survivors about following tradition bring to light two problems:

- People traditionally identified as leaders might not make *good* leaders.
- It is sometimes hard to know what tradition to follow.

> *"Every civilization begins with theocracy and ends with democracy."*
>
> Victor Marie Hugo

Theocracy

An additional problem involved in making Father O'Connor the leader is that it could make the island a theocracy. A **theocracy** is government by religious leaders appealing to religious principles to determine secular law. This would create friction between religious and non-religious people on the island, and among those who are religious, between Catholics and other faiths. In fact, Father O'Connor might reject this option himself. While every major religion contains some who oppose the separation of church and state, these are increasingly minority opinions.

Government by the Best

An alternative to rule by tradition or theocracy is that those thought to be best at governing should govern. As described in Chapter 13, this is the meritorian view of Plato. Of course, several people could claim to be the best, so a way is needed to determine which of them really is.

This would be a serious problem on the island. Once an autocratic leader is chosen, he or she is not responsive to democratic control or recall, and the island would be stuck with him or her indefinitely, or would have to resort to revolt to try to get a different leader.

There is also the more directly philosophical problem of deciding what counts as good leadership. Plato thought that philosophers should rule, since they are the most profound thinkers. When, however, Plato himself was briefly empowered to make actual political decisions (as advisor to the king of Syracuse) he found that philosophical wisdom was not enough and specifically political skills were needed.

This problem would be compounded on the island, since several candidates might be offered for leader, but each with very different qualities: the physically strongest, the smartest, the most popular, the best at organizational skills, the best speaker, and so on.

> *"Let's face it: However old-fashioned and out of date and devalued the word is, we like the way of living provided by democracy."*
>
> Eve Curie

Democratic Forms of Government

The most enthusiastic student politician, Anil, is pleased to see the survivors reject undemocratic options. He suggests that they set up an island parliament, divide themselves into political parties, and run candidates in elections. But the others reject this approach as both unnecessary and undesirable. It is unnecessary, they say, because so far the survivors have been doing well enough making decisions by talking through different options together, usually reaching agreement and sometimes resolving a disagreement by taking a vote. It is undesirable, most think, because it would divide their small group into professional politicians and ordinary citizens of the island and replace cooperation with competition among the political parties.

Participatory Democracy

The disagreement between Anil and the other students demonstrates an important fact about democracy. It is one thing to favour a democratic form of government. But it is another thing to decide how a democracy will operate.

Democracy literally means rule by the people, but this might be accomplished in more than one way. If the survivors reject Anil's suggestion but want a democratic form of government, they might decide that they should all make decisions together by discussions, where everyone tries to reach consensus about what is best for the entire group. This is called **direct** or **participatory democracy**.

Rousseau championed this form of democracy. When it is properly functioning, people do not compete. Instead, they try to figure out what is in the public good. The prisoners' dilemma would not exist in such a democracy. In a small society, as on the island, or in neighbourhood associations, clubs, and friendship circles, participatory democracy is often feasible, and it seems to achieve the aims its advocates claim for it.

For participatory democrats, the best way to make decisions is by talking through an issue until consensus is reached, rather than by taking votes. This helps to solve another problem raised by social choice theorists, the "cyclical majority problem." This problem is most easily explained using an example.

Cyclical Majority Problem

Imagine that the thirty survivors are voting on which of three people will be the leader.

- Ten survivors prefer Anil to Silvana and Silvana to Marvin.
- Another ten survivors prefer Silvana to Marvin and Marvin to Anil.
- The remaining ten survivors prefer Marvin to Anil and Anil to Silvana.

If the vote were taken by giving each survivor a ballot with the three candidates' names on it, and each is to vote for his or her top candidate, each candidate would receive the same number of votes. Even if each survivor were asked to rank the candidates in order of preference, the candidates would receive the same total rankings. Therefore, no matter what kind of vote was taken, nobody would win.

Social choice theorists say there is no way to guarantee that such a distribution of voter preferences will not ruin any attempt to make democratic decisions by means of majority voting. Participatory democrats maintain that, by using their method, this problem is avoided. Instead of voting, all the survivors would talk about who would be the best leader until they reach agreement. They might even decide that there should be no leader at all or that Anil, Silvana, and Marvin should take turns being leader.

Despite these advantages of participatory democracy, many political philosophers see problems with it.

Does Participatory Democracy Force Conformity to Group Opinions?

Suppose that the group is trying to decide if they should divert material and energy to constructing a boat for escape from the island. Even after hearing everyone's opinion, John thinks that this is a doomed and wasteful idea. But he remembers that Mei-Yu had refused to back down when pushing her opinion that the pilot should be leader. As a result, the other students criticized her for not being a team player. She was then excluded from discussion or cut short when she spoke. John does not want to be in the position of either hiding his opinions or voicing them and enduring Mei-Yu's treatment.

John's solution to this problem is this: a rule should be agreed to that anyone can express any opinion, even if it is unpopular, and not be punished, either obviously or subtly. This means that John wants to introduce "rights" into the democracy of the island—specifically, freedom of speech and opinion.

Some of the participatory democrats on the island think that this right can be accommodated, but others believe that it is dangerous. It would encourage people not to try to reach agreement, but to be quick to take independent positions that might destroy group solidarity. Also, it might lead to demand for other rights, such as the right to form political parties as Anil wished, which would be even more destructive of the group.

How is the student government organized in your school? What do you consider to be its greatest strengths and greatest weaknesses? Are there opportunities for participatory democracy? If so, how effective is it and how might it be improved?

Participatory Democracy in Large Societies

To illustrate another challenge to participatory democracy, assume that the survivors have been rescued and returned to the large town where they live. Silvana was one of the most enthusiastic supporters of participatory democracy on the island. She would like to continue this form of democracy, starting in the school and then in the city, the province, and the entire country.

Silvana is aware of a main objection to this idea. Participatory democracy, its critics say, requires face-to-face discussion, but this is impossible in any society larger than the 30 or so people on the island.

Silvana thinks that one answer is to use the Internet. Very large numbers of people could carry on extensive discussions on-line. Another option is to divide the school, city, or even the country into local "councils." These could be organized by grade in a school and by neighbourhood or workplace in a city.

These councils would be small enough to allow for direct-democratic decision-making. Each would delegate one of its members to a higher-level council, which would also be small enough for participatory-democratic deliberation and would delegate members to yet higher-level groups, until a national leadership is formed. This leadership would be directly responsible to the councils below it and therefore indirectly responsible to all the other councils.

WEB CONNECTION

Participatory Democracy at School

Do you think participatory democracy could work in your school? Search the Web for information on participatory democracy and consider its advantages and disadvantages in a school setting.

Schemes such as Internet-based or council-based democracy have been proposed from time to time. There is a lot of debate about whether they are practical. But there are other, more philosophical objections to trying to import participatory democracy into a large society. Consider the two key ideas behind participatory democracy: people directly govern themselves, and in doing so they aim at serving the public good. One objection is that in a large, complex society neither of these things can be achieved. If citizens are going to discuss issues on the Internet, someone will have to identify the issues to be discussed and decide when enough agreement has been reached to make a decision. These people, and not ordinary citizens, the critics say, will be the real leaders of the society.

Similarly, in Silvana's council scheme, people in the first level do not actually govern themselves but are governed by those they have delegated to higher councils, and the members of the top council are the major political leaders. It is therefore not really a form of direct democracy. Instead it is a form of **representative democracy,** where leaders are supposed to govern while respecting the interests of the citizens.

The idea that in a democracy people can and should try to discover and promote what is in their common interests—that is, the public good—is also challenged.

In a large society, people have many different interests and opinions about what is good for the society as a whole. As a result, it is argued, there is no one public good on which they could all agree. On most issues, a vote will have to be taken, but even people who vote the same way may do so for different reasons. For instance, both Anil and Silvana might vote that the authority of Ms. Jenkins should be limited. Anil votes this way because he wants the head of a "Students First" party he has organized to have more

POINT OF VIEW

Joseph Schumpeter

Joseph Schumpeter (1883–1950) was an Austrian theorist who lived in the United States. He maintained that people do not literally govern themselves but are governed by politicians and that the idea of a single public good is a myth. He therefore defined "democracy" as nothing but the competition among politicians for the popular vote. Followers of Schumpeter call this the **realist** approach to democracy, because they think this is the only practical way to think about it.

authority, while Silvana does not want anyone to have authority over anyone else. Therefore, the fact that they vote the same way does not mean they share an idea about the common good of the school.

> *"The hand-to-mouth existence of the casual labourer ... do not permit the development, in the individual or the class, of the qualities of democratic association and democratic self-government. "*
>
> Beatrice Potter Webb

> *"In looking at models of democracy—past, present, and prospective—we should keep a sharp look-out for two things: their assumptions about the whole society in which the democratic political system is to operate, and their assumptions about the essential nature of the people who are to make the system work ..."*
>
> C.B. Macpherson

POINT OF VIEW

C.B. Macpherson

Among the critics of Schumpeter was the Canadian political philosopher C.B. Macpherson (1911–1987). He agreed that the realists' view matched the way societies called democratic actually function. He thought, however, that this means modern democracy has become divorced from the people and that a more participatory form of it should be regained. Macpherson was best known for criticizing approaches to democracy that assumed humans to be selfish and consumerists, or what he called **possessive individualists**. He taught at the University of Toronto where he also campaigned to make the University itself more democratic.

Liberal-Democratic Pluralism

Probably Central High, like Canada as a whole, would adopt some form of representative democracy, as in an elected student council. Also, it would ensure in school rules that students' rights are guaranteed, for instance, to express their opinions freely. The school might also allow or even encourage direct participation where it is appropriate, for instance, in the student clubs or on sports teams.

This combination of representative democracy and protection of rights illustrates a form of democracy called **liberal democracy**. It was this form that John Stuart Mill defended. He thought that representative democracy was necessary due to the size of modern societies and because not everyone has the ability to make good political decisions. As noted in Chapter 14, he also insisted that democratic societies be governed in accord with rights to protect such things as free speech and association.

Unlike some (but not all) liberal democrats, Mill also encouraged participatory democracy where feasible (for instance in town or neighbourhood meetings), because he thought that this would enable more and more people to learn how to make political decisions wisely.

An important part of liberal democracy is **pluralism**, which means that people should, as far as possible:

- try to achieve goals they have chosen for themselves;
- use methods of their own choice in furthering these goals; and

- be tolerant of those whose goals and methods of pursuing them differ from their own.

Government, according to liberal-democratic pluralists, ought not to dictate what goals people should have. Rather, liberal democracy's role is to protect people's right as far as possible to pursue their lives as they wish. Further, through elected bodies like Parliament, liberal democracy provides places where politicians negotiate and try to pass laws in the interests of their constituencies or at least of those who voted for them.

Critics of Liberal Democracy

Some political philosophers are highly critical of liberal democracy for creating political passivity, promoting relativism of values, and encouraging competition among individual citizens. Other political philosophers recognize a problem with liberal democracy concerning multiculturalism.

Anarchists

Anarchists especially object to the emphasis of liberal democracy on representation. In their view, this turns politics over to professional politicians. It gives too much power to a state distanced from the people. Therefore, anarchists advocate participatory democracy. They believe that political power should be located in places where people live, work, and study, and decisions should be made collectively. One of the early advocates of anarchism was a Russian nobleman, Peter Kropotkin (1842–1921). A more recent anarchist philosopher is Murray Bookchin (born 1921) from the United States.

Civic Republicans

Civic republicans criticize the moral relativism they see in liberal-democratic pluralism. Instead, they think that a democratic society should actively encourage attitudes of **civic virtue**, where citizens take seriously an obligation to promote the good of their society.

They also object to the emphasis liberal democracy places on "negative freedom" as that term was discussed in Chapter 14. Liberal democrats favour this form of freedom to protect the ability of people to do what they wish without the deliberate interference of others. But civic republicans maintain that people are not truly free if, for instance, nobody stops them from devoting themselves to watching TV and pigging out on junk food, even if they want to do these things. Civic republicans contrast such negative freedom with "positive freedom," which requires leading a moral and socially responsible life.

Civic republicans refer to the ideas of Aristotle, the Roman philosopher Cicero (106–43 BCE), and, on some interpretations of his thinking, the Italian Niccolo Machiavelli (1469–1527), for support. Modern-day civic republicans include the British philosopher, Quentin Skinner, and Michael Sandel, from the United States.

> *"To be a citizen is more than just voting every four years, it's more than just registering your self interest in politics."*
> Michael Sandel

Deliberative Democrats

Deliberative democrats claim that in a liberal democracy citizens look to government mainly for what they can get out of it for themselves. This promotes competition among citizens, and nobody tries to do what is good for the society as a whole. Deliberative democrats agree with participatory democrats that people should try to reach consensus, and they agree with civic republicans that they should try to advance public goods. They believe that these goals can be met if people deliberate with each other in a spirit of mutual respect and from positions of equality. A major defender of this view is the German philosopher, Jürgen Habermas.

What Is the Relation between Politics and Economics?

In deciding what would be a good political society, the survivors needed to select ways of distributing talents and possessions. This is an economic decision. They also needed to select the best way they might be governed. This is a political decision. This poses questions about the relation between economic and political aspects of a good society.

Political philosophers ask what economic arrangements go together with what political ones. The answers are not straightforward. For instance, anarchists, such as Kropotkin and Bookchin, along with libertarians like Nozick, share a dislike for strong governments (and in fact, Nozick described himself as an anarchist). However, these classic anarchists are also anti-capitalists and egalitarians in their economic views, while the libertarians are strong supporters of capitalism.

> *"In common with all socialists, the anarchists hold that the private ownership of land, capital, and machinery has had its time; that it is condemned to disappear."*
>
> Peter Kropotkin

Liberal Democracy and Socialism

A common viewpoint is that liberal democracy and egalitarianism, especially socialism, cannot be combined. Socialism, on this viewpoint, cannot be liberal because it must deny people the freedom to do what they wish with their talents and possessions. It cannot be democratic, because it must force people to conform to long-term egalitarian plans. The collapse of socialism in the former Soviet Union and countries of Eastern Europe beginning in 1989 is supposed to illustrate this incompatibility.

Socialists in the Marxist tradition usually agree that socialism and liberal democracy are incompatible. They think that liberal democracy is too individualistic and is biased against citizen participation.

However, social democrats, and even some socialist theorists, such as Macpherson, disagree that liberal democracy must be economically capitalistic. They maintain that the economic inequalities of capitalism are themselves the most serious threats to individuals' liberties. Further, they maintain that a socialist government could be democratic if it had majority support and was prepared to relinquish power if it lost this support in free elections.

In your view, what combinations of politics and economics would be most effective in dealing with the following problems and issues: health-care costs, homelessness, environmental problems, crime, another issue of your choice?

How Should a Democratic Society Deal with Multiculturalism?

Canada is officially a multicultural country. This means that the government is supposed to promote tolerance among people from different national, ethnic, and religious backgrounds. The government must also encourage people to retain and nurture their various, unique traditions. However, supporting multiculturalism is not always easy as the following imaginary story illustrates.

Liberal Individualism

John's view of how to resolve the festival problem is an expression of a strong version of the liberal-individualist position in social and political philosophy. This position rejects the idea that public institutions, whether of countries or schools, should privilege the religious or other values of any one group of people. These individualists often appeal to the views of Immanuel Kant and John Stuart Mill.

PHILOSOPHY IN EVERYDAY LIFE

Does Multiculturalism Work?

Central High always has a festival before the December/January break. This year the student council will decide how it should be conducted. In the past, the festival was a celebration of Christmas. This year, however, some Jewish students on the council suggest that the festival should not be exclusively Christian, but include Jewish celebrations as well. The Jewish students find support among Buddhist and Islamic students who would like to make a multi-faith festival.

Other members of the council reject this proposal for two different reasons. (1) John thinks that there should be no religious content to the festival at all. Religion, he says, is a personal matter, and the school, being a public institution, should not associate itself with any religion. (2) Silvana objects to the multi-faith proposal for the opposite reason. She says that the majority of students in the school come from Christian backgrounds, and that, from its founding, the school has had a tradition of celebrating Christmas. So Christmas should continue to be the centre of the festival. How would you solve this problem?

Communitarianism

Silvana's view of the festival problem is that of the philosophical **communitarians**, such as the 19th century German philosopher Georg Hegel (1770–1831), or more recently the civic republican Michael Sandel. They claim that individualists fail to understand that religious, national, ethnic, and other traditions of the groups to which people belong make them what they are even as individuals. So if individuals are to be respected, then so must their traditions.

The individualist/communitarian debate is a lively one among contemporary political philosophers. Each side in this debate draws upon the liberal-democratic principle of pluralism to criticize the other side. Silvana can say to John that if pluralism means people should be able to pursue their own values as they see them, and if pursuing religious values for many students includes celebration of their faiths in the school, the liberal pluralist should respect this. Meanwhile, John can point out to Silvana that there is not a single tradition in the school, so to give Christianity a privileged place in the festival runs against the pluralist principle of tolerance.

Two of the important philosophers in this debate are Canadians: Charles Taylor and Will Kymlicka. Each of them recommends positions in between pure individualism or pure communitarianism.

POINT OF VIEW

Will Kymlicka

Will Kymlicka (born 1962) teaches philosophy at Queen's University in Kingston, Ontario. He argues that individualists should understand that the groups and traditions with which people identify are important for the meanings they give to their lives. Therefore, they should respect multicultural and group rights, provided the traditions or groups respect the right of individuals to be critical of them. In this way, Kymlicka starts from individualist premises but draws conclusions similar to those of the communitarians.

POINT OF VIEW

Charles Taylor

Referring to Quebec and English-speaking Canada, Charles Taylor (born 1931) also insists that people's traditions are vitally important to their identities. This fact should, he maintains, lead to what he calls a "politics of recognition." Instead of being hostile to or fearful of those from different national, ethnic, or religious traditions, people should try sympathetically to understand and learn from them. Like the communitarians, Taylor advocates sympathetic study of the different world's traditions. This study shows, he maintains, that there can be agreement among the main traditions on most values favoured by liberal-democratic individualists, even though they are expressed in different ways among the various traditions. Taylor taught philosophy at Oxford and more recently at McGill University in Montreal.

What Do You Think?

If you were stranded on a desert island, what kind of a political society would you create? If everyone on the island pooled his or her resources and talents, you would have a socialist society. On the other hand, if you view talents and possessions as personal property, you would have a neoliberal capitalist society. In between, you might achieve a society of welfare capitalism or social democracy. If you chose to operate a democratic state, what form of democracy would you choose? Once you established a form of political society, who would lead it, and how would that person(s) govern? You could have government by tradition, a theocracy, or be governed by the best person for the job. In a multicultural society, there is sometimes a tension between protecting the rights of individuals and promoting the traditions of society's many cultures. How should these tensions be dealt with?

Unit 6

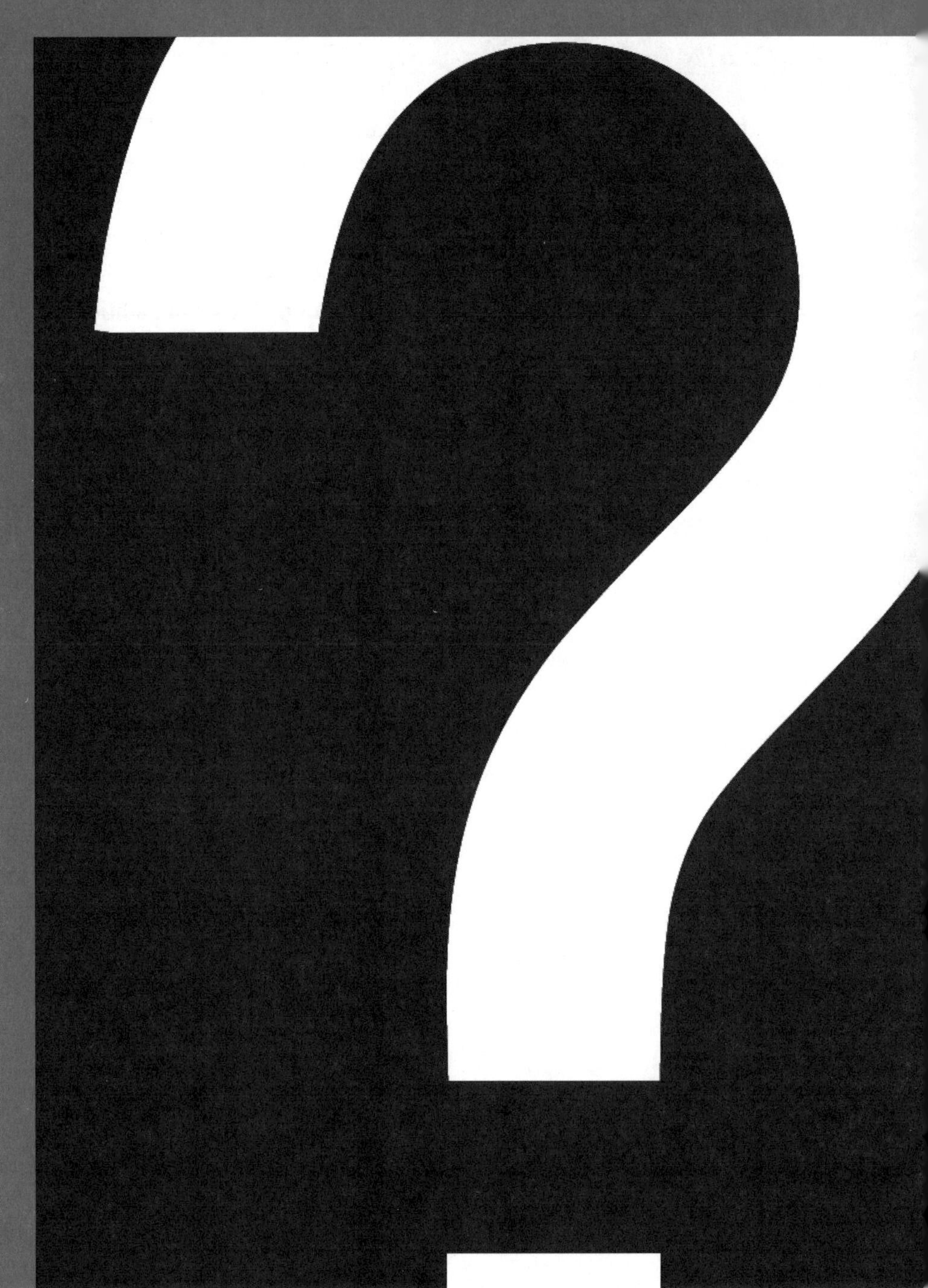

What Is Human Knowledge?

What does it mean to say that something is true? How can we justify our beliefs? Is all knowledge based on perception? Is knowledge relative? These are essential and important philosophical questions. The study of the nature of human knowledge is called **epistemology (**from the ancient Greek word for *knowledge*). Naturally, there are many different philosophical views about how to answer these questions. An understanding of epistemology will acquaint you with these views and give you critical thinking skills.

Chapter 16 What Are Knowledge Skills?

Key Words
Intrinsic value
Critical thinking
Factual claim
Appeal to authority
Informal fallacies
Induction
Deductive arguments
Valid arguments
Sound arguments
Modus ponens

Key People
John Stuart Mill
Aristotle

What Are the Skills of Knowledge?

> *"All men by nature desire to know."*
>
> Aristotle

What do swimming, riding a bicycle, playing a guitar, and cooking a meal have in common? They are all activities that people deliberately do. However, the most important similarity is that these activities all require skill. As with all skills, there are rules to learn for using them. They can be done better or worse, and improved upon through practice.

Knowledge is also a skill—one that is used for acquiring reliable beliefs about human beings and other things. Knowledge skills, too, involve learning rules that people can improve upon.

Most skills are valued because they enable people to accomplish other goals. Swimming, for example, is a useful way to get exercise or to avoid drowning. Similarly, knowledge skills are vital for human survival and well-being. Humans could not have survived at all if our distant ancestors did not possess farming and hunting knowledge. Modern technology, medicine, communication systems, and nearly everything else on which people depend are based on centuries of accumulated scientific knowledge.

At the same time, just as swimming or playing the guitar are rewarding on their own, knowledge can have value for its own sake, or have what philosophers call **intrinsic value**. Pursuing philosophical knowledge is useful for other things, for instance, confronting ethical or political problems as discussed in earlier chapters. But sometimes it is pursued simply in response to wonder about the big questions.

In this chapter, you will learn about some of the basic knowledge skills that philosophers have identified and sharpened. These are **critical thinking**, **induction**, and **deduction**.

Critical Thinking

The term "critical thinking" does not mean just being critical or negative. It refers to the skills of clarity and precision in examining reasons given by people to support their conclusions. These skills are divided into three major groups:

- *Identifying someone's point.* Simple as it may seem, this may be the hardest part of critical thinking.
- *Identifying the reasons given for conclusions.* This can also be difficult, since reasons are not always spelled out clearly, and sometimes they are not given at all, but just presupposed.
- *Evaluating the reasons.* This requires: (1) determining whether the reasons are *relevant* to the conclusions they are supposed to support; (2) identifying *fallacies* in reasoning; and (3) examining the *grounds* on which the reasons themselves are or could be justified.

What Kinds of Grounds Support Conclusions?

Another important part of critical thinking is figuring out what *kinds* of grounds are being given to persuade someone to agree with a conclusion. The following story provides an example of three kinds of grounds (among many others).

Suppose your school is trying to decide whether every student should have a free reading hour every day in the school library to do homework. The following reasons are given in favour of having such a policy:

1. Unlike at home, there is nothing else to do in the library but study, so more is accomplished in a shorter time.
2. According to the English teacher, Mr. Luca, to improve reading comprehension, it is much better to read books in a school library than at home.
3. It is unfair to students who must work after school that they have less time to study than other students. The school should provide the free time to help them.

The first reason is based on a **factual claim** about how much more efficient it is to study at school than at home.

The second reason looks like the first one, but it is really of a different sort. It is an **appeal to authority**, namely that of the teacher, Mr. Luca.

The third justification is an appeal to **moral norms**, resting on the view that students ought to be treated fairly. The use of the word "ought" indicates that the reason given does not appeal to facts about how much time is needed to study but to the moral view that it is unfair that students who need to work are disadvantaged in their studies.

To see the difference between these kinds of grounds, think of what you would have to do to question them. For the first reason, you might log your

RESEARCH AND INQUIRY SKILLS

Applying Critical Thinking

Do you believe everything that you read? Most people rely on the media to learn about what is going on in the world. Most newspapers provide editorials and have columnists who provide opinion towards current events. Do you always agree with them?

Use the critical thinking skills described on page 264 to help you read articles. The main steps for evaluating arguments are:

- identifying the main idea or point of the article, that is, its conclusion;
- identifying the reasons given to support the main idea;
- evaluating these reasons—that is, determining whether the author's arguments are good ones.

Practising Your Skill

Read an editorial, column, or article. Follow the steps above to critically examine its ideas. Write a letter to the editor or author of the piece that outlines whether or not the author's argument is good. Also present your point of view in response to your chosen editorial, column, or article.

time and ask other students to do likewise to show that it is not more efficient to study in a library than at home.

To challenge the second reason, you would have to show that Mr. Luca may not be a good authority. You might review other opinions of his about studying. Or you could note that Mr. Luca has not been a high school student for decades and, therefore, it is doubtful that he understands changes in home environments (more pressure from parents to study) and in school libraries (more rowdy).

To challenge the third reason, you could deny that it *is* unfair. For instance, someone could argue that students know that they will have less time to study when they take a job, so the choice is theirs. Or, you could grant the unfairness, but maintain that there are other ways to remedy it; for instance, by giving students who work more time to complete their homework.

What Are Fallacies in Reasoning?

Philosophers have identified several common fallacies encountered in ordinary thinking and writing. These are sometimes called **informal fallacies** to distinguish them from mistakes in formal or "deductive" logic, which is summarized later in the chapter.

Examples of common informal fallacies, and their Latin names, are on page 267.

Induction

Even if you are not a scientific expert, how do you know that thunder follows lightning, or that day follows night?

> *"The induction which proceeds by simple enumeration is childish; its conclusions are precarious, and exposed to peril from a contradictory instance; and it generally decided on too small a number of facts, and on those only which are to hand. But the induction which is to be available for the discovery and demonstration of sciences and arts, must analyze nature by proper rejections and exclusions; and then, after a sufficient number of negatives, come to a conclusion on the affirmative instances."*
>
> Francis Bacon

When you see lightning in the sky, you know that a few moments later you will hear a thunderclap. If you enjoy one particular music recording by a certain performer, you know that you will probably like another recording by the same performer. Philosophers call the skills that people use to know in this way **inductive**.

Rules of Inductive Arguments

Induction involves reasoning by the use of arguments. When philosophers speak of arguments, they do not mean shouting matches. Rather, an argument for philosophers is an attempt to derive conclusions from premises following reliable rules. Much of the philosophy of induction is the identification of these rules.

THINKING CRITICALLY

Informal Fallacies

- **Argument to the person** (*argumentum ad hominem*). Example: Marvin maintains that it is only fair to people with jobs to have a study period, but Marvin has a vested interest, since he is famous for never getting his homework done.
  This argument criticizes Marvin's conclusion by criticizing Marvin, not by giving arguments that a study period is required to be fair.

- **Begging the question** (*petitio principii*). Example: To have a free hour would prevent general unhappiness among students, because having free hours tends to make people happy.
  The conclusion is that free hours prevent unhappiness, and the reason given is that having free hours makes people happy. Since one of the things that being happy *means* is not being unhappy, the reason presupposes the conclusion it is supposed to support.

- **Irrelevant conclusion** (*ignoratio elenchi*). Example: There should not be a free study hour, since members of the football team use all their spare time practising football and would not make use of it for studying.
  The reason given—that football players would not study if given more free time—does not relate to the conclusion. The conclusion is not about whether everyone in the school would use the free hour, but about whether there should be a free hour for those who would use it. (As with many informal arguments, whether this one commits a fallacy depends on the specific circumstances in which it is given. If *everyone* in the school were a football player, the argument would not be fallacious.)

- **Argument from ignorance** (*argumentum ad ignorantium*). Example: The only reason to provide the free hour is to improve students' grades, but no study has ever shown that a free hour would have this effect.
  This is not a good reason to reject the policy, since it only says that we don't know that it would be a good policy, not that we know that it is not a good policy. A conclusion that might follow from this reason is that more time is needed before making a decision.

- **Appeal to force** (*argumentum ad baculum*). Example: Having a free hour is not a good idea, because the principal would never allow it.
  The fact that the principal has the power to prevent a free hour does not mean it is a bad idea in general. Reference to the principal's force is appropriate if arguing for the different conclusion that: It is a waste of time to try to get a free hour.

POINT OF VIEW

John Stuart Mill

The process of determining what may or may not be the cause of thunder is one application of the method called *agreement and difference*—a term coined by English philosopher John Stuart Mill (1806–1883). *Agreement and difference* is based on this rule of inductive reasoning: relevant correlations must be found and irrelevant ones ruled out. Inductive rules are not always as easy to follow as in the lightning example. Most things in nature are so complex that reliable inductive reasoning requires sophisticated scientific experiments and laboratory controls. Mill applied his method to the natural sciences, psychology, and economics.

So why is it that even people with no scientific understanding of weather know that lightning is followed by thunder? It is because this sequence of events has happened so many times in the past that a person can conclude that lightning is involved in causing thunder. Similarly, when you like a music recording of a performer, you will probably like another recording by the same performer because you have learned that similar circumstances have similar results. These conclusions are reached by applying rules that also apply to more complex situations. It is not enough for someone to experience just one instance of a thunderclap following lightning to conclude that another thunderclap will follow the next lightning strike. *Repetition* is an important rule for inductive reasoning.

But repetition is also not enough. Suppose that you had experienced this correlation many times, but always in the Spring when there are a lot of birds, and the birds always chirp at the beginning of an electrical storm. You would have to rule out the possibility that bird chirping is the cause of thunder (where a cause is taken as a necessary and/or a sufficient condition for its effect). This is not hard to do in the example: very often thunder is not preceded by birds chirping, while sometimes birds chirp and there is no thunder.

PHILOSOPHY IN EVERYDAY LIFE

Opinion Polls and Inductive Reasoning

Opinion polling is one complex example of inductive reasoning. Suppose a political party wants to know whether women voters prefer maintaining social services, such as health care, to paying lower taxes. To ask a few random women voters is not enough. To establish a correlation between being a woman and having a voter preference for support of social services over tax cuts, a large and representative sample of women needs to be polled. However, deciding *how large* a sample is enough requires mathematical calculations based on the science of statistics.

Deciding which people to poll to get a representative sample is also difficult. If, for example, a poll is taken only in a large city and only among women with university education, the polling results may indicate a correlation between these specific things and voter preferences. However, the poll will not reveal a correlation between women in general and the preferences. So inductive rules dictate that it is also necessary to poll university educated men from cities and women from small towns without university education. This enables a comparison to establish that it is being a woman that is relevant to preferring the social service option.

The politicians will also want to know if they can appeal to a preference likely to be shared by all women. So they will want to take polls to rule out the possibility that being university educated or living in a large city is necessary for preferring the social service option. And there are many other traits shared by women and men: age, income, ethnic background, state of health, and even such things as eye colour or eating habits. Reliable inductive reasoning involves figuring out which of these issues to take into account and devising the poll accordingly. What is more, it cannot be ignored that it might make a difference *how* the poll is conducted—by phone, by mail, by personal interview, or a combination.

Why Is Induction Uncertain?

A major feature of inductive arguments is that they can, at best, justify a belief that their conclusions are *probably* true. Inductive reasoning is based on past experience and is typically used to give people knowledge of the future. But no one can experience the future, nor can anyone be completely sure of having had enough past experiences to give reliable information about it.

Politicians sometimes find that voters do not act as the opinion polls predict. Similarly, when trying to decide whether you will like a particular music recording, the fact that you liked one by the same performer before is a good, inductive reason for confidence. But you could still buy the recording and be disappointed. The reason for this is that no two events are absolutely identical. The second recording may have been made in a studio with inferior recording equipment or a different band may have backed up the performer. Or, *you* may have changed, and this, too, will affect whether you enjoy the song.

Deductive Reasoning

You know that you will probably like the next recording by your favourite music performer, but you cannot be certain of this knowledge. You also know that 2 + 2 = 4, but you are certain of this. What is the difference between these two types of knowledge?

> *"In deduction we are engaged in developing the consequences of a law. We learn the meaning, content, results or inferences which attach to any given proposition. Induction is the exactly inverse process. Given certain results or consequences, we are required to discover the general laws from which they flow."*
>
> W.S. Jevons

Think about these questions: (1) Is the sum of the angles of any triangle equal to 180 degrees? (2) Is Fred, the bachelor, unmarried? You do not have to measure the angles of a lot of triangles to see if they all equal 180 degrees or decide whether Fred is sufficiently similar to other bachelors to conclude that, like them, he is probably unmarried. Induction is not needed to discover these things at all. Rather, you can *deduce* the conclusions. You may have proven the conclusion about the sum of a triangle's angles in a geometry course. That Fred the bachelor is unmarried can be known by looking up the meaning of the word *bachelor* in a dictionary.

Unlike inductive arguments, the conclusions of **deductive arguments** are known with certainty. Once the proof in geometry is understood, you are sure that all triangles, past, present, and future, will have angles equal to 180 degrees. Once it is known that Fred is a bachelor, and what the word *bachelor* means, you know that he and all other bachelors must be unmarried. Like inductive arguments, deductive ones follow rules, but their rules are different. Philosophers of logic, or **logicians** have devoted a lot of attention to these rules, and the ways of formulating them have changed over the centuries.

Aristotelian Syllogisms

The ancient Greek philosopher Aristotle (384–322 BCE) was one of the first to identify some of the rules of deductive logic. He applied these rules to forms of arguments called **syllogisms**. An example he used is:

1. All humans are mortal.
2. Socrates is a human.

---

3. Therefore, Socrates is mortal.

The statements 1 and 2 in this argument are its **premises**, and statement 3 is its **conclusion**. Philosophers of logic are only interested in discovering rules of deductive arguments (also called formal arguments) such that, when they are followed, the conclusions will be true *if* the premises are true. These arguments are called **valid**.

From the point of view of formal logic, it does not matter whether the premises (and therefore the conclusions) of arguments really *are* true, since this logic is mainly concerned with discovering rules of inference. For example, the argument above would still be valid even if you replaced the word *mortal* with *two-headed*.

A valid deductive argument that has true premises will necessarily also have a true conclusion. These arguments are then said to be **sound** as well as being valid. Because logicians are mainly interested in the forms of valid arguments, they often use symbols instead of words. For instance, the argument above is symbolized:

1. All M are P
2. S is M

---

3. Therefore S is P

Aristotle and his followers (called "Aristotelians") studied ways that valid inferences are made from premises to conclusions. Some of these inferences are easy to identify and can be made directly. For example, if it is assumed that "All humans are mortal," it can be directly inferred that "Some humans are mortal." Or from the statement that "Some people are vegetarians" it follows that "Some vegetarians are people." Most arguments represented in syllogisms are more complex. For example:

1. All of the students who are successful in school enjoy studying.
2. Nobody who enjoys studying is tempted to watch TV.

---

3. Therefore, no student who is tempted to watch TV is successful in school.

The validity of this argument is less obvious than the one about Socrates being mortal. It also illustrates the importance of distinguishing between validity and soundness. If the conclusion seems wrong, this is not because the argument is invalid, but because the second premise (and maybe also the first premise) is most likely false. That is, the argument is valid, but may not be sound. To know whether or not it is sound, you would have to apply *inductive* reasoning skills to determine whether the first two premises are probably true or probably false.

Aristotelian logicians list several rules for determining when an argument is valid. One of these is the "law of distributed middle." This refers to the term in a syllogism that links its premises to its conclusion. Consider again the first example:

1. All M are P
2. S is M

---

3. Therefore S is P

In this example, the middle term is "humans" (symbolized by "M" above), and it connects being mortal and Socrates in such a way as to make a valid argument. Here is an example of an invalid argument due to the middle term not being distributed:

1. All cows are four-legged animals.
2. All dogs are four-legged animals.

———

3. Therefore all cows are dogs.

This is symbolized:

1. All S are M
2. All P are M

———

3. Therefore All S are P

Note that the middle term, M, appears in the same location in each premise. The term M is not distributed as the subject in one premise and the predicate in the other, which is required for a valid syllogism.

Even though arguments that violate the law of excluded middle are easily recognized as invalid, they are often encountered. For example, some politicians criticize their opponents using guilt by association:

1. Totalitarians favour state censorship.
2. In advocating the banning of pornography, my opponent favours censorship.

———

3. Therefore, my opponent is a totalitarian.

1. Change the first premise of the argument above to make it valid. Discuss in class what kinds of inductive arguments are needed to establish the truth of the first premise as you have changed it.

Modern Logic

> *"Logic, which is, as it were, the Grammar of reasoning... [is] a test to try the validity of any argument; in the same manner as by chemical analysis we develop and submit to a strict examination of the elements of which any compound body is composed, and are thus enabled to detect any latent sophistication or impurity."*
>
> Archbishop Whateley

Today, Aristotelian logic has been largely replaced by versions of deductive logic based on mathematics. One of these is called the **propositional calculus.** This branch of logic is concerned with the formal relations among statements or propositions (though the term "calculus" might be misleading, since the mathematics on which it is based is set theory, which is much closer to algebra and geometry than to differential calculus). Philosophers of the propositional calculus lay down rules of valid deduction for getting from some propositions or statements to other propositions. For example, this is their way of formulating the argument about Socrates:

1. If someone is human then that person is mortal.
2. Socrates is human.

———

3. Therefore Socrates is mortal.

Modern logic is sometimes called **symbolic logic**. Philosophers of symbolic logic do not use sentences but symbols standing for sentences, such as "p" and "q" or "A" and "B." Similarly, they use symbols to represent the *relations* between propositions. There are several different systems of symbols used by the modern logicians. Here are some examples from one system:

- "and" is represented by a dot, for example: **p.q** (the statement represented by "p" is true and the statement represented by "q" is true)
- "or" is represented by a small v, for example: **p v q** (p is true or q is true, or they are both true)
- "if... then" is represented by ⊃, for example: **p ⊃ q** (if p is true, then q is true)
- "not" is represented by ~, for example: **~p** (p is not true)

- “therefore” is represented by ∴, for example: **p.q ∴ p** (p and q are both true, therefore p alone is true)

Arguments with the same form as the one about Socrates are symbolized thus:

1. p ⊃ q (if the proposition “p” is true then the proposition “q” is true)
2. p (the proposition “p” is true)

———

3. ∴ q (the proposition “q” is true)

Symbolic logicians identify this argument form as a basic rule of inference. Any argument of this form—called **modus ponens**—will be valid and may be appealed to when testing the validity of more complex arguments. Some other basic rules of inference are:

p.q
∴ p (**Simplification**)

p
∴ p v q (**Addition**)

p
q
∴ p.q (**Conjunction**)

p **v** q
~ p
∴ q (**Disjunction**)

Deductive proofs using these symbols proceed much as proofs you will be familiar with from mathematics courses. For instance, suppose it is given that A.B is true (this is **premise 1**) and that (A v C) ⊃ D (**premise 2**) is also true. You are to prove the truth of A.D (**the conclusion**). Referring to the rules of inference above, here is the proof:

3. A (from premise 1 and the rule of simplification)
4. A v C (from step 3 and the rule of addition)
5. D (from premise 2 and the rule of modus ponens)
6. ∴ A.D (from step 3, step 5, and the rule of conjunction)

DOING LOGIC

1. Using the rules of inference listed above, construct a proof for the following:

   Given:

   Premise 1: (A v B) ⊃ (C.D)

   Premise 2: A

   To Prove: C

(Hint: You will need three steps and will use the rules of addition, modus ponens, and simplification in that order.)

1. (A v B) ⊃ (C.D) (first premise); 2. A (second premise) To prove: C (conclusion); 3. A v B from premise 2 and addition; 4. C.D from premise 1, step 3, and modus ponens; 5. C from step 4 and simplification

There are many more rules of logic, and there are many techniques for effective deductive reasoning. A Web search or a trip to any university bookstore or library will reveal a large number of textbooks in logic.

What Do You Think?

In this chapter, you have learned some basic skills of knowledge designed to produce valid inductive and deductive arguments and to spot fallacies. These skills are, however, of limited use unless they are combined with knowledge that produces sound as well as valid arguments. But what do you think are the origins and nature of knowledge? Are there limits to what can be known? What methods are available to critically assess whether knowledge is valid and true? In Chapters 17 and 18, you will explore some answers to these questions.

Chapter 17 How Do Philosophers Think Critically about Knowledge?

Key Words

Epistemology
Justified true belief
Causal theory of knowledge
Correspondence theory of truth
Coherence theory of truth
Pragmatic theory of truth
Principle of non-contradiction
Scepticism
Epistemological relativism
Linguistic relativism
Paradigm analysis
Epistemological realists

Key People

Edmund Gettier
Bertrand Russell
John Dewey
Georg W.F. Hegel
Dharmakirti
Pyrrho
Benjamin Whorf

What Do Philosophers Ask about Knowledge?

Philosophy helps people think critically and develop inductive and deductive skills. Philosophy also applies critical thinking to these and other forms of thinking themselves. This self-critical feature of philosophy keeps it from becoming dogmatic or complacent, and it drives philosophers always to improve their theories and skills.

In this chapter, you will explore some of the main questions that philosophers have brought to this subject:

- What are knowledge and truth?
- Does deductive logic misrepresent the world?
- Is induction reliable?
- Can philosophy avoid complete scepticism?
- Is knowledge relative?

> *"The question you were asked, Theaetetus, was not what are the objects of knowledge, nor yet how many sorts of knowledge there are. We did not want to count them, but to find out what the thing itself—knowledge—is."*
>
> Plato (using the voice of his teacher, Socrates)

What Are Knowledge and Truth?

The topics of knowledge and truth are at the centre of the philosophical study of knowledge, or **epistemology**. Philosophers of knowledge, or epistemologists, propose various conceptions of knowledge and truth.

What Is Knowledge?

Common sense suggests that you have knowledge—that you know something—when you have a true belief about it. But this view does not stand up well to critical examination. Imagine that you are at a racetrack, and there is a horse about to run named "Aunt Millie," which happens to be the name of your own aunt. Being superstitious, you are confident that Aunt Millie will win the next race, and, in fact, the horse succeeds in doing this.

In this case, even though you had a true belief, it was just an accident that the belief was true. Nobody would say that you *knew* it would be true.

There are many examples of people who stumble onto true beliefs for reasons that have nothing to do with them being true. So philosophers from the time of Plato and Aristotle have tried to figure out what needs to be added to a true belief, or what Plato called "opinion," to make it genuine knowledge.

Do you believe that the world is a sphere and not a square box? Can you justify your belief?

Justification

Justification is the favourite candidate for what to add to true belief to make it genuine knowledge. That is, I know something: (1) when I have a true belief about it, and (2) when my belief is justified—a justified true belief. Of course, there are many ways to justify beliefs.

There are many ways to justify your belief that Aunt Millie (the horse) will likely win the race. For example, you could come to this belief by studying racing sheets and learn how well she performed in the past against the same horses with the same riders on similar tracks. You could ask the advice of a friend who is a recognized authority on horse racing. Or you could have contacts in the underworld who inform you that the "fix" is in. In any of these cases, you have reasons that are generally reliable for making good predictions in this matter; so, even if your prediction turns out wrong, your belief is justified. If the belief is also accurate, you have knowledge about the chances of Aunt Millie.

Critical thinking about what knowledge is does not stop here. One debate is over what kinds of justifications are required to say you have knowledge. For example, are there basic truths on which all knowledge is ultimately founded? In Chapter 18, you will see that some philosophers think that all knowledge is built up out of simple sense perceptions. By contrast, Plato thought that humans must base knowledge on direct understanding of non-physical, eternal truths. Other philosophers think that there are no basic truths; so there are no rock-bottom justifications—all justification is incomplete. This raises the question of whether humans can have knowledge based on incomplete justification.

Does Justification Define Knowledge?

Another critical question to ask about knowledge is about whether justification makes true beliefs count as knowledge. Twentieth century American philosopher Edmund Gettier (born 1927) does not think so. Imagine that, unknown to you, your teacher has an identical twin. Seeing her at the front of the class, you believe that your teacher is in the classroom. This belief is justified, because seeing someone who looks exactly like your teacher is a good reason to conclude that the teacher is there. Now suppose that your actual teacher *really is* in the classroom, but at the back where you cannot see her. Now you have a *true* belief, which is also justified, but, Gettier claims, it would be peculiar to say that you *know* that your teacher is in the room.

Causal Theory of Knowledge

Gettier's view and similar critical questions have given rise to different theories about what you must add to a true belief to make it count as knowledge. Some argue that a more complex version of the "justification" interpretation of knowledge is needed. Others, such as the English philosopher Bertrand Russell (1872–1970), maintain that, for a true belief to count as knowledge, someone's belief in it must be (directly or indirectly) caused by the same thing that makes the belief true. This is called the **causal theory of knowledge**. It would rule out the mistake about your teacher, since what caused you to believe your teacher was in the room was not the fact that your teacher was in the room. Instead, you mistook your teacher's sister as your teacher. This view has also been subjected to critical analysis by epistemologists, and defenses of the traditional view have been produced; so this debate among philosophers continues.

What Does "Truth" Mean?

Correspondence Theory of Truth

Is there one thing that you can say for certain is true? If yes, what is it? If no, why not?

A common sense notion of truth is that beliefs are true when they are about the world as it really is, or, to be more precise, when statements expressing the belief are true. On this view, the statement, *snow is white*, is true if (and only if) it corresponds to a fact of snow being white. This is called the **correspondence theory of truth**. It is the conception of truth held by most philosophers up until recent times. But this conception has been challenged.

One problem is that many true statements do not seem to correspond to facts in the world. For example, consider this statement: *it is not snowing now.* It is strained to regard negative statements like this one as corresponding to a fact, since this would mean that a negative fact (not snowing) somehow exists. Now consider this statement: *snow is white.* Even simple statements like this may not correspond to facts that exist independently of people's beliefs. Inuit peoples have many different words for *snow*. So whether the statement *snow is white* is true for them may depend upon just what sense of *snow* is used. The point of this example is that there is no single fact of snow being white; rather, what counts as this fact depends upon people's experiences and beliefs, and these are not the same for everyone.

> *"A belief is true when there is a corresponding fact, and is false when there is no corresponding fact."*
>
> Bertrand Russell

Coherence Theory of Truth

> *"[I] have contended that coherence is in the end our sole criterion of truth."*
>
> Brand Blanchard

Some philosophers try to meet such examples by developing more sophisticated versions of the correspondence theory of truth. Others suggest alternative theories. One of these is the **coherence theory of truth**. On this view, to say that a belief or statement is true is to say that it fits in harmoniously (or coheres) with a network of other beliefs. To use the snow example, Inuit people have a unique way of thinking about the weather. When a belief about one of the things they call what we translate as *snow* fits in with the other beliefs that make up this way of thinking, it is regarded as true by them.

Pragmatic Theory of Truth

Another theory of truth focuses on the idea that beliefs are guides to action: beliefs about the weather guide decisions about how to dress; beliefs about

WEB CONNECTION

The Complications of Truth

Go to the *Internet Encyclopedia of Philosophy* (www.iep.utm.edu) and look up the word *truth.* Be prepared for a hard read!

how fast race horses will run are useful in placing bets; and so on. A theory that follows this thinking is the **pragmatic theory of truth**. According to John Dewey (1859–1952), one of the founders of the school of philosophical **pragmatism**, beliefs should be considered true when they are useful for some purpose.

A problem for the coherence theory of truth is that the discovery of new and revolutionary truths, as in scientific breakthroughs, call into question former beliefs precisely because they are *not* harmonious with them. Pragmatists have trouble interpreting trivial beliefs or beliefs about bizarre matters, which, though they seem true, have no obvious practical value. Still, these philosophers, like supporters of the correspondence theory, have developed ingenious arguments in defense of their views.

This topic is one of the most challenging and difficult for epistemologists. Most of the points made in the rest of this unit could apply to "knowledge" and "truth" on almost any interpretation, but they will be used in the mainstream senses of "justified true belief" (knowledge) and "corresponding to reality" (truth).

Which of the truth theories that you have studied up to this point do you think has the greatest merit and why?

How Does Deductive Reasoning Relate to the World?

As explained in Chapter 16, deductive reasoning is concerned with formal demonstrations of validity rather than with the truth of premises and conclusions. But this does not mean that deductive logicians are entirely indifferent about what the world is like. They presuppose that the principles of logic can apply to reality. Among the most basic of these is the **principle of non-contradiction**. As modern logicians put it, a statement cannot be simultaneously true and false—in symbols, **~(p.~p)** or its equivalent principle, **p v ~p** (either a statement is true or it is false). An Aristotelian formulation makes clear that the principle of non-contradiction is meant to apply to reality: "a thing cannot both be and not be at the same time and in the same respect."

One challenge to this is by logicians who take exception to the "p v ~p" formulation. Some of these critics worry that this encourages people to think of any proposition as either true or false, but that, especially when talking of the future, it is better to estimate probabilities. For example, commentators on the weather very seldom say that it will rain (or that it will not rain); rather, they assign any of a large number of probabilities to the likelihood of rain. Other critics maintain that the principle fails to account for the fuzziness of reality. For instance, if it is drizzling, then the statement *it is raining* or *it is not raining* is false, since drizzling weather has features both of raining and not raining.

Even more challenging to traditional deductive logic are the criticisms of G.W.F. Hegel and other defenders of **dialectics** in philosophy. On their view, Aristotle and the other formal logicians presuppose a static conception of reality. For the dialectical philosophers, this makes it unsuitable for application to things that are changing, or as Hegel put it, are in the process of "becoming" something else.

> *"Neither in heaven nor in earth, neither in the world of mind nor of nature, is there anywhere such an abstract 'Either—or' ... Contradiction is the very moving principle of the world, and it is ridiculous to say that contradiction is unthinkable."*
>
> G.W.F. Hegel

POINT OF VIEW

Georg Wilhelm Friedrich Hegel

Georg Wilhelm Friedrich Hegel (1770–1831) was a German philosopher. He opposed the view, which has been dominant in Western philosophy since the times of Plato and Aristotle, that ultimate reality is made up of things that are unchanging, such as substances or eternal forms. For Hegel, reality is always in a state of change. Aristotle's syllogisms were designed to help understand static reality, but were not suitable to understanding the dynamism of things. Hegel's "dialectical logic" aimed to accomplish this by showing how things are always turning into their opposites and transcending their own limits. He applied this logic to physical nature, history, morality, human perception and knowledge, politics, and religion.

© Bettmann/CORBIS/MAGMA

Hegel violated his own theory that everything is dynamic in holding that in the East (i.e., South and East Asia) history had stopped. This is ironic, since many aspects of his dialectical logic had already been developed in detail eleven centuries earlier in India.

The reason for this is that if something is in transition between what it has been and what it will be—that is, if it is becoming something else—it can be correctly described both as what it was and what it will be. For example, an adolescent person is in transition from childhood to adulthood and has elements of each. So an adolescent is both a child and not a child, both an adult and not an adult. In each case, the law of non-contradiction—~(p.~p)—is violated. For the dialectical philosophers this is not an exceptional case. Things are all changing, and they are changing *because* they contain contradictory or opposing elements within them: adolescents feel conflicted because they are propelled toward adulthood by biological and psychological feelings and thoughts that are literally in conflict. Some contradiction-driven

POINT OF VIEW

Dharmakirti

Dharmakirti (c. 7th century) was a Hindu philosopher who explained and developed theories of nature, perception, and especially logic as set down by earlier Buddhist philosophers (prominently Dignaga and Vasubandhu). The logical theories of this tradition, fully recorded by Dharmakirti in his *Seven Treatises*, are thoroughly dialectical. For instance, while both Aristotelian logic and the propositional calculus assign only the values of true or false to statements, the Buddhist dialectical logicians added "true and not true" and "neither true nor not true." His works, including the *Seven Treatises* and the *Nyayabindu* (The Drop of Logic), were preserved by Tibetan Buddhists and remain influential in Indian philosophy today.

changes are obvious, but, for the dialectical philosopher, everything is always changing—individual people, societies, organic nature, even things such as mountains and planets.

Whether criticisms of the dialectical philosophers are damaging to the reliability of deductive reasoning is a matter of dispute. Challenges that appeal to the fact that most predictions are expressed in terms of probability or to the "fuzziness" of things do not lead to rejection of deductive reasoning, but to its revision. An example is Buddhist logic, which includes a "many valued" logical system that allows for more possibilities than that a proposition is either true or false. Some dialectical philosophers do not reject the law of non-contradiction, but insist that qualifications that recognize the changing nature of things must always be added when applying the law.

Can Induction Be Relied Upon?

In Chapter 16, it was stated that inductive reasoning involves basing beliefs about things that have not been observed (typically in the future) on things observed in the past. If done carefully, this is a reliable way of gaining knowledge, but unlike deductive reasoning, it can sometimes fail.

One critical conclusion is that failures in induction can result even when its rules are carefully followed. Recall this example from Chapter 16: you like one past music recording by a performer, and based on this, you form a belief that you will like the performer's future recording. It was noted that you might be disappointed because the new recording was prepared in a studio with inferior equipment, or there had been a change in the band. In principle, you can allow for these sorts of things by careful application of inductive rules.

You could review many of the performer's recordings by reading the labels. Doing this, you can determine that the ones you liked were produced in the same studio and with the same band, and that the recordings you did not care for had not been produced in that studio with that band. But, even if you were very careful in this test, and the performer you like had made many recordings, you could not rule out the possibility that producing so many recordings in the same circumstances at some point leads to an inferior production simply due to the performer getting bored.

Consider the example of the music performer making an inferior recording. Can you make up and describe a test that determines whether or not the inferior recording is the result of the performer becoming bored with the process of making recordings?

Is Inductive Reasoning Justifiable at All?

A good solution to the problem posed in the above exercise is to broaden the application of the inductive method. You could review the recordings of many different performers similar to the one you like, all of whom had produced even more recordings than your favorite. If the review shows that, after a certain number of recordings, the quality of the performances declined, you would have inductive support for belief in a boredom factor. Accordingly, your caution about buying future recordings of your favourite performer without listening to them first is justified.

This inductive study may be difficult and time-consuming, but as long as there are many performers similar to your favourite, it seems that there is nothing *in principle* to prevent such a study giving you reliable expectations. However, philosopher David Hume called into question the general reliability of induction.

POINT OF VIEW

David Hume

David Hume (1711–1776) was a Scottish philosopher who subjected the major philosophical ideas of his time to critical challenges. Regarding ethics: he questioned philosophers' abilities to justify claims about what is moral on the following grounds. Any justification would require deriving views about what *ought to be* from views about what *is*, and that these inferences are illegitimate.

Regarding religion: Hume listed the major arguments for the existence of God and wrote, what he considered, decisive refutations of them.

Regarding science: Hume subjected belief in the reliability of induction as summarized in this chapter.

> *"Whatever be the most proper mode of expressing it, the proposition that the course of nature is uniform is the fundamental principle or general axiom of induction."*
> John Stuart Mill

To draw reliable conclusions from the inductive study about the music recording, the performers observed for boredom must be *similar to* the performer you like. You need to be confident that there is sufficient similarity to draw reliable conclusions from your inductive study. Hume pointed out that, in addition, you have to have confidence that the past will be broadly similar to the future. To draw a conclusion from observations in the past regarding the music performers (or anything else about what will likely happen in the future), you must suppose that there are no radical differences, in general, between the past and the future. For instance, you must assume that all the laws of physics or psychology will not suddenly change. As Hume put it, confidence in induction supposes that nature is *uniform* through time or that, in general, the future will resemble the past.

POINT OF VIEW

Immanuel Kant

Immanuel Kant (1724–1804) was a German philosopher who set out to rescue religion, morality, and science from Hume's challenges. For Kant, it was obvious that successful scientific thinking and everyday knowledge are possible, as is evidenced by the very survival of human beings, who depend on them. So the question to ask, for Kant, is not *whether* people can reliably employ inductive reasoning, but *how* it is possible to do this.

© Bettmann/CORBIS/MAGMA

Kant concluded that, at the most basic level, human perception and thought are such that belief in things like the uniformity of nature make possible experiencing anything at all; so once this is realized, this, these essential beliefs, cannot be seriously doubted. Philosophers can discover this, according to Kant, neither by inductive reasoning nor by deductive reasoning, but by what he called "transcendental" reflection on the possibility of human experience.

The problem is in *justifying* the belief that the future will resemble the past. There is nothing in the idea of the past that suggests with certainty that the future will resemble it. The situation is, therefore, not like the example of the bachelor, where you can know that bachelors are unmarried just by thinking about the meaning of the word *bachelor*. So justifying belief in the uniformity of nature cannot be by deductive reasoning. According to Hume, this leaves inductive reasoning as the only way to justify this belief, since he thought induction and deduction are the only two ways of justifying beliefs. But to conclude that the future will resemble the past, because it always has before, presupposes the very principle you want to justify. This reasoning is an example of the fallacy of begging the question, described in Chapter 16.

Hume's conclusion was that although people presuppose the uniformity of nature as an unthinking habit, it cannot be rationally justified. For some epistemologists, the fact that nature instills this habit in humans, and that people are usually successful in basing their activities on inductive reasoning, means that induction needs no justification. Others have tried to show that an inductive defence of induction does not involve the question-begging fallacy. The most influential attempt to meet Hume's challenge was by the philosopher Immanuel Kant. Kant rejected Hume's view that induction and deduction are the only two ways to justify beliefs.

Scepticism

In the everyday sense, people are called sceptical when they express doubts about claims that other people make and demand proof from them. Scepticism, in this sense, is an important part of critical thinking. Philosophical **scepticism** carries such doubt to a radical extreme. It is the view that no beliefs whatsoever can be justified, neither by induction, nor by deduction, nor by any other method.

Scepticism has existed almost as long as philosophy itself. It was central to a school called Pyrrhoian Scepticism, named after its founder, Pyrrho of Ellis (365–270 BCE). A general argument for radical scepticism by a member of this school, Sextus Empiricus (3rd century) is summarized thus:

1. Justifying any belief requires employing a principle of justification, for instance by induction or by deduction. Call the principle **X**.
2. This means that someone depending upon **X** must believe that it is a reliable principle. Now, the sceptic asks, how is *this* belief justified? There seem only two possibilities: to appeal to **X** itself or to some other principle, call it **Y**. But to

appeal to **X** is to beg the question or argue in a circle by using the principle to justify belief in itself. To appeal to **Y** raises the question of how to justify the belief that this new principle is reliable, and the same problem recurs—to justify **Y** by reference to itself or to yet another principle, and so on forever.

3. Therefore, any attempt to fully justify any belief leads either to circular reasoning or to an endless regress of justifications. Since these things are rationally unacceptable, no belief can be justified.

Refuting Scepticism

Scepticism is both very hard and easy to refute. It is hard because, as the sceptic sets up the argument, there seems no answer to it. One approach is to look for rock-bottom principles that are self-justifying. In the next chapter, you will encounter the attempt of René Descartes, who took this approach. Another reaction is to deny that there is anything wrong with an endless regress of justifications. Perhaps one of these approaches can succeed in defeating philosophical scepticism, and a lot of ingenious arguments have been developed along these lines, but the very extreme nature of the sceptical view makes it a difficult position to refute.

Some philosophers argue that scepticism contradicts itself. The sceptic uses rational arguments to conclude that rationality is impossible or claims to know that knowledge is impossible. This does, indeed, challenge the sceptic, but it is not a conclusive disproof. As Hume observed, philosophical sceptics have the luxury of *not caring* whether they contradict themselves, since their use of reason is just to undermine it. As Hume put it, "the sceptic enters the house of reason" but only to bring it down by using reason's own tools against it.

A much easier refutation of scepticism is offered by life itself. Very little that human beings accomplish could be explained by blind instinct or sheer luck. The achievements that humans have made in science would have been the result of incredible luck if no beliefs were justified. Humans would have rocketed to the Moon by accident, deluding themselves in thinking that the extraordinarily precise calculations employed by teams of scientists and technicians had reliably guided them.

Even such simple things as riding a bicycle are incompatible with philosophical scepticism. *I believe that I can stop my bike by pressing on the hand brakes.* The basis for this belief is elementary inductive reasoning: *because this has always worked to stop the bike before, I trust that it will again.* If the sceptics were right, then you would be no more justified in believing that pressing the brake would stop the bike than shouting out threats to it or praying to the stars. In everyday life, nobody is or can be a radical sceptic.

It seems easier to refute scepticism through everyday life than through purely philosophical arguments. However, this does not mean that philosophical scepticism is nothing but an exercise in useless abstract reasoning. Precisely because it is so difficult to refute by purely philosophical arguments, it has forced imagination and rigour on philosophers in their development of theories of knowledge.

> *"The main principle of the Sceptic system is that of opposing to every proposition an equal proposition; for we believe that as an consequence of this we end by ceasing to dogmatize."*
>
> Sextus Empiricus

Relativism

In the movie *Atlantic City*, a character reports that she has no fear at all of flying in an airplane because she does not believe in gravity. This is an extreme version of **epistemological relativism**. In this form, beliefs are true *for* the people who have them. For most people, the statement *things as heavy as airplanes will fall to the earth unless kept up by some method* is true, whether everyone believes it or not; for the character in the movie the statement is false just because she believes it to be false.

Relativism in this extreme form comes to the same thing as thoroughgoing scepticism.

Certainly, if something can be made true simply by believing it, or be made false simply by disbelieving it, the justification of beliefs would be easy, but it would also be completely useless. What is more, just as in the case of scepticism, nobody could sincerely be an extreme relativist in his or her actual lives. Let someone who claims that the law of gravity is not true prove this by making a heavy object levitate or by jumping out a window.

Because such an extreme view is so implausible, almost all epistemological relativists qualify the position. The main qualification is to specify that it is only certain *sorts* of beliefs that are relative. The main sorts are: beliefs about what is *moral* (for example, that some animals have moral rights or that only humans have rights); general *world views* (for example, the world view of the religious believer or of the secular humanist); and very general *scientific theories* (for example, Newton's physics or Einstein's theory of relativity).

Also, most relativists do not claim that believing something automatically makes it so. Rather, they hold that, for instance, both the religious believer and the secular humanist may be justified in holding their views; however, neither can, even in principle, rationally persuade the other that his or her world view is objectively wrong. This is because people will only accept reasons that make sense to them, and it is just such things as general viewpoints on the world that determine what makes sense and therefore is an acceptable reason.

For example, consider especially brutal and apparently pointless crimes. A secular humanist might interpret these crimes as simply the actions of individuals who lack a sense of morality or who take pleasure in harming others. The secular humanist would look for psychological or social explanations of the conditions that create violent individuals. From some religious points of view, such crimes are also, or instead, seen as the result of the presence of evil in the world. From this view, the evil must be understood in religious terms. According to the relativist, the same activities make equal sense from each of these two, incompatible world views. The relativist believes that there is no way to prove that one of the interpretations is superior to the other.

Pick an example of an actual crime from a newspaper or television report and construct a debate over its causes from a religious perspective and a secular humanist one. Try to find a way that one side could be proven right or wrong.

POINT OF VIEW

Benjamin Whorf

The linguist Benjamin Whorf (1897–1941) defended a simple version of what is called linguistic relativism. **Linguistic relativism** is the view that general viewpoints are determined by the languages people use. Beliefs consistent with these viewpoints make sense to those who share the language and not to others. It was Whorf who called attention to the richness of Inuit language described earlier in this chapter. Whorf maintained that, as a result of their language, Inuit peoples experience nature differently from non-Aboriginal city dwellers. More philosophically sophisticated versions of linguistic relativism are found in works by the Austrian philosopher Ludwig Wittgenstein (1889–1951) and the French philosopher Jacques Derrida (born 1930).

PHILOSOPHY IN SCIENCE

Paradigm Analysis

Another view of relativism is found in the sciences. In the history of science, **paradigm analysis** maintains two things: (1) the major scientific theories are each based on some model or "paradigm" of the essential nature of reality; (2) scientific thinking takes these paradigms for granted and is guided by them. The main examples are: the Ancient and Medieval *Aristotelian paradigm* of reality as composed of matter and form and having unique potentialities; the *Newtonian paradigm* of matter in motion within the expanse of the neutral continuums of space and time; and the *Einsteinian paradigm*, where space and time interact with one another and with matter. In other words, an Aristotelian theory about the nature of the universe makes sense from an Aristotelian point of view. However, the Aristotelian theory may not hold up from a Newtonian view of the universe, just as a Newtonian view will not hold up from the point of view of Einstein. This is because the Aristotelian, Newtonian, and Einsteinian paradigms base their concepts on different fundamental beliefs.

American philosopher of science Thomas Kuhn (1922–1996) first presented paradigm theory in his book *The Structure of Scientific Revolutions.*

Epistemological relativists have called attention to the ways that beliefs fit into general systems of thought and language. These have the advantage of making sense of the world, but the disadvantage of making communication and rational debate among those with different systems of belief difficult, if not impossible. The relativists' views are most compatible with the coherence theory of truth described earlier.

Critics of epistemological relativism, sometimes called **epistemological realists**, admit that rational communication among people with different world views, basic scientific theories, or conceptions of morality is often difficult, but deny that it is impossible. They also claim that, if pushed, epistemological relativism turns into thoroughgoing scepticism.

What Do You Think?

In this chapter, you have seen how philosophers use critical thinking to consider knowledge and truth. Some philosophers think that justification is what true beliefs need to count as genuine knowledge. Other philosophers challenge this idea. In the same way, philosophers differ about what truth is. Perhaps, as some philosophers reason, truth and knowledge are relative—based perhaps on the different languages people speak. Some philosophers question the core principle of deductive logic, the law of non-contradiction. Sceptical philosophers question knowledge in the extreme: they state that no beliefs can be justified either through deduction, induction, or any other means. Do you think that any genuine knowledge or truth is possible, or do you, like the sceptics, doubt that this is possible?

Chapter 18 What Are the Origins of Knowledge?

Key Words
Direct perceptual realism
Representative perceptual realism
Empiricism
Philosophical idealism
Solipsism
A posteriori
A priori
Rationalism
Ontological argument
Pragmatism
Mysticism

Key People
Aristotle
John Locke
George Berkeley
David Hume
Vasubandhu
Bertrand Russell
Plato
René Descartes
Gottfried Wilhelm Leibniz
Baruch Spinoza
Plotinus

What Are the Bases of Knowledge?

Think of one thing you know. Can you describe the basis for this knowledge? Did you come by it through inductive or deductive reasoning, or some other means?

Here are three things that the author of this chapter knows:

1. *I know that the temperature of the room I am in now feels warm.*
2. *I know that when water is heated to 100°C it boils.*
3. *I know that the sum of the angles of a triangle is 180 degrees.*

The author can also explain *how* he knows these things:

1. *I know that the room feels warm to me because this is how it feels.*
2. *I know about the temperature of boiling water both from being taught this in a science class and also by running an experiment in the class.*
3. *I was also taught the fact about the angles of a triangle in school, and one of my exercises in a geometry class was to prove this fact.*

Philosophers of knowledge (epistemologists) can accept these explanations, but regarding these or any other examples, they ask the more general questions: how *reliable* is the knowledge, and on what is it *based*?

From Chapter 16 you know that knowledge about the boiling point of water is an example of knowledge by induction; while knowledge about the angles of a triangle is an example of deductive knowledge. This means that that the knowledge about the triangle is certain, and hence, the most reliable form of knowledge. Knowledge about the boiling point of water depends upon experiments that result in probable knowledge. So even if the probability is very high, this will not be the same thing as absolute certainty. Moreover, inductive knowledge is only approximate. Only completely pure water heated just at sea level would boil at 100°C, so the author's knowledge about his tap water is not exactly correct.

Even if I had not performed the experiment or done the geometry proof in classes, I would have good bases for knowledge about water and triangles, namely the authority of my teachers and textbooks. However, epistemologists are not satisfied with authority as a basis for knowledge, and want to know on what the knowledge of the authorities is itself based. In the two examples, the authorities' knowledge is based on inductive reasoning in the one case and deductive reasoning in the other.

In this chapter, you will review some philosophers' theories about the bases of knowledge and about how reliable they are.

Can Perception Provide Knowledge?

Do you believe that your sense perceptions give you accurate knowledge of the world? Why?

The most common source of knowledge is human perceptions of the external world gained through the use of the five senses: sight, sound, taste, smell, and feel. The example of the room feeling warm is this sort of knowledge. Its basis is the human ability to feel degrees of heat or coldness, and it is an example of very reliable and even certain knowledge. *If I feel warm then I know for sure that this is how I feel.* But epistemologists still raise several questions about the general reliability of perception as a basis for knowledge.

The Relativity of Perception

Suppose you enter the author's room wearing a heavy sweater, and he tells you that you may wish to take it off, since the room is warm. In thinking about his advice, you need to be aware of two senses of the word *warm*. In one sense, something is warm for someone if it feels warm *to* him or her. This is a *relative* sense of warmth. But in another sense, being warm is an *objective* fact. It might be said that if the temperature of a room is between about 18 and 22 degrees, it is warm; below 18 degrees and it starts to get cool; above 22 degrees, it is hot. It is an

objective matter whether the room is in the 18 to 22 degree range. The author's feeling of warmth is sometimes a good indicator of objective warmth, but he might also be mistaken. If, for example, he had a slight fever, the room may feel warmer to him than it really is.

Philosophers ask whether *all* beliefs gained through perception are relative. For instance, to test the accuracy of a person's feeling about the temperature of the room, you can place a thermometer in it and look at its register. But this raises the same question at different levels. For one thing, at some time some people had to determine what degrees of temperature corresponded to feelings of warm, hot, cold, and cool. This means that the determination of temperature is relative to the feeling of *these* people. Also, even in looking at the thermometer's register, how can two people be sure that they are seeing the same thing? One or both may have poor eyesight, or the register may be colour coded, and the two may see colours differently.

Perception and Interpretation

Many philosophers have challenged the idea that there are simple, raw perceptions. Rather, they say, perception always involves an element of interpretation. In hearing a sound, you always hear it *as* something—for instance, as a door slamming, or as something dropping, or even just as an event happening outside of your head—but never as a pure sound. The same thing applies to the other senses. **Epistemological relativists**, as described in Chapter 17, draw from this view of perception some sceptical conclusions about the ability of our senses to provide us with objective knowledge of the world.

The problem as the relativists see it is that perception cannot provide objective standards of how to interpret the world, since it is always infused with interpretations itself. For example, a multimillionaire sees a building *as* a modest house, while a pauper sees it *as* a luxurious home. Which is it *really?* The relativist claims that this is entirely a matter of interpretation depending on someone's point of view—there is no right answer to such a question.

The relativists sometimes illustrate the point about the relativity of perceptual interpretations with "reversible figures," that is, pictures that can be seen in two different ways.

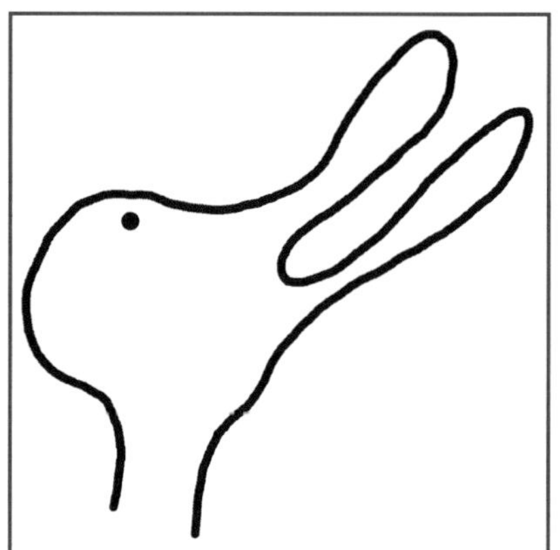

There are two views of this illustration: a duck looking up or a rabbit looking forward. The Austrian philosopher of language Ludwig Wittgenstein (1889–1951) used it in arguing for a subtle form of relativity of knowledge. Philosophers call it a *duck-rabbit.*

Is the drawing really of a duck or a rabbit? If you agree that there is no correct answer to this question, then do you think that this proves that perception cannot give us objective knowledge?

What Do Humans Perceive?

Direct Perceptual Realism

Aristotle disagreed with the sceptical conclusions of relativists since he thought that perception involves gaining direct knowledge by means of the senses. His view is one example of **direct perceptual realism**. The view is realistic because it holds that human senses give people beliefs about the world as it really is. It is called direct because it holds that, in perception, there is an immediate connection between things in the world and the beliefs that perception of them give people. In holding that the connection is direct, Aristotle did not mean that perception alone gives us all the knowledge we need or that our senses never deceive us. Rather, he thought that, carefully employed, our sense organs provide reliable information about the world.

Other philosophers challenge the directness of perception. One problem is that this theory has difficulty explaining how perception can be misleading even when there is nothing wrong with someone's sense organs. For example, a stick half immersed in water will look to be bent, even though it is in fact straight.

Philosophers with a different theory of reality than Aristotle raise another problem. For Aristotle, physical reality is made up of *substances* composed of *matter,* or the stuff of which things are made, and *forms*, which make the substances what they are—a human, a dog, a table, a tree, and so on. When you see a table, your mind takes in its form and this is how you know that there is a table in front of you. Even in his own times, not every philosopher agreed with Aristotle's theory. From around the 17th century, Aristotle's concept of reality was being replaced by the theory that what exists are particles of matter (atoms) moving and combining in accord with the laws of physics. On this view, what *really* exists are complexes of atoms, which themselves do not at all resemble things as humans perceive them. For instance, a table looks and feels solid, but once its physical composition is understood, it is known that the table consists of vast spaces between its atoms.

Representative Perceptual Realism

Philosophers such as John Locke (1632–1704) argued against direct realism and in favour of one now called **representative perceptual realism**. This theory is still realistic because beliefs derived from the senses usually yield knowledge of things in the world. But people do not directly perceive these things. Rather, people perceive *representations* of things in their minds. Locke called these representations "ideas." **Direct realists** say there are two components of perception: things in the world and minds that perceive them. **Representative realists** say there are three components of perception: (1) the perceiving mind; (2) the ideas or representations of things in the world, which it directly perceives; and (3) things in the world themselves, which cause the representations.

On this theory, the fact that things do not resemble a person's ideas (for instance, in appearing solid when they are mainly empty space) is not a problem. The ideas are caused by things we perceive rather than being copies of them. Also, mistakes in perception are explained as distortions in a person's ideas. *I think that I am seeing a bent stick because the representation I directly perceive is bent, though what it represents is not.* One job of science (and of careful perception generally) is to discover such distortions and allow for them.

POINT OF VIEW

The empiricists

Empiricism is the theory that all knowledge comes from information gained through the five senses. Though some version of this view has existed from ancient times and in several cultures, its best-known development was by British philosophers in the 17th and 18th centuries. These were: the Englishman John Locke (who is also famous for his theories in political philosophy); George Berkeley (1685–1753), a bishop of the Anglican Church in Ireland; and the Scottish philosopher David Hume (1711–1776), whose critical theories about induction were referred to in Chapter 17.

For the empiricists, the mind at birth is what Locke called a "blank tablet," which begins accumulating perceptions. When these perceptions come together often, they are associated by the mind. For instance, when lightning is seen (that is, when you have an idea representing it), you expect the idea of thunder to follow. Thinking involves the combination of simple ideas into complex ones, which are sometimes purely imaginary. All complex ideas are built up out of simple ones. Empiricists hold that knowledge requires analyzing these ideas into simple ones and tracing them back to original perceptions. This method does not provide certain knowledge, but it is the only knowledge available to people, and it is generally reliable.

> *"Let us then suppose the mind to be, as we say, white paper, void of all characters, without ideas: How comes it to be furnished? When comes it by that wide store which the busy and boundless fancy of man has painted on it with almost endless variety? Whence has it all the materials of reason and knowledge? To this I answer, in one word,* experience. *In that all our knowledge is founded; and from it ultimately derives itself."*
>
> John Locke

Problems with Representative Realism

Empiricists themselves recognize some problems with representative realism. One is this: if the only way of knowing things is through sense perception, and if what is directly perceived are ideas of things, then people have no

way of comparing the things in the world with the ideas of them, which are in their minds. In fact, there is no way of knowing for sure that there *is* a world outside of the mind. For example, when you perceive the idea of a table, the only way to know that there is a table outside of your mind causing you to have this idea is to compare the idea and the table. But this requires you to perceive the table itself directly, and this is just what representative realism denies is possible.

George Berkeley pointed out that you cannot know what things outside your mind are like, and you cannot even know that there *are* physical things outside of your mind at all. What are called things may in fact be nothing but ideas in your mind. In this case, the existence of what is taken for things independent of the mind is nothing but perceptions in the mind. Berkeley's conclusion was that people do not need to believe in physical causes of perceptions. What exists are just perceptions. As he put it in a provocative phrase: "to be is to be perceived."

> *"It is indeed an opinion strangely prevailing amongst men, that houses, mountains, rivers, and in a word all sensible objects, have an existence, natural or real, distinct from their being perceived by the understanding."*
>
> George Berkeley

Some students of Berkeley were in the habit of whirling around very quickly, hoping to catch the nothingness that on his theory would be behind them as long as they were not perceiving it. Explain why this effort was doomed to failure on Berkeley's theory. Try to disprove the theory that to be is to be perceived.

POINT OF VIEW

Vasubandhu

The derivation of philosophical idealism from representative perceptual realism is not unique to British empiricism. Several centuries earlier, one stream of Indian philosophy went through the same process of reasoning. In the 4th century, the philosopher, Vasubandhu reacted to an earlier school (the Sautrantika) that upheld a theory of perception like Locke's. Vasubandhu drew the same conclusion as Berkeley did much later: that since there is no way to know that external objects cause human perceptions, it is best to give up the idea that they exist.

Philosophical Idealism

This theory—that only minds and ideas in minds exist—is one version of the view called **philosophical idealism**. It is a difficult theory for empiricists to disprove. Say, for example, a teacher wants to prove that the now empty hallway outside her office exists even though neither the teacher nor anyone else perceives it. The only way she can prove this is to open the door and look outside. But then she would *perceive* the hallway, thus making it exist.

Berkeley, himself, was not disturbed by this implication of empiricism—philosophical idealism—since it fit in with his religious views. He concluded that *only* minds exist, which means human minds and the mind of God. What are thought of as things existing outside of human minds and about which people need to have reliable beliefs, are in fact ideas in the mind of God, who ensures they are orderly and dependable. For example: my chair and table are only ideas. God sees to it that I can depend upon my having the right perceptions (seeing the chair, feeling it under me as I sit, and so on) at the right time to achieve my purposes.

Can you prove that your classmates actually exist, that they are not just figments of your imagination?

Solipsism

David Hume did not believe it possible to know that there *is* a God, so he could not accept Berkeley's view. He took a more sceptical position: a person can never know whether there are things outside of him or her causing his or her ideas (or "impression" as he called them). Further, Hume claimed that nobody can know whether there are any minds other than his or her own. This position, called **solipsism**, is the thesis that only I exist, and everyone and everything else is a figment of my imagination.

> *"Solipsism may be more drastic or less drastic; as it becomes more drastic it becomes more logical and at the same time more unplausible."*
>
> Bertrand Russell

Ockham's Razor

The later empiricist Bertrand Russell (1872–1970) gave an argument against both Berkeley's idealism and against solipsism by using one of Berkeley's own principles against him. Berkeley thought that if two theories are equally good at explaining all the facts they are meant to explain, but one of them is simpler than the other, it should be preferred to the more complex theory. All the empiricist philosophers agree with this principle, which is called "Ockham's Razor" after the medieval philosopher William of Ockham (1285–1347), who first expressed it. Russell maintained that the simplest explanation for a person's beliefs about the external world, including other people, is that they exist independently of each person's perceptions. Other philosophers think that the fact that empiricists must find arguments to defend belief in the existence of the external world counts against it.

How Do Perceptions Become Knowledge?

A third problem relating to perception, applies both to direct and representative theories. Ancient Greek philosopher Plato (427–347 BCE) raised this problem many centuries before the British empiricists. He asked how perception can give people knowledge at all. Sense perception cannot provide knowledge of things like goodness or justice, he thought, since these are not the sorts of things that can be perceived. But perception alone also cannot give knowledge of such things as horses or chairs. The reason for this is that a person cannot perceive something *as* a horse or a chair unless he or she already has an idea of these things. In thinking of perception this way, Plato was agreeing with the view described earlier in the chapter about all perception involving interpretation, but he did not draw sceptical consequences from it.

Chairs and horses come in many different sizes, shapes, and colours. When you see one particular example of a chair or a horse, there is nothing about that particular example that tells you it is an example of a horse or a chair. The point may be put like this: people can perceive particular things recognized as horses or chairs, but cannot perceive the essence—the *horseness* or *chairness*—of these things that makes it possible to recognize them as horses and chairs.

Plato's conclusion was that, in addition to the world of material things, there is a world of nonmaterial essences, called "Forms." Forms are not accessible to human sense organs, but are understood by human reason. Reason then makes it possible for people to perceive particular things as examples in the material world of their prototypes in the world of Forms. While everyone must have some knowledge of Forms, for Plato, most grasp them incompletely and imperfectly. They are like people in a cave who see shadows of things on its walls without understanding that the shadows are produced by the Sun's illumination of things outside the cave.

However, Plato thought that *philosophers* are able to get outside of the cave and understand the true origins of human perceptions in the world of Forms. On this point, Plato's student, Aristotle, disagreed with him. Aristotle held that, if properly used, our sense organs are not obstructions to knowledge, as Plato thought, but can function with our intellect directly to comprehend the essence of physical things.

Can Reason Provide Knowledge?

Many philosophers, also disagreeing with the epistemological relativists, think that perception can help to produce knowledge provided it is guided by reason. However, there are differences among them about what kind of knowledge reason can provide and its usefulness.

A Posteriori Knowledge

For the empiricists, reason plays two roles, each relating to a kind of knowledge. The five senses only provide knowledge of particular facts. To gain general knowledge, people have to make repeated and careful observations and try to discover general laws, for instance, about causes and effects. Inductive reasoning, as reviewed in Chapter 16, is indispensable for this. The kind of knowledge this reasoning provides is called ***a posteriori***, from the Latin (*after*) to refer to knowledge gained as a result of (or following) sense experience.

A Priori Knowledge

The other kind of knowledge empiricists recognize is ***a priori*** knowledge, or knowledge gained without or "prior to" sense experience. One example is knowledge of things that are true by definition. As noted in Chapter 16, you do not have to quiz or otherwise experience bachelors to know that they are unmarried. This fact follows from the meaning of the word *bachelor*. You know that a bachelor is unmarried before you meet him. Other examples are truths of deductive logic, such as the truth of the claim that if all humans are mortal and Socrates is human, then he is mortal. If the premises are assumed to be true, then you can know without reading a biography of Socrates' life and death that he was mortal. (Although, if you are interested, you can read the story of Socrates' death in the *Phaedo,* a dialogue written by Plato.) Reasoning is useful both in figuring out the meanings of words and in doing deductive logical proofs.

According to empiricists, the advantage of *a priori* knowledge is certainty. Its disadvantage is that such knowledge provides no information about the world. Just knowing that bachelors are unmarried does not tell you how many bachelors there are, whether they are happy, or who of the people you know is a bachelor. Similarly, the syllogism about Socrates does not tell you whether all humans are in fact mortal or whether Socrates was a human. For these things, knowledge based on experience is required. This is *a posteriori* knowledge, which is informative, but it can never be certain.

Do you believe that you have knowledge that does not depend at all on perceptual experience? If yes, provide examples.

Do you believe that human beings are capable of proving certain things to be undeniably true? Can you give an example?

POINT OF VIEW

The Rationalists

The rationalist philosophers of Continental Europe in the 17th and 18th centuries gave reason a much more important role than did the empiricists. The father of rationalism is the French philosopher, René Descartes (1596–1650). Other leading rationalists were Gottfried Wilhelm Leibniz (1646–1716), from what is now Germany, and Baruch Spinoza (1632–1677), born in the Netherlands of Portuguese Jewish ancestry. He was expelled from the Amsterdam synagogue for heresy due in part to supporting Descartes' philosophy. Descartes is also the founder of analytic geometry, as Leibniz is of calculus (independently developed by him and by Newton). Spinoza was one of the first Western philosophers to defend **pantheism** or the view that God and the universe are identical.

Against empiricism, **rationalism** holds that reason provides knowledge that is both certain and informative. Thus, Leibniz disagreed with Locke that the mind is a blank tablet waiting to be filled by information from perception. Each person's ideas of the basic natures of humanity and other things are in the mind prior to any experience. In principle, according to Leibniz, the cause of an effect can be known with certainty, since he thought that the ideas of causes are *contained* within the ideas of their effects.

Spinoza deduced an entire theory of the nature of humans, the world, and ethics from a few definitions. (The key one is of a "self-caused being," defined by Spinoza as a being whose "essence involves existence.")

One of Descartes' proofs for the existence of God is derived from his definition of "God" as "the being than which no greater can be conceived."

WEB CONNECTION

Rationalists vs. Empiricists

Go to the *Internet Encyclopedia of Philosophy* and look up some of the concepts discussed in this chapter. When reading the entries, notice how rationalists' views differ from those of empiricists.

PHILOSOPHY IN EVERYDAY LIFE

An example of Descartes' use of reason is his revival of an earlier proof for the existence of God, the **ontological argument.** First given by the archbishop of Canterbury, St. Anselm (1033–1109), the name for this argument is taken from the Greek word for "being" (*ontos*). Like St. Anselm, Descartes claimed that God's existence can be demonstrated just by considering the definition of the word *God*. Once the meaning of this word is understood, God's existence can no more be doubted than it can be doubted that a triangle has three sides—once the meaning of the word *triangle* is understood. One version of the ontological argument follows.

Whatever else God is, God is the perfect Being. Because He is perfect, God is a Being than which no greater can be conceived. If God only existed in people's minds and not also in reality, something greater could be conceived of, namely, something that exists both in people's minds and in reality. Since God is, by definition, the greatest thing imaginable, God must, therefore, exist.

> *"It is now some years since I detected how many were the false beliefs that I had from my earliest youth admitted as true, and how doubtful was everything that I had constructed on that basis; and from that time I was convinced that I must once and for all seriously undertake to rid myself of all the opinions which I had formerly accepted, and commence to build anew from the foundation, if I wanted to establish any firm and permanent structure in the sciences."*
>
> René Descartes

Descartes' Proof of His Existence

Descartes wished to provide a basis for all of science and religion by means of principles that are certain. To this end, he employed the method of doubting all of his beliefs to see whether any of them could *not* be doubted. If he found such a belief, it would be something he would know with certainty (because he was incapable of doubting it), and it could be used to discover other things that can be known with certainty.

This method would only work if the doubt was complete, so Descartes imagined these things: that when he thought he was experiencing things, he was really asleep; that what he thought were people around him were really perfectly designed robots; and even that an evil but very powerful genius was dedicated to deceiving him in all ways. By this method, his previous beliefs fell, one by one.

He could not trust any of his senses, since he might be asleep or hallucinating. He could not trust elementary mathematical beliefs, because the evil genius might have tricked him into believing false rules of mathematics. And so on. However, Descartes concluded, one belief escaped his most energetic efforts to doubt: his belief in his own existence. The reason for this is that the very fact that Descartes was thinking (in his case by trying to doubt his existence) *proved* his existence. In one of the most famous pronouncements in philosophy, he concluded: "I think, therefore I am."

Descartes examined this proof of his own existence to see what made it certain. He came to the conclusion that it was because of the complete "clarity and distinctness" with which he knew that he existed. He then examined his other beliefs to see which of them shared the same clarity and distinctness. This enabled him to reintroduce many of the principles he had earlier doubted. These included the belief thatprovided they are subjected to rigorous scientific control and direction the senses can be trusted and that deductive principles, such as of mathematics, are reliable. He also developed the ontological argument for the existence of God plus two more arguments for God's existence, each supported by his criterion of clarity and distinctness.

Traditional and Non-Traditional Views about Knowledge

For rationalists there are, in principle, no limits to what humans can know. Once first principles of reality are discovered, the careful and thorough application of reason, employing perception and scientific experimentation when required (but always under the guidance of reason), should allow for the indefinite accumulation of knowledge about all things.

Empiricists are more modest about what can be known, since this must be limited to what is learned from perception. Perceptual knowledge depends upon inductive reasoning, and inductive knowledge is never certain or complete.

Meanwhile, epistemological relativists, as discussed in Chapter 17, consider knowledge as limited to those who already share common principles of knowledge, for example as determined by their language or their general world views. Sceptics, of course, go the furthest in seeing no scope at all for knowledge.

These are some of the main traditional approaches to knowledge by philosophers. The chapter concludes by noting two approaches that do not fit into this framework. The two approaches are very different from one another.

Pragmatism

Pragmatism is a mainly U.S. philosophical school first developed by Charles Sanders Pierce (1839–1914), William James (1842–1910), and John Dewey (1859–1952). They thought of knowledge not as an abstract, philosophical matter, but practically as a number of tools for solving problems as in the sciences and everyday life. The test of the reliability of knowledge tools, such as specific applications of inductive or deductive reasoning, is how well they help people to solve problems. What is more, in the process of being used, the tools themselves are improved upon as lessons are learned from successes and failures.

Like the empiricists, pragmatists are modest in limiting the use of knowledge to specific problems, but they do not insist that all knowledge must be reduced to sense perception. Like rationalists, the pragmatists are optimistic about the possibilities of reason, which they think can always be improved. But since there will always be new problems to solve in all realms of life and thought, they do not think the project of knowing everything could ever be successful.

In viewing knowledge as an ongoing, practical project for which perception and reason provide tools even while they are themselves improved upon, the pragmatists think they can avoid having to choose from among traditional theories of knowledge—rationalism, empiricism, and relativism.

> *"Pragmatism has sometimes been charged with oscillating between two contrary notions; the one, that experience is 'through and through malleable to our purpose,' the other that facts are 'hard' and uncreated by the mind. We here offer a mediating conception."*
>
> C.I. Lewis

Mysticism

Mystic thought has existed in all religious traditions, such as the Christian mysticism of Meister Eckhart (1260–1328) or mystical readings of the Bhagavad-Gita in Hinduism. Mystic thought has also had non-religious expressions, as in Indian Jainism and some versions of Buddhism. The relation of mysticism to knowledge as studied by epistemologists may be seen in the thinking of Plotinus (205–270). A philosopher inspired by Plato (a **neoplatonist**), he was born in Egypt and later started a school in Rome.

Like the rationalists, Plato was optimistic that some people—the philosophers—could come to full understanding of things, in his case, by knowing the world of Forms. Plotinus drew on some puzzling statements in Plato's later writings to develop his ideas further. On Plotinus's view, there is a world beyond the Forms and even beyond being itself, called "the One." He further held that it is possible for people's consciousness to merge with, or more precisely, actually to become the One.

Plotinus's views are typical of most mystic writing: a world is posited—sometimes described as beyond being, sometimes as pure being, sometimes as God, sometimes as pure nothingness, and sometimes as combinations of these—with which it is possible wholly or partly to merge. It would be misleading, however, to describe such merger as a way of knowing in the sense of traditional epistemology. In epistemology, knowledge is pursued by a subject or a self that wishes to acquire true beliefs about objects of knowledge. But for the mystic, *that which knows* and *that which is known* become the same. The result, for mystics, is a form of knowledge that is beyond both reason and experience, and in which the distinction between knowing subject and known object disappears. In fact, some mystics do not think the result should be described as knowledge at all.

> *"The* Tao *is not classifiable as either knowledge or non-knowledge. Knowledge is illusory consciousness and non-knowledge is blind unconsciousness. If you really comprehend the indubitable* Tao, *it is like a wide expanse of emptiness ..."*
>
> P'u-yüan

What Do You Think?

In this chapter you have considered two major schools of thought that address the origins of human knowledge. On the one hand there are the rationalist philosophers who believe that reason alone provides access to important knowledge. On the other hand, the empiricist philosophers think that all useful knowledge must ultimately come from sense perception. Pragmatist philosophers avoid taking sides in this debate. They see knowledge as a tool to solve practical problems, which draws upon either perception or reason as needed, and which can be reliable, even if it is never perfect. Whose views do you think are better able to describe the basis for human knowledge: the rationalists, the empiricists, or the pragmatists? Or, do you disagree with all of them, preferring instead the sceptical theory that nothing can be known, or the mystical view that shuns knowledge in any traditional sense in favour of a merger of self and non-self?